THE TRUTH OF MY SOUL

To Janet

Be the Woman you Are!

Love,

Bonny Billan

TRILOGY- BOOK 1

A STORY TO EMPOWER FEMALES & GIVE AWARENESS TO MALES

DOES BEING A FEMALE DETERMINE YOUR LIFE?
DO YOU HAVE THE COURAGE TO CHANGE YOUR DESTINY?

DESTINY – FATE OR CHOICE?
WHO... Creates Yours?

THE TRUTH
of
My Soul

*A Woman's Journey of Gender Inequality & Male Dominated Challenges,
& her "Spiritual Awakening" & "Heavenly Healing Path," for her soul's freedom.*

BONNY BILLAN

Order this book online at www.trafford.com/07-0258
or email orders@trafford.com

Most Trafford titles are also available at major online book retailers.

The Truth of My Soul, Trilogy - Book 1.
Copyright © 2005 – 2007 by Bonny R. Billan.

Note for Librarians: A cataloguing record for this book is available from Library and Archives Canada at www.collectionscanada.ca/amicus/index-e.html

Printed in Victoria, BC, Canada.

ISBN: 978-1-4251-1849-5

We at Trafford believe that it is the responsibility of us all, as both individuals and corporations, to make choices that are environmentally and socially sound. You, in turn, are supporting this responsible conduct each time you purchase a Trafford book, or make use of our publishing services. To find out how you are helping, please visit www.trafford.com/responsiblepublishing.html

Our mission is to efficiently provide the world's finest, most comprehensive book publishing service, enabling every author to experience success. To find out how to publish your book, your way, and have it available worldwide, visit us online at www.trafford.com/10510

 www.trafford.com

North America & international
toll-free: 1 888 232 4444 (USA & Canada)
phone: 250 383 6864 ♦ fax: 250 383 6804 ♦ email: info@trafford.com

The United Kingdom & Europe
phone: +44 (0)1865 487 395 ♦ local rate: 0845 230 9601
facsimile: +44 (0)1865 481 507 ♦ email: info.uk@trafford.com

10 9 8 7 6

I Dedicate this book to the Female Gender
Past, Present, and Future of Every Culture
Around Our Universe.
I Honor Your Courage, Strength, and Wisdom
on the Battlefields of Life, in Choosing to be Born a Female.

Together We Have Power, Divided We Lose Strength,
Transform Our Beliefs and We Change Our Destinies.
Love and Unite with One Another the World Over
and We Have Truly Conquered and All Won.

Soul Sisters from Sea to Sea,
Remember What You Have Lived Through.
Never Forget, Who You Are.
Never Forget, How Strong You Truly All Are!

Women... a Goddess with Inner Beauty,
I Honor The Truth Within Your Souls.

Contents

A Special Recognition

$\mathcal{I}$ wish to give a special thanks to you Oprah Winfrey, for changing my world. My journey to self-discovery began many years ago with one of your premiere shows, and 4:00 p.m. on weekdays has become much more to me than just a time. I've had much laughter as you've share your joyful spirit, and the positive manner which you radiate has given me strength especially during my times of pain. I have also improved myself while becoming greatly aware of the many issues plaguing our universe.

Miss Winfrey you are a great role model and your down-to-earth personality has endeared you to many. You are a courageous woman who I realize has experienced your own share of personal pain which many can relate to.

Millions of lives all over our world have benefited from your extensive array of inspirational guests, and the knowledge which they have imparted for the progression of all. Women, men, and children have been affected and changed forever in response to their messages, as they have aided many people in truly realizing their paths of pain within the far reaching regions of their beings. Many of us have greatly healed by understanding our stumbling blocks and truly accepting the truth within our spirits. As well as, delving deeply within our ruins and reinventing ourselves within our hearts and souls, as we continue to learn, change, and expand our awareness.

Your great undertaking regarding the enormous amount of information concerning important global issues, and the extremely horrendous plights that others have endured, has informed us and increased our love, compassion, and actions towards our fellow man. With this new consciousness we are going to exceed many of our old beliefs as to what we can accomplish in this lifetime for ourselves, our families, and for many people around our world, as we reach out to touch hands with theirs.

Our universe will continue to be a finer place because of your love and kind heartedness which you have extended to many. We are fortunate to have been a recipient of the insight and fortitude which you have given. How very proud you must feel to have had such a strong impact on so many lives, for you have left a great legacy which will continue to generate positively for future generations to come.

Please know Miss Winfrey, that I never would have had the courage to venture out and write my story, if my soul had not been touched and continued to be nurtured so profoundly by your encouragement, vision, and show of strength. You have been a great inspiration and helped in keeping me strong throughout the past years. Much of the power in my actions came from a spark within me, which you contributed in growing into a flame and your optimism has kept my dream alive.

I in turn, am passing on my awareness by writing this book to assist females of all ages. I wanted to help in Awakening their Spirits, Challenging their Society's and Family's Beliefs, and Increasing their Actions towards making courageous and positive life altering changes within their lives. I also wanted to convey to them, that they must never give up in their efforts and strength towards themselves or any others.

My story is one that I hope may empower many females while offering awareness to various males of all cultures and walks of life. If both genders can use the knowledge which they have accumulated, in addition to understanding my struggles, growth, and miracles within my journey, they too may be able to change their destinies. And all of this will lead towards a higher development, safety, and happiness for their souls and the greater good of their families.

Miss Winfrey, I am a stronger, healthier, knowledgeable, and more compassionate woman, for welcoming you and your world into my life. God Bless You.

From My Heart to Yours,
Bonny Billan
Feb. 2001/2006

My Message To Readers

Guidelines to Empower Females
While Offering Awareness to Males

MY INTENTION FOR WRITING THIS STORY IS TO ALERT FEMALES OF ALL AGES AND CULTURES, TO RECOGNIZE THAT REGARDLESS OF THE NATIONALITY THAT THEY ARE BORN, THEY HAVE CONSTITUTIONAL RIGHTS AS HUMAN BEINGS OF OUR WORLD.

ALL FEMALES AROUND OUR UNIVERSE MUST BE AWAKENED TO COMPREHEND, THAT THEY ARE ENTITLED TO BE TREATED AS AN EQUAL TO ALL MALES. THEY MUST ALSO BECOME AWARE AND UNDERSTAND, THAT THEY HAVE THEIR OWN HUMAN RIGHT TO LIVE DAILY WITHOUT ANY FORM OF ABUSE IN A WORLD OF FREEDOM.

THEY MUST COME TO KNOW, THAT THEY ARE ENTITLED TO CHOOSE THEIR OWN PATHWAYS AND TO STATE THEIR OPINIONS WHILE BEING TREATED WITH THE UTMOST OF RESPECT AND EQUALITY. AS WELL AS, USING THEIR VOICES TO STAND UP FOR THEMSELVES AND OTHERS, WITHOUT ANY FEAR OF BEING SUBJECTED TO DISGRACE, HARM, OR VIOLENCE.

I REALIZE THAT THE SUBSERVIENT ROLES THAT MANY FEMALES ARE THRUST INTO ARE INTERTWINED WITH EXTREME CREULTY. HOWEVER, THEY MUST BEGIN TO FIND THE STRENGTH TO START SAYING "NO" TO ANY MISTREATMENT OR DISRESPECT IN WHICH THEY ARE EXPERIENCING. THE FEMININE GENDER MUST MAKE EVERY EFFORT POSSIBLE, ESPECIALLY THROUGH THEIR OWN CHOICES, TO NOT SUBJECT THEMSELVES TO ANY OF THESE OFFENCES WHICH ACTUALLY GOES AGAINST THEIR VERY SOULS.

THERE ARE BILLIONS OF WOMEN AND CHILDREN WHO ARE BEING TREATED HORRENDOUSLY WITHIN THEIR SOCIETIES. IS THIS OCCURRING BECAUSE IT IS TRULY A PART OF THEIR FAITH, OR IS IT JUST ANOTHER ATTEMPT BY ONE GENDER TO CONTINUE ASSERTING THEMSELVES WITH POWER OVER ANOTHER?

ONE MAY FIND, THAT IF THEY ACTUALLY RE-READ OR SIMPLY READ THEIR CULTURAL SCRIPTURES FOR THE FIRST TIME, THAT THEY MAY HAVE MISUNDERSTOOD ITS TEACHINGS. AS A RESULT, WHAT THEY HAVE ESSENTIALLY CARRIED ON FROM ONE GENERATION TO ANOTHER, AND INFORCED RATHER SEVERELY IS THEIR LACK OF KNOWLEDGE TOWARDS THEIR OWN RELIGION.

WHY WOULD THE HOLY MEN WHO FORMED THE BELIEFS IN DIFFERENT CULTURES WANT TO HARM A FEMALE'S SPIRIT AND JOY FOR LIFE? IS IT NOT MORE LOGICAL, THAT THEIR SAINTLY WORDS WERE CREATED WITH WISDOM AND INTENDED IN TRUTH, TO NURTURE AND POSITIVELY BOND THE RELATIONSHPS BETWEEN WOMEN AND MEN?

HOWEVER, OVER THE CENTURIES THEIR SACRED WORDS HAVE ACTUALLY BEEN MISINTERPRETED, MISUSED, AND DISTORTED BY BOTH GENDERS, MUCH TO THE DETRIMENT OF FEMALES EVERYWHERE AROUND OUR UNIVERSE!

IN ADDITION AND I SAY THIS WITH THE UTMOST OF RESPECT, PERHAPS SOME OF THE TRADITIONAL PRINCIPLES WHICH WERE FORMED HUNDREDS AND EVEN THOUSANDS OF YEARS AGO, SIMPLY DO NOT APPLY IN THIS DAY AND AGE. SOME BELIEFS MAY NEED TO BE RE-EVALUATED AND CHANGED, SO THEY DO NOT BELITTLE, CRUSH, DESTROY, OR TAKE AWAY ANY FEMALE'S SPIRIT, SELF ESTEEM, AND SOMETIMES... EVEN HER LIFE! EACH AND EVERY

FEMALE AROUND OUR GLOBE HAS THE HUMAN RIGHT TO WALK EQUALLY BESIDE EVERY MALE, WHILE ALSO STANDING PROUDLY BY HERSELF.

IN TODAY'S WORLD, WHY WOULD ONE GENDER BELIEVE THAT THEY ARE MUCH MORE SUPERIOR OVER THE OTHER? WHY MUST IT BE, THAT WHATEVER REGULATIONS MEN ESTABLISH FOR WOMEN, THESE LIMITATIONS ARE TAKEN AS THE GOSPEL TRUTH AND MUST BE FOLLOWED AS THE ABSOLUTE RIGHT THING TO DO? WHY IS IT, THAT ONLY THE MALE GENDER SEEM TO BE BENEFITTING FROM THE MANY INFORCED RESTRICTIONS, THAT ARE PUT INTO ACTION TO HALT A FEMALE IN HER GROWTH TO KEEP HER MANY STEPS BEHIND THEM. WE MUST ALL ASK OURSELVES THESE QUESTIONS, AS WE STRIVE TO ALTER THIS WAY OF THINKING AND THE PERCEPTION OF SOME, THAT WOMEN ARE UNINTELLIGENT AND WORTHLESS POSSESSIONS.

DAILY LIVING MUST CHANGE FOR BILLIONS OF PEOPLE AND WE NEED TO BOND TOGETHER IN SUPPORT FOR ONE ANOTHER. MANY OF THE FEMININE GENDER NEED TO BE SHOWN AND TO ACCEPT, THAT THEY HAVE THE RIGHT TO BE SAFE AND HAPPY IN A DIGNIFIED MANNER. THEREFORE, WE MUST ALL CONTINUE IN THE BATTLE TO FIRSTLY, SEIZE AND RETAIN THE OWNERSHIP OF OUR OWN LIFE'S AND THEN LEND A HAND TO OTHERS!

WOMEN THE WORLD OVER, CAN ALSO BE A GREAT ASSISTANCE IN EMPOWERING FEMALES OF ALL AGES. IN MOVING FORWARD TOWARDS BELIEVING IN A DIFFERENT FUTURE, OTHER THAN THE ONE WHICH HAS BEEN PROJECTED ONTO THEM. WE MUST HELP THEM TO UNDERSTAND, THAT THEY ARE ENTITLED TO HAVE POSITIVE FULFILLING LIVES, WITH WANTS OF THEIR OWN. AS WE

ALSO AID OTHERS IN REMEMBERING, THAT THEY MUST NEVER CAST ASIDE OR FORGET ABOUT MANIFESTING THEIR HEARTFELT DREAMS. AS WELL AS, CONTINUALLY STRIVING TOWARDS THE CREATION OF THEIR MOST SACRED DESIRES.

IF YOU HAVE DISCOVERED YOUR FREE WILL, YOU MUST ALWAYS GRASP IT IN YOUR HANDS, USE IT, AND NEVER LET IT GO. IF THIS IS NOT WITHIN YOUR REACH AT THIS MOMENT, YOU MAY HAVE QUITE A CHALLENGE IN ACHIEVING IT. HOWEVER I ASK YOU TO NOT GIVE UP, BUT TO CONTINUE WITH ALL OF YOUR INNERMOST STRENGTH AND WILLPOWER TOWARDS THIS GOAL. IT IS ALSO ONE OF YOUR HUMAN RIGHTS TO OWN.

THESE ISSUES HAVE NO BARRIERS OR BOUNDARIES FOR THEY CROSS OVER AND TOUCH EVERY NATIONALITY, CULTURE, AND CREED THROUGHOUT EVERY NATION. ALTHOUGH, THEY MAY BE MORE COMMON IN SOME SOCIETIES OVER OTHERS.

THESE GUIDELINES SHOULD BE THE INITIAL MAJOR POINTS WITHIN THE VERY FOUNDATION TOWARDS THE FREEDOM, EQUALITY, AND DIGNIFIED RESPECT OF EVERY WOMEN AND CHILD IN OUR UNIVERSE. AND WITH THE CREATION AND THE SINCERE DETERMINATION OF EVERY LEADER AROUND OUR GLOBE ON BEHALF OF THESE STRATEGIES, THIS COULD INDEED BE A WINNING FORMULA. IN DOING SO, THE MOST PROMISING AND PEACEFUL EXISTENCE FOR FEMALES WITHIN EVERY BRANCH OF LIFE, MAY BE POSSIBLE WITHIN OUR LIFETIMES.

WE MUST ALL BEGIN OR CONTINUE TO LOOK AT THE PAST AND THE PRESENT, SO WE MAY CREATE A MORE COMPASSIONATE AND LOVING FUTURE FOR ALL HUMAN BEINGS.

In sharing my life story I have touched upon my deepest hurts, beliefs, and desires as a female living within my male dominated family and culture. I am not trying to cast any blame upon my parent's regarding my upbringing. I recognize that they too were born into families which highly accepted inequality between the genders, as a normal way of life. As well I realize that their childhoods were extremely disciplined and at times very cruel. I can also appreciate that they raised me to the best of their ability, as they honored the principles which they greatly believed in, with the understanding that they had from within themselves. However, the following is the reality of what I lived through, and as we each chose a different pathway to walk, this is my truth as it took place for me.

I was born and raised in Canada and since my surroundings, dress, and language reflected quite a non-traditional way of life, most of the time I felt like I was a foreigner in my own culture. Everywhere that I went in my society, females were segregated from the males while being treated like second class citizens. And were looked down upon with the least amount of regard than anybody else. I absolutely despised how we were considered to simply not be good enough and unequal to males. Let alone, the looks of disapproval, sadness, and death on the faces of both genders whenever a baby girl was born.

I found it very difficult to embrace my background for it was something that I was not able to agree or identify with. Therefore I took the similarities in my strict upbringing and my ethnic culture, and I grouped them together as something I desired to distance myself away from. I believed within the core of my heart, that any situation which took away from a female and categorized her of not being on an equal footing with a male, was not something that I could happily or truly be a part of. As a result, the origin of my inequality issues with my culture began decades ago.

In my writings I am not trying to criticize my ethnic background or religion, but this is how I as a child perceived the world which I was born into. However, my beliefs changed drastically in the year 2006 after I took the opportunity to research my society's faith. It was at this moment, that I truly came to the realization that Sikhism is a great religion, and significant misunderstandings had been made along the way by a great amount of people. I began to understand the basis of Sikhism, and I also discovered one of the most important principles which greatly pertained to all females within our culture.

The first Sikh Guru and founder of the Sikh religion was Guru Nanak Dev Ji. (1469-1539) He challenged the values of his societies appalling beliefs towards the dreadful treatment and disrespect of womanhood. He tried to raise females from the lowest most horrible points of humiliation to the highest points of praise, as he voiced his support for EQUALITY BETWEEN FEMALES AND MALES.

Guru Nanak gave women, the title "Daughter of God" as he brushed away the old and negative expressions which were used to criticize women. He composed a verse which said, "It is by woman the condemned one, that we are conceived. And from her that we are born; it is with her that we are betrothed and married. It is woman we befriend; it is she who keeps the race going. When one woman dies, we seek another; it is with her we become established in society. Why should we call her inferior, who gives birth to great men? A woman is born of a woman, none is born without a woman. O Nanak, only the one True Lord is without a woman."

He gave WOMEN THE SAME RIGHTS AND PRIVILEGES that were already given to MEN, which enabled them to take part in religious, cultural, social, and political activities. He also worked toward changing the cast system. Guru Nanak stomped on traditional values and advocated equality for women and equality for all human beings. He also taught that the whole of humanity is one brotherhood and God is the only Father of all of us. And anybody could have a connection to God without going to any type of formal service.

Nine more Gurus would follow him and continue to develop the Sikh religion and society, as all of their battles for freedom and independence would make up this now, five hundred year old religion. Guru Gobind Singh who was the tenth Guru, gave an honor to the Sikh holy book, the Guru Granth Sahib. He gave it the tribute, of being the eleventh and final eternal living guru of the Sikhs. These Holy Scriptures are given great honor and respect in our Gurdwaras, which is the name for our temples.

He also gave Sikh women the surname "Kaur" which means princess. Men were given the surname "Singh" which means lion. He appreciated the two different genders and made this distinction in regard to these names with respect.

I was truly amazed when I heard what Guru Nanak was trying to achieve for women, that it brought tears to my eyes. This also happened when I read what Buddha's teachings were in regard to the various handicaps and drawbacks that a woman has to endure. For the first time in my existence, I had been led to two leaders who understood something that I had been feeling and fighting for my entire life, and it drew me to them. It deeply touched my heart to know that Guru Nanak worked so hard to raise and enhance the status of women, and I was suddenly so very proud of this religion.

Over the years, I have felt some sort of connection to Guru Nanak for I have a necklace of him which I often held when I prayed. I've had it since I was ten years old and my children all once wore it. It now has a place on my bedside table and I sometimes still hold it close to me as I pray.

On a subconscious level, had my soul remembered a previous bond to Guru Nanak? Further on in my story, I speak about the soul's past life memory. However oddly enough, one of my sons has the same name as one of the Gurus and they both happen to be born on the same day. I also named him at his birth.

Throughout the ages, if others in my culture had heard, listened, and lived by the Guru's words, then life for so many females would not have been such a hell. These are some of the teachings of the great masters during Sikh history, but how many other religious scriptures in various cultures have been misunderstood by their followers? When I read about the struggles that the Gurus and their soldiers fought and died for, I felt very proud for being a Sikh, but also rather foolish for not knowing about their beliefs and sacrifices before now. I had fought a concept my entire life and maybe, I was one of the most unaware and ignorant of all!

I also discovered in the gathering of my information that Sikh history had been made by Sikh women too. Many females did their share of battling for various causes, as well as the wives and families of the Gurus. There were many people to be highly commended for their courage and determination in carrying out the Gurus teachings.

One of the most significant teachings in Sikhism to me was the ruling regarding equality between females and males. However this was something that I rarely experienced especially while I was growing up, and the same held true for the females that grew up around me. Since this was one of the main beliefs that Guru Nanak established I truly needed to ask, WHAT HAPPENED TO THIS EXTREMELY IMPORTANT GUIDELINE?

Did it disappear because people simply lacked the education and couldn't understand and accept this truth, let alone embrace it, and pass it on to their children and the next generation? Perhaps this belief which over the centuries would affect billions of females was used for awhile, and then its meaning gradually changed and became distorted over time, until it was completely disregarded and tossed aside.

Throughout the centuries, how many people truly took the time to read and live the truth in the Sikh holy book which is filled with so much wisdom? I realize that many people didn't know how to read the languages within it or even read at all, and they had to rely on others for the interpretations of its teachings. However, it was very shocking and sad to me that this huge recognition for females did not filter through, and reach the minds and hearts of the majority of citizens within my culture, a hundred years ago and even fifty years ago?

How long did it truly take after the Gurus passed on, for their absolute life altering message of equality between women and men to become LOST AND BURIED? I say it is NOW TIME, for this TRUTH TO BE DUG UP, HONORED, and LIVED BY ALL SIKHS whether one is MALE or FEMALE!

Remember, that the Gurus and their soldiers sacrificed their very souls, as they courageously battled through many crusades and much blood shed. And some of their tortured bodies even died lying in their own blood. Do we, who are Sikh, all have it within us to honor and pay tribute to their ultimate wishes, to always be and do our very best? And make every effort possible to live with one another in equality and harmony?

Also, as we go to our places of worship to pray and listen to our holy book of songs and prayers, we must remember that we are listening to their words. Above all else, since the Guru Granth Sahib is a living Guru, they are still existing and speaking through each and every one of us, as we go through each second of our daily lives. For their messages of love and compassion are flowing through all of our hearts and souls. It's up to us whether or not, we will truthfully honor their struggles and desires for freedom and equality for all human beings, in forming the religion of Sikhism, which I am sure Sikhs are very proud to be a part of.

The word "Guru" means going from the darkness and into the light, or leaving ignorance behind and walking into enlightenment. Whatever culture you are from… think about how you live your life. Do you regard both genders and every race, creed, and color of human beings with the utmost of respect and equality? Have you walked out of the gloom of darkness and into the illumination of the light yet?

Other cultures would surly benefit and do themselves proud, if they were to truly consider and perhaps adopt some of the teachings of Sikhism. I believe it was created by one of the most insightful and wisest spiritual leaders of all time.

The word "Buddha" means "Awakened" one. I ask everyone the world over, have you allowed your soul to truly awaken or is it still… deep in sleep?

Every human being the world over deserves a great existence, and there are vast amounts of people who need to transform their philosophies. Each gender must pause and reconsider their beliefs, so they may truly honor another person's life.

Can we as human beings, possibly take a chance and help others by allowing them opportunities for their souls to grow and fly? And perhaps manifest their absolute destiny which they came to earth to create and live?

Let us all, whatever our gender and nationality, do our best to be the utmost loving and kindhearted person, that we possibly can be towards all mankind and all forms of life and energy here on earth and in heaven.

My story reflects my opinions of what I lived, believed, and experienced in my life and as God is my witness, this is the solemn TRUTH OF MY SOUL.

This is also my life and I own it.

I also wanted to clarify to anyone who is included in my true account, that if they aided in the shaping of the person that I became by either touching my soul positively or negatively, then they are mentioned in my story. I have not used any names or occupations and I have tried my best to protect all identities. My purpose is not to intentionally hurt or blame anyone. If my writings come across that way, I truthfully regret that, but as I looked back upon my passage, this is simply how my existence occurred.

My life was deeply agonizing for me to write about and relive repeatedly, but my commitment to it was for the greater good of anyone who might benefit from my experiences. In sharing my past years, I wanted others to see that gender inequality and abuse needs to be stopped, for on some level if these hurts continually happen, one begins believing in them. And this devastating reality eventually becomes etched within their very soul.

I deeply apologize if any of my story harms the memory of my parents, or brings discomfort to my children, my siblings, my ex spouse or his family. I needed to tell my entire account and one may not understand my reasoning, unless they follow through with my entire trilogy.

I have struggled with the publishing of my book for the past couple of years because I certainly didn't want to cause any of them any pain. In the end, my soul would not relent in its endless fight for my voice to be heard, because it knew and continuously reminded me, that this was a huge part of my destiny. I needed to speak out on behalf of other females who were powerless to do so, and to also show our world, that there is another way to create and live in peace.

We are all on earth for a purpose, and at some point in time, we must take a daring leap of faith and dive in, in order to take charge and be the creator of our own destinies.

In concluding, as we deal with our personal histories and we grow and shift, we must allow the newfound knowledge within us to change our negativities, our thoughts, and our life's into that of an empowered person, instead of being a lifelong victim of our circumstances. We can rise above and beyond, heal and forgive, and gain momentum from our pasts, even though, it may take decades for us to accomplish this feat, for that is how strong our hearts, spirits, and souls… truly are.

Bonny Billan
July 5, 2006
Victoria, British Columbia

TRILOGY

Book One

Preface

$\mathcal{I}$ finally came to the realization today, on October 28, 2000 at precisely 10:05 a.m. that the time was ripe at last. Yes, the moment had ultimately arrived for me to seriously begin the intense task of writing a book.

My endless burning desire to fulfill this wish was so deeply embedded within me, and this yearning had penetrated its cravings down to the great depths of my immortal soul. This creation was something that I wanted to give birth to for many lonely and agonizing years, and my delivery of it would encircle my lifelong battle for equality. It would also lend a voice to my cries of being spiritually hurt and unloved throughout many parts of my marriage. While also cautioning other women to be more aware than I had been, and not let this situation happen to them or continue to be a part of their lives.

My spirit had been constantly whispering to myself in a manner of a deafening awareness to pursue this venture. The more that I pushed the idea into the hidden recesses of my mind, the more that it leapt and pounced out at me. This haunting created an uneasiness in my soul which plagued me endlessly for almost a decade.

My dilemma continued alongside of my inner and outer worlds which had collided into each other screaming out repeatedly. I truly needed to determine the chaotic situation which was uprising deeply within me, and to understand all of the deep rooted facets of my past which had provoked this. The honest reality of my life had surfaced at last, as the aftermath of my nonstop mistreatment had erupted by thrusting itself from within the confines of my bruised and battered spirit. My harsh years had catapulted and ripped its way throughout my emotional and spiritual sense of wellbeing, and branched into my internal system before it finally burst out externally in a fierce explosion. I needed to uncover the untamed feelings which resided inside of my anguished mind, my fragmented heart, and my unloved pain filled body. The moment had come for me to confront all of the harsh judgments and injustices which had set my soul aflame, as it would no longer accept being hushed.

My struggles had actually begun upon my first breathe into this world, and have led me into a lifelong conflict and rebellion against my male dominated upbringing. I had been wounded over a matter of four decades, and I was angry from the constant accumulation of inequality between the genders which I had inhaled. Now my hurts and the aftermath of my deadly inflictions were demanding to be dealt with. Furthermore, I was equally and continually outraged, whenever I heard about any discrimination or anguish which other females had endured. As a result, of the ancient beliefs

3

of their ancestors and the authoritarian males who were living within their worlds.

Many of my issues would lead me back to my beginnings which were entwined within a one-sided masculine society. One which I have always felt while I was growing up had many rules and regulations, which were directed towards the oppression of women and the enforcement of this concept. Therefore because of this, I needed to expand the content of my writings, to include my childhood with all of its harsh realities which I had become so accustom to.

I started this undertaking to share my life story because I wanted females everywhere, to undoubtedly take note of the painful lessons which I had experienced. And I wanted them to comprehend, consider, and never repeat some of the choices which I had made, as they saved themselves and possibly others from what I had endured. While also vowing to deeply ingrain and arm themselves and their children with the knowledge, that they must never let anyone abuse them in any way, shape, or form. I wanted females to realize that they must never relent on having the courage to stand up for themselves. And to honestly be true and listen to what their hearts and souls were saying to them!

I was being commanded from beyond to fulfill my dream and end my years of silence. And as I did so, I embarked on a spiritual journey which I soon discovered I would have little control over. Furthermore I hoped that as I was frantically searching for any clues which might lead to the truth within my soul's past lifetime, this unique pathway would also help me to understand myself, so I could calm and change my spirit and release its deep heartache.

Once I realized that this new passage was getting to the root of my problems by enlightening me in regard to my inner self, my desire then became one of sharing that part of my life also. Lastly I wished to share my new found awareness and the miraculous situations which I encountered on a gifted pathway granted to me by God.

Over the course of the next ten years, the astounding "Awakening of My Soul" was very important for me to impart to others. I wanted to assist them in understanding their present and overcoming their past. And to recognize the spiritual side of themselves and others, while creating their future in a new reality of living within our universe.

My wish to create one book has become a trilogy which deals with cultural issues, gender inequality, male dominance, my childhood, marriage, joys, loneliness, abuse, betrayal, despair, strength, divorce, single parenting, courage, creating self-love, spiritual occurrences, gifts, Angels, miracles, heaven, accepting love, healing, the discovery and acceptance of my soul's purpose, and lastly, happiness and freedom for my soul while creating my heart's deepest desires.

Book 1- "The Truth of My Soul." This trilogy begins by focusing my hope, support, and encouragement for all females around our universe, as I honor and pay tribute to their soul's beauty and human rights for freedom, equality, and respect. I wanted to empower females of all ages while I offered awareness to males in all walks of life.

My story leads its way into my parent's harsh upbringings, my challenging childhood, my multifaceted marriage, and divorce. It covers this from the perspective of my life intertwined within my culture.

It also explains, "Why heaven first reached out to me," and "Why I began a spiritual pathway to search for my truth." Also included are my inspirations in a collection of poems, which I hope will stimulate others in regard to their Unique Journeys of Self-Discovery. While also increasing their Insight into the Awareness, the Awakening, and the Purpose of Mankind on a Human and Spiritual level.

Book 2- "The Truth of My Soul II," continues in "Conversations With A Tibetan Monk." My journey proceeds as my spiritual growth expands in the healing discussions which took place between my spiritual teacher and I, over a ten year period. (1995-2005) This was in regard to my life lessons, struggles, astonishing spiritual experiences, transformations, and discovering the intellect of a soul and its link with the human body, that it lives within.

Our conversations took place through trance channeling which involves a qualified person going into a trance, and one from the spiritual realm speaks through them. In my consultations, a gifted woman named Emily went into a trance and a 300 hundred year old Tibetan Monk emerged, and spoke through her to me. He knew all about me, even though, I had never met either of them before.

Within this section of the story, the monk's words of wisdom are explained in correlation with the mind, body, and soul connection. It clarifies some of the many stages a soul travels in relation to living as a human being, in regard to life and life after death. And it displays this by using the aspects of my life, as a model to help others in understanding their soul's passage in heaven and on earth. It also gives an insight into the deep level of healing that needs to take place after years of hurt and abuse.

My experiences will undoubtedly show, that one's soul never dies, as love from heaven continues to touch my world even further in huge proportions. Many people will truly appreciate the GREAT LOVE and the MAGNITUDE OF BLESSINGS which came to me, as they witness the events and the loving souls who reached out from beyond, to help heal my soul.

The MIRACULOUS CONNECTION and WISDOM from this realm, will greatly assist others in their search and understanding between THE

HUMAN BEING AND SOUL RELATIONSHIP. This is especially in regard to, WHO THEY TRULY ARE, WHAT A SOUL REALLY CONSISTS OF, and WHAT A SOUL'S PURPOSE IS?

My healing concludes as the revelation of my soul's purpose is uncovered and as I stand before the gates of heaven, my decade long search for my deepest truth comes to light.

Continue with me in "Book 2" if you would like a better understanding of your soul's journey and the heavenly world of love, healing, and growth from a intriguing realm. Begin to walk in the light and discover how to create your own miracles and one day, you too, may connect with heaven.

Book 3- "The Truth of My Soul III," concludes in "Desires, Destiny, and Love." My rebirth begins as I embrace my newly discovered destiny and I truly begin to live "The Truths Of My Soul." New astounding situations flow from heaven, as my God given gifts continue to reveal themselves. I also share my heart's desires, healing, and miracles in an array of poems which I wrote to highlight my journey.

Finally, as my deepest desires and long awaited reunion with a destined soul mate seems to be on the horizon, my heart joins my mind, body, and soul in a unified loving connection, as it truly considers loving another again.

My story continues as God grants me the chance to re-unite with two of the greatest loves of my soul's entire existence. Would my heart truly desire one of these men for this lifetime or would I be guided towards a new love? Follow along as our hearts and souls re-connect, and thrusts me into a head spin as my senses whirl out of control for both of them.

Join me with anticipation in the finale of my passage, as my heart dives into the happiest and most turbulent sensations that any soul can experience... love, lust, and sensuous desires.

From the start of this journey, I was in pursuit of absolute independence from my past. I was not about to surrender, until I had won in my enduring saga for my complete and supreme freedom victoriously in an emotional, spiritual, mental, verbal, intuitive, and physical manner. My determination was to continue until my heart, mind, body, and soul were truly united and positively connecting on each and every one of these levels, for only at this point, could I breathe easily. And I'd carry on until I had triumphantly conquered and released all of the ghosts within the deepest parts of my soul, and discovered the whole purpose of my birth. However long it took me, I was going to persevere until I achieved a final outcome of happiness and peace.

It was the utmost of importance for me, to not only create and guide my destiny, but to awaken and beckon others to the transformation of theirs also, so they would be the ultimate reigning force within their lives today and tomorrow.

Allow this trilogy to inspire you to truly awaken and begin to search for the truth within the heart of your soul, so one day, you may Discover the True Purpose of your Birth, Begin to Live your Soul's Promise, and Create your Deepest Dreams and Desires with Love.

Introduction

I had a powerful force within me to produce a book which would alert and inform other females in regard to my male dominated life experiences. This underlying theme had constantly forced itself onto me, but I never seemed to be able to put aside the great amount of time which was needed to accomplish this tenacious task. I thought about this endeavor every day, as I hoped that the journals which I had kept over the past fifteen years would at some point in time, be the book that my screaming soul desperately wanted, needed, and someday would create.

One day recognizing, that my moments on earth were quickly slipping away and I was no closer to composing the project that my soul was crying out for, I asked God for help.

I said, "Please help me find the time to write my book."

Little did I realize that my life was about to come to a halt. Two hours later while I was sitting in my parked car conversing with one of my sons, an older woman backed into the rear end of my vehicle and fled from the scene. The result of this, left me with quite a bad case of whiplash and I was bedridden for weeks. I had a non-stop stinging pain on the side of my neck, shoulder, and back area which was accompanied by terrible headaches and nausea. And to add insult to injury, the insurance corporation said that, "There was not a sufficient amount of impact to have caused such an injury," so there was no compensation from them!

My son was also in the car and he was even closer to the accident than I was, but he suffered no injuries at all, for the incident was sent directly to me from God!

It was suffice to say, that my prayer had been answered and the saying, "Be careful what you wish for," rang in my ears.

Three weeks later, I propped myself up in bed armed with a heated bean bag for my neck, a water bottle, Tylenol 3, and a pain relaxant for my back, and I seriously began writing my book. I was either high or crazy, I don't know which, but nothing was going to stop me from my project.

My dream had begun and I hoped that as I shared my story it would be beneficial and caution other women about matters of the heart. I wanted to enlighten them about my negative experiences relating to my relationships with the opposite gender. Furthermore I had a deep desire to warn other females in regard to the inequality, domination, and unjust behavior which I had endured in my marriage.

Once I began writing, it forced me to look at my earliest years as a child and to re-evaluate them with an open honesty of truly seeing, the truth of my family dynamics in which I was influenced. I had to admit out loud, just how harmful my childhood truly was for me and not ignore the reality, that the females in our home were not treated equally to the males. This disturbing way of life was the ultimate belief of most of the adults within my community. And the traditional mindset that women and men were never equal in any situation, was how many of us were raised. The idea that MALES WERE SUPERIOR to FEMALES was the unsettling basis of my youth, and my refusal to accept this turned into a lifelong battle which I fought against in every way possible.

I had grown up being a strong female who was outspoken at times, and I distinctly remember how my father tried his best to keep me silent. It was his mission to put me in my place and he carried it out by belittling me every chance that he had. Years later I realized, that much of the same had taken place with my spouse.

Two of the most important males in my life turned out to be the cruelest people that I had ever met. And at times, they did their utmost to try and break my spirit and sense of well being. Thirty-eight years later, all of the pain which I had experienced began to rapidly surface as my spirit began to scream out. My heart was shattering to the center of my very soul, as my body began drowning in a cesspool of sludge from the spiritual, emotional, verbal, and mental negativity which I had endured for almost four decades.

The passion to write about my life was spurred on because I wanted my voice to be heard by females and to support those, who were powerless to speak up for themselves. And to bring an understanding to some of the dilemmas that they were living through. I wanted to speak out on behalf of women and children who have endured and tolerated dictatorship, under the controlling rule of their own ethnic societies, families, and men which they had come into contact with.

I had a desire to express myself on behalf of the female population, whose destiny at birth was to have their exclusive right to equality, fairness, and freedom, snatched away from them because of the gender that they were born. I needed to speak for people who had their virtuous spirits crushed and stampeded on, down to the deepest depth of their souls. And I wanted to recognize, the women and children who are in debilitating situations and have experienced great hopelessness, gut wrenching pain, and sadness throughout their everyday lives.

I truly wished to seek out females whose spirits had been ripped away from them. Thus leaving them devastated, down trodden, and broken, only to face the reality, that their life's had been tossed into the carefree winds to be carried millions of miles away from them. I wanted to speak out towards anyone, who had a somewhat duplicated scenario as myself, and to those who had experienced even the slightest amount.

I also needed to inspire women with the thought that being born a FEMALE also GIVES THEM THE RIGHT TO LIVE AND

BREATHE FREELY. I wanted to help them to understand that they have the right to exist without the bindings of outdated beliefs and teachings, which are constantly being subjected towards them. All because of the out of touch reality and sometimes, selfish behavior of many males within their lives.

Females of all ages have had their very souls tortured and shredded apart throughout this great world of ours, and this is completely unacceptable especially in this day and age. The atrocious rituals that females are being forced to endure must somehow be stopped and completely discarded. In certain societies, this gender has undergone extremely incomprehensible acts that are so hard to even imagine. One of these atrocities is female circumcision which is often compared to male castration. Genital mutilation is the act of young females having all or part of their genitals cut off as part of an ancient tradition. And even more inconceivable, are the many young babies and children that are being raped because of some males who believe, that if they are with a virgin, they will be spared from having aids.

I recently saw a documentary about a certain country, whereby if a woman is raped, she must produce four eye witnesses to this invasion of her body, before the offender can be tried for the offence. She can have him charged for the crime, but if it is not proven to be correct, she can then be charged with adultery. Furthermore, any woman that speaks up for herself or other women, and attempts to change the rules of this country, are often humiliated in public for trying to support other females.

In parts of India some males are taking extremely selfish and unbelievable advantages of women. They are doing this by marrying them, only after their parent's have scrimped together a huge dowry for their daughter's upcoming marriages. Once they are wed, their groom takes all of the assets and abandons his wife and returns back to the country where he resided before his marriage. He leaves his bride heartbroken and hugely disillusioned, as he's shattered her beliefs towards a happy union. While also destroying her reputation and everyday life, for these women usually never remarry again.

Are all of the brutal measures which are taken against women, beliefs that are being passed down from one generation to another, or are the regulations being changed along the way? If any hard edged men put themselves in women's shoes for even a day, would any of them ever want to be dealt with in the same way that they treat females? Would any of them welcome inequality, male domination, or abuse in its many deplorable forms? Would they like their self esteem and souls torn to shreds?

Have the leaders of certain countries honestly tried to change outdated laws and introduce new ways of thinking regarding the treatment of females, or on some level, have they simply been trying to silence outspoken women, who are trying to transform the lives of others?

What is it, that many in the masculine gender are so worried about concerning women? Why do we pose such a threat to them? Could they be worried, that if the female gender are given the same opportunities, the same education to increase their awareness, and expand their thoughts, that women may go beyond and eventually outrank them?

I know that when I began writing my story years ago, in certain countries it was felt that females didn't need to be schooled. And education for them was practically non-existent. If by chance females were fortunate enough to come into contact with a teaching institute, quite often their educational process had to be hidden in order to not offend their oppressors. Once again, this repressive role of women having to live within this concept was that of utter male domination and intervention was greatly needed. It's wonderful that this has changed for several females the world over, but there is much more change that needs to take place in other countries regarding education for females.

My deepest desire is to get the attention of as many disrespected young girls, teenagers, and women as I can from around our world, and to somehow, convince them, that their current abusive life is not acceptable in any way, shape, or form. And they must try to do all that they can to help bring about major positive changes by discontinuing to accept their lives the way that they currently are.

I am hoping that my story will reach those who most need to hear it at this point in time. And in some way, something from my life may touch a part of their souls and urge them to not give up on themselves. I will continue to have faith that they may be embraced by my kindred spirit. And as my strength sinks into their psyche, they will begin to be stirred, so that a spark ignites within them until a tiny flame grows. As a result, one day they will realize that they have a full-blown fire raging and racing within, to spur them on to considering improving their lives from the painful situations that their souls have forced them to face.

Most importantly is that I wish for everyone, whatever their age, gender or ethnicity, is to hear my pleadings and begin to scream out and say, "No! I will not live like this anymore! I will not, even for one second longer, live and accept anymore mistreatment! My pain will stop now and I will put an end to the lack of respect and inequality that you have shown me! I am not the person that you are trying to shape and mould me to be! I have a brain of my own to think with, even though, I have been told for many years that I do not!"

All females must also get to the point of believing and repeating a certain phrase to themselves from this moment forward, "I will never subject myself to any abuse nor will I be in the company of anyone who shows me any disrespect whatsoever, FOR I DESERVE AND DEMAND, KINDNESS AND RESPECT!"

This new action will begin to change their destinies forever.

I realize that this is very difficult to do, but females of various ages must begin to believe and dig deep within themselves, to find their inner might and hold on a bit longer to their sparsely scattered spirits. After that point, they can very slowly ease themselves forward and progress towards making drastic life altering changes, because their souls have truly begun to awaken and their power is becoming alive. This will inject a new possibility and intent into their world, which they long ago realized was spinning deeply and sadly out of control. No one deserves the irrational behavior of others selfish and ancient reasoning which is mainly for their own personal gain.

Everyone needs to comprehend, that change does not happen overnight and that their recovery may take quite a long time to achieve. This will depend on what they have endured and for however long it has occurred. One also needs to decide, exactly how deep they wish to go with their healing.

Does one want a complete recovery or just a band aid solution on the surface because unless they go to the root of their dilemmas, certain issues will continue to repeat themselves throughout their lives. They will continue to draw to themselves the same types of individuals and situations which they tried to break away from, unless they deal with it once and for all.

I am hoping that by considering my story, females will recognize that they will eventually proceed onto a state of recovery from the callous and vindictive insensitivities of their plights. And along with their determination, they will continue to be propelled towards a new way of living which they have never really encountered before within their lifetimes.

However, as hard as one tries to heal their wounds, will the complete violations of the scars on their souls and the inflictions which were thrust upon them as unequal female counterparts, ever disappear? Will females who have endured male dominated situations ever think of themselves as being equal to men? Will they ever come into contact with and enjoy the company of the opposite gender, who respectfully and sincerely believe that females are honestly their equals? Will we as a gender, ever be able to completely rid ourselves of this human injustice which is plaguing billions of females every second of the day around our world? If not, will this biting and imposing thought follow women coldly to their graves? Will your destiny have the same inevitable ending as that of your great, great ancestors, your grandmothers, and perhaps even your mother or will your ending be different?

The choice is yours! It all starts with you, as you begin to change your way of thinking and set yourself in motion to make the necessary changes in creating your new life.

If you don't attempt to transform your world, whose vision are you really living out? Is it your parents, your husbands, or someone else's beliefs and wishes that they had for you? When was the last time that you truly considered, what you wanted out of your life? Are you going through the motions of everyday living just to get you by? Are you happy at all or do you wish that you were dead? We each have a life to live and we each deserve the right to enjoy it and get the most out of it. Perhaps your moment is now here to begin your pathway of discovering your true inner spirit and its calling, so you can above all else, create your dreams one by one. And manifest only those wishes, which will truly make you happy.

I know that a lot of women have chosen to stay at home and raise their families, but at the same time they need to start thinking about what they want out of their lives. They need to begin with small steps and make a plan to put into motion for when they are able to carry it out. Also even though, one's family consumes so much of their time and energy, just thinking about what they want will put a bright and new force into their days.

Every so often, do something to create your vision and your dreams may become a reality, sooner than you think. I realize that having children is also a dream come true, but one can have an even richer life when they are also fulfilling the promise that they gave to their soul.

Therefore, how long will you be able to survive in your prison of inequality? Will you ever escape? It takes a great amount of courage to start, but even more than that, it takes the act of starting to love yourself enough to begin this climb up your highest mountain. For without self-love, what do we really consist of? You need to initiate your changes now, for you have a destiny which is close to your heart to accomplish.

Beginning in my childhood and through to my adulthood, my consistent trait is that I have always spoken up for myself, no matter how badly I was treated afterwards. And even though my strength often led to unkindness, bullying, and misery, and my words may have fallen onto deaf ears, I would not, nor will I ever, relent and silence my voice for respect towards myself or anyone else.

We must all learn to speak up for ourselves for everything begins within us and if we don't, who will come to our rescue? We must try to do this and change the situations that we are in, and learn how to nurture and love our souls, before the spirit within us completely dies.

Every human being has a story to tell and many are filled with unhappiness, inequality, abuse, and domination. When will your injustices stop, and when will your soul's story change? Only you, hold the power to do this, deep within your soul.

Many males around our world believe that their feelings of superiority towards females is actually their right, and that they are without a doubt, the cleverest and absolute ultimate. However, how much of our world will be destroyed because of wars, bombs, and the battling which is raging against millions of innocent people because of the selfish and destructive mentality of others? I have to wonder, that if more women were to take the lead and rise to the highest positions in the world, would it be in such a catastrophic state of devastating proportions? What do you think?

Women from all around our communities, our cities, our countries, and our entire globe must embark on a journey to equal freedom. This can begin by introducing love, new beliefs, dreams, support, and kindness especially towards all womanhood. We must come together and connect ourselves in harmony, so we can invade on the trespassers of our lives, our souls, and of our worlds. This will be the moment in your history to remember, that you made a difference not only throughout the sisterhood within your lives, but also for future generations. As your energy lends support and hope for our entire universe.

I often think about how awful life is for so many people and in those moments, more than ever, I pray for them. I pray for the less fortunate whether their plight is because of poverty, medical disabilities, misfortune, or because they were born in a certain part of our world. Whenever I am out driving and I see any child, teenager, woman, or man walking alone, I pray for protection for them. Each night I ask GOD to encircle our world from the bottom to the top with pink healing love and the white light of protection for all. I continue praying for that love to reach everyone, and I ask for that love and light to continue up throughout our universe.

I realize that there are so many kind individuals around our world who have helped a great deal of people. However, is it not possible for many more to unite together to make a true difference into the unjustified and miserable existence of others? We can all further the help which we give with our prayers, if we join together with others to blanket our world with that love. This will create a huge difference because our positive warmth and thoughts, will send even bigger shimmering beams of love and light towards healing all. With the time differences throughout our universe, there should never be a moment that our world is not protected by many loving people.

I have opened my heart and shared it with you, for I feel my years must have had a greater purpose contained within them, other than the growth to my soul. I am sharing the hardships of my past and the lessons which I learnt upon my journey, with a desire for my life to touch many females. I wish to give them hope, light, and an abundance of my love, which transfers into giving them the strength and the power to carry on, until they too can find their path to freedom.

The formatting of this book reflects my personal vision. I self published my work, so my messages could not in any way be altered or stifled, but rather continue to flow in all honesty from my heart to yours.

I apologize for any grammatical errors, I am simply a woman who decided to write a book and do it her own way.

Herein lies the unfolding chapters of my soul which contains my tears and sorrow, along with the miraculous evolution which took place down to the core of my very being, so I could discover "The Truth of My Soul."

Tribute to Women

This book is a tribute to all of the courageous women who have endured hardships
and the misery of existence throughout our history.
They are our ancestors and our mothers, who grew to be great pillars of strength.
I praise this special gender, who have held their own against the mighty forces
around them, so future generations would have a higher quality of life.
Women that I applaud, who have dared to be different
and stood up to much opposition.
I also give my respect to the bold and brave females from around our world,
who are currently suffering horrendous injustices.
As well as, to the diligent women who have battled through life in order
to raise their families when in fact, it was almost unbearable for them to do so.
Females have persevered on behalf of their children because the lives that
they have created and sustained within, are as much a part of them as their limbs.
Women of all nationalities have carried the brunt of the male's ego for centuries.
Many have been the tormented recipients of the harmful beliefs passed down
from their predecessors, while continuing to support the males within their worlds.
These females never give up, even though, their daily living is a complete agony
and is often filled with many abuses and deplorable treatment.
Millions of people have realized the urgency to halt the deep rooted beliefs
of long ago, and know that it must cease to exist.
We as females, must never stop finding the ways to change the behavior
of many of our male counterparts.
We must continue to work towards building a new equality
between the two genders, that several of us have never known.
Women of all cultures need to be proud of themselves
as they have experienced numerous trials throughout their lives.
They have survived to carry on because deep within them
is a powerful mountain of courage and fortitude, filled with a massive
amount of unselfishness which beckons them to never surrender.
God created females and a great many of us have had first hand
experience in knowing, that we are not meek or mild and perhaps,
the more gallant gender in the universe.
As a female... I ask you, how often have you given your power away?
The time is now here, to take back, what is rightfully yours!
What will you teach your daughters about being a female in today's world?
Courage, Strength, Self-Respect, Love, and Compassion...oh yes,
but perhaps more importantly... Respect and Equality from all!

Bonny Billan

What Is The Truth Of Your Soul?

Our moments here on earth, should be filled with love, joy, and peace.
Each one of us has a specific intention for being here,
 which has a significant meaning within it.
 We have all come to learn our different lessons, increase our knowledge,
 and share the wisdom which lies deep within us.
  All of which we gain within this lifetime will further the development
  of our souls and will continue to be apart of us, as we are constantly reborn.
   What is your purpose for existing in this universe?
   Have you discovered it yet?
   If not, will you take the chance to explore and fulfill your destiny?
    Every human should strive to add to the world
    and our kindness should touch many.
     The heart of our spirit above all else, beckons us to love and respect,
     but we must first be true to ourselves and then to others.
      We need not settle for anything less for we all deserve the very best.
      We must realize, that in all of our relationships whether it is with family,
      partners, or friends, it should feel right and be filled to the brim
       with trust and free of any type of abuse.
       Don't be silent; let your voice be heard.
       Too many of us are in intolerable situations and we have
       lost our way, our spirits, and forsaken our souls.
        We have forgotten our dreams.
        We have let go of what we truly wanted within our lives,
        and what we wished to create and achieve.
         What was your heartfelt desire?
         Search and find your beckoning star.
          Let your voice be heard.
          Exhale… who you really are.
          Live out the truth of your soul.

Bonny Billan.

19

Have You Found Your Beckoning Star?

A moonlit night,
gaze up to marvel.
A sky filled with glistening stars…
too many to count.

There's a bright one in the distance.
It's calling out to you, as it is coming closer.
Listen… it knows your name.
Ahhhhhhhhhh it's beautiful.

There is a reason, why it found you.
Your moment is now here.
Reach out and take hold.

Bonny Billan

Dreamer

Set sail for a new journey.
Be a dreamer and never relent.
Visualize something much greater then you ever thought possible,
and as a different pathway begins to manifest itself,
realize that your life is truly changing.
Step out into your world which you created,
your new destiny awaits you.

Bonny Billan

Beauty

Beauty is in the eye of the beholder.
Many times it is only skin deep.
Our soul and what it consists of… is our beauty.
It is that, which one should truly be concerned with.
The depth of our soul and what flows from it… love,
kindness, generosity, and unselfishness
are the attributes of our true soul's beauty.
What is the beauty of your soul?
What is your beauty?

Bonny Billan

25

Judgment

One of the strongest characteristics of a human being is in judging others.
When we are doing this, we should stop and ask ourselves,
"Why am I being so critical?
What gives me the right to think, that I am so much better than them?"

If we truly consider life, and all that has passed before us,
we may have already experienced the same situation
which someone else is going through now.
It was just in a different time, in a different place, in a different lifetime.

We need to remember that this time around, we have not stood in the
worn out shoes of anyone else or crept along their weary miles.
Nor have our hearts felt the stabbing of their pain
or the weight that they carry within their life.
We have not felt their fears, wept their tears,
or gone through the despair within their tattered spirits.

Have we forgotten all of which we truly have… our children, family,
friends, good fortune, a home, safety, protection, love, and light?
All of which equals, much abundance within our lives.

Is it not possible to send people in need, our compassion
instead of our negativity, gossip, or ridicule?

Why not ask for love and healing to surround them and be a part
of their everyday life, and then ask for it to come into yours.
Ask for your soul to wake up and send only that positive energy
onto the four corners of our universe!

Bonny Billan

What Is A Soul?

Did you know that your soul is inside of you?
If you look deep into your eyes, you may experience the feeling
of something looking back out at you… this is your soul.

Everyone's eyes are the surest way to peek at their souls,
you can tell a lot about a person by peering into theirs.
One can see truth, mistrust, hurt, depression, or fear
and who to beware.

Why do we have a soul?
It is within to inspire and guide us to a smoother life,
as it tries to help us deal with our past life strife.
This is often quite a task, and if you start this path,
you may one day say, "Why did I even begin to ask?"

Your soul wants to continue in its growth,
so it is constantly being reborn.
Once true enlightenment has been achieved,
it will remain from whence it came,
to help many in heaven on their stairways.

Now and then, I get an uncomfortable feeling,
this happens if I am with one, who is untruthful and needs healing,
or if they're not with me for my higher good and learning.
It is in these times, I find it hard to look into the mirror,
for I can sense that my soul wants me to steer clear.
Other times I get a terrible feeling deep within me,
and it is awfully loud as can be.

At times I ignore my spiritual help, because I don't want to hurt
anyone's feelings, and I am practicing my free will.
However my soul is trying to caution me and say something big,
I need to honor it more, for it's always with me and never out of range.
Its deepest desires are for me to STOP, LISTEN, and CHANGE!
Guess I need to stop being such a human being,
and take the loving help that God has provided me,
so I can live this life as a true spiritual being.

Bonny Billan

The Mirrors Of Your Soul

When you look at your face in the mirror,
do you like what you see there?
Do you ever wonder, how it became so full of sadness and fear,
or if the answers will ever become clear?

Really gaze at the image in the mirror.
If you look deep within your eyes,
truly all your answers lie in there.
Your soul is calling out and it wants to be heard,
it's urging you, to wake up and listen.

As you look through these windows to your soul,
truly connect with the inner guidance that is speaking out to you.
Deep down, you know that things could be better.
Take a leap of faith and challenge yourself
to create the life you truly desire.
Then proceed with all the courage and strength
you have, in order to succeed.

One day when you look at the reflection in the mirror,
you'll see, that much of your pain has actually disappeared.
I promise you, you'll even see some relief and happiness there.

If you have a decision to make, look into the mirror,
for you now know, all your answers lie in there.
Look into those eyes, the greatest mirrors that we have,
and peak into the deepest depths of your entire being.
Listen to what your soul is saying to you... yes... sight unseen.

Bonny Billan

Endless Possibilities

What do I visualize as I gaze out to sea?
I see peace, hope, and endless possibilities.
This is what this scene does for me,
for at these times, I know I can be absolutely everything.

What landscapes do you need around you,
so you can imagine your dreams too?
Reach out and grasp them deep within your palms,
know you can achieve anything before very long.

As I look high above the ocean blue,
I touch God's hands and see heaven in its beautiful hues.
I also see you standing right beside me,
and you are looking very happy.

Just one more thing before I go,
we are surrounded by Angels, who want you to know,
they are proud you had the courage and the guts,
to show yourself and others, what you are truly made of.

Bonny Billan

Dream, Wish, and Believe

I once wished upon a star,
this I sent right from my heart.
Little did I truly know,
that God was listening in on me too.
He spoke to Angels near and far,
who had always been protecting my star.
To truly bless and help me manifest,
all that I needed to achieve my best.
So they sprinkled stardust all over me,
now I could be absolutely anything.
I must never forget, that as my desires come true,
that they were actually guiding me through.
MIRACLES happen for those,
who dare to DREAM, WISH, and of course... BELIEVE!

Bonny Billan

*It doesn't matter, what gender you are born
or whatever your circumstances may be.
Your destiny is not set in stone,
take a chance and change yours!*

– BONNY BILLAN –

"A Chance"

Chapter 1

$\mathcal{I}$t was a beautiful sunny Saturday morning on February 5, 1955 and even though the dawn had barely opened its sleepy eyes, it promised to be a brazenly gorgeous day.

Birds chirped throughout the awakening city as delivery vans began their daily routes. The hustle and bustle on the public streets of Vancouver, British Columbia had just started, but the day had already begun elsewhere for quite sometime. The calm and hushed atmosphere here had long ago disappeared, as the large room with its beaming, bright lights, and cool metal instruments was full of lively activity. The staff at Vancouver General Hospital had taken the necessary precautions and were now awaiting the piercing sounds to come forth, as the delivery room was about to surrender its sterile setting to the birth of twins.

The first birth occurred quite easily and a healthy, hardy baby boy weighing almost 7 lbs. was born bellowing away. His mother barely had time to catch her breath, when the next birth began a few seconds later. It did not go as well.

This delivery was strenuous and it was apparent that something was wrong. The infant was in distress and it seemed to be suffocating while trying to emerge through the birth canal. After three minutes of intense struggling, a baby girl weighing 6 lbs. 7 oz. arrived at exactly 5:53 a.m. to join her brother.

She was gasping as she fought for her first breath and her coloring was anything other than normal. The doctors rushed about trying to save the newborn, but the situation was grave and it showed on their faces. They explained to the infant's parents, that the diagnosis was that it would be very difficult for her to overcome the possibility of survival. The next forty-eight hours would be crucial in determining her fate and they classified her as, "A Chance Baby."

The infant fought to live. She made it through the first two days and each day after that she showed her strength and will to survive, as she became even stronger. By the end of their hospital stay, the baby girl had beaten the odds and together the twins went home.

They joined their parents, two older sisters, two older brothers and their black and white spotted dog Sporty, at their home which was at 3162 Grant Street. It was a few blocks away from the future dwelling of the Pacific National Exhibition Park.

One of the babies had hazel eyes and the other dark brown eyes and they both had a mop of unruly jet black hair on their tiny heads. These two innocent babies were of East Indian descent. And they would have distinctly different upbringings, even though, they were brought up by the same parents in the same home for the first twenty years of their lives. The great distinction in the way that they were to be raised would be astronomical and at times very heartless, all because they were different genders.

The male child would be shown an enormous amount of love, attention, and favoritism and his every wish would be granted. Unfortunately the female child would not experience anything remotely resembling the kindness which was bestowed upon her brother and she asked for nothing!

He was a great source of pride to his parents and he was praised, pampered, and highly regarded, but she was constantly demeaned, criticized, and considered inferior. She felt left out and didn't receive much love or attention from either of her parents. As well as, for many years her two older sisters were not very kind to her either. While this female was growing up she was constantly called names that she didn't like or even know the meaning of, but she knew that they were not words of love. She often wondered what she had done to deserve all of their unkindness and she wanted it to stop.

As she got older, she was told that when she was a baby and her family went away for a few days, she was often left behind to stay at their housekeeper's home while they all went off together. She questioned from time to time, if she was actually born into this clan. Her older sisters had told her many times, that she was adopted and of Oriental descent since her eyes were smaller than theirs. She can remember going through the family album to see if there were any baby pictures of her and there were. However that didn't prove anything, for they had also told her twin that he too was adopted. The difference was that he received so much kind heartedness while she was often the recipient of her family's ridicule.

She noticed all the consideration which was given to her brother. He was showered with toys and received different bikes during the various stages of his childhood. He was even given a new car upon his high school graduation. She was never given one bike and she was the only child in the family who would never receive one. Also for her graduation she was given nothing, but she too wanted something special to mark this milestone in her life. Hence she told her mother that they were going to Birks jewelry store and once there, she was going to buy her daughter a silver charm bracelet and an engraved charm to honor this occasion. Her mother was surprised, but she smiled and agreed to the request. A couple of the siblings were married by this time, and she and her mom had become quite close.

The seeds which were vital to the nurturing of her soul had been planted and for twenty years, they were nourished with a harsh sense of rigid negativity. And although the molding of her self-esteem was cast in stone, her self respect was still very evident and the smothering of her flame had failed to be extinguished. Her soul had fought through much to survive and she remained strong and fairly happy, as her laughter could always be heard. This child's father had constantly tried to stifle her and take away her strength, but he never succeeded and his callousness only gave her even more power and determination.

Throughout her childhood, she always felt that she was very different and her feelings of not really belonging to this family had greatly intensified. She had not been accepted in many ways, and a part of her always felt like an outsider looking in on them from her world. The contrasting ways that the infant's relatives and others within their male dominated community had embraced these two babies differed greatly. This significant distinction presented the twins with very different destinies, as the male would be greatly received and the female would have to repeatedly prove herself.

I am that female baby. Little did I know that the foreshadowing of my birth would only be the beginning of the struggles which would lie ahead for me, as my life as a fighter had begun. Over time, my battles would vastly increase as the female inequality and war cries throughout my existence, would eventually scream and twist its way to the surface of my very being. Now decades later, this is my heartfelt story, but first let's go back to the start with my parent's beginnings.

Bonny - 2 years old

It all begins here as you will read,
what my parents lives were like, before I was even a seed.
They both had very rough beginnings,
and lived in a time period, where no one considered their needs.

– BONNY BILLAN –

My Parents

Chapter 2

*M*y father, Gurdave (Dave) Singh Billan was born in India on September 10, 1918 in a small village named Raipur Dabba. He lived there with his parents Bunthi Kaur and Baudharm Singh and his two siblings, a brother and a sister. There were also other children, but unfortunately they passed on at quite an early age. My grandfather was a hard worker as he toiled in the sugarcane fields and sugarcane was my dad's all time favorite treat.

In 1932 at the age of thirteen, my dad began an amazing new journey as he said goodbye to his family and traveled by ship to live in Vancouver, British Columbia. This was a very brave thing for him to do since he was so young and he had never been on a ship before, let alone, a huge one. He must have been very frightened to not only leave his country, but his family and home behind too, not really knowing when he would ever reunite with them again.

Just imagine in that day and age, what it would have felt like to sail off into the deep blue waters not really knowing, what to expect as the ocean surrounded the moving vessel which you were on. As well as, when you looked back to the shoreline, you slowly saw your family and home land disappear, till you eventually saw no land anywhere at all.

His passage was very rough and the accommodations for him and all of the Sikh immigrants were of the bare minimum and the least desirable. The ship stopped for a layover in Hong Kong, and somehow my dad lost the money that he needed for the continuation of his voyage. Consequently he had to live for awhile at the Sikh Temple in this city until more money could be sent to him.

When my dad finally arrived in Vancouver he went to live with his tough, disciplinarian uncle and his family. Upon entering his home, this man beat him because of the loss of his fare. My dad used to say that his uncle was a very tough man and one had to tow the line with him or else.

My father was put into a grade one class at Henry Hudson School, even though, he was thirteen years old. This may have been done to enable him to learn to speak and write English from the very beginning stages. He left school a short time later to sell wood with his uncle on his truck and they worked for very long hours. My dad labored a lot harder at this job than he ever would have had he continued in school. His new destiny had begun as mine was still in the making.

My mother Malchete (Mary) was born on June 28, 1928 in New Westminister, British Columbia. She was the second eldest of five children that consisted of three girls and two boys and they all lived on the family's farm in Queensborough. Her parents Naranjan Kaur and Rama Singh had emigrated from India to Canada, and her mother was one of the first women from India to take this huge step to a uncharted life.

My grandfather had a trucking business and one day while he was working on his truck, it burst into flames. As a result, the ghastly incident was fatal as he caught on fire and died. After this happened, my mother's life changed dramatically. She had to stop her education at Queen Elizabeth School to help out on their farm. The livelihood of her family needed to take precedence over her schooling, even though, she was only twelve years old. On that day her life as a child stopped, as her cruel fate stepped in and she quickly became a young adult. Since my grandfather's horrible accident, my grandmother had a hard life as she raised her five children alone.

My parents wed on August 4, 1946 in an arranged marriage which was held at the Sikh temple in New Westminister. My dad was twenty six years old and my mother was eighteen years old. They lived in Queensborough for awhile and before long my father bought a home on Grant Street in Vancouver.

They began their family with a son, and eleven months later my mother gave birth to her first daughter who they named Nana. She was a beautiful baby with quite fair skin, hazel colored eyes, and curly dark brown hair. Unfortunately she was born with a hole in her heart. This condition classified her as a "blue baby" and regrettably months later, she passed on from it.

Their third child was a daughter, and thirteen months later, their second son was born followed by another daughter eleven months after that. Three years later, my brother and I were born and my mother now had six children to take care of. She was fortunate enough to be able to hire a housekeeper to help her out around the house.

My father left early in the morning for work and he was back late at night. Over a period of time, he became a business man who climbed his way up the ladder of success. Needless to say, my mother and all of the mothers of that era raised their children single handedly. The demands of their home life, family's wellbeing, and nurturing fell completely on the shoulders of these persevering and strong hard working women.

My Dad's Parents - Dec. 28, 1951

My Mother's Parents & My Mom - Nov. 1928

My Mother 18 years old — 1946

So many children, where will I fit in?
I don't know, maybe I won't.
I'll try my best and see what will be,
but one thing is for certain, one day I shall truly be me!

– BONNY BILLAN –

My Beginnings

Chapter 3

One day in the summer of 1959, my dad asked all of the children in our family to vote on whether we wanted to move or not.

We all said, "Yes."

He had already made the decision to do so and this was just his way of telling us about it.

I was only four years old, but I'll always remember the day that we moved into our big and beautiful new home. It was in a prominent area in Vancouver and my parents bought all new furnishings for most of the rooms. There were four levels which provided a lot of space for all of us, and that was a good thing because my mother was expecting her eighth child. Four months later, she gave birth to a daughter which completed their family of nine.

My mom was always a very strong and determined woman and her main goal in life was the complete dedication to raising her family. She was the hardest working person that I had ever met and throughout our childhood she enforced that trait in all of her children. She was up at the crack of dawn cleaning this and that, while her china teacup filled with Nabob Tea was cooling on the kitchen counter.

Our home was absolutely immaculate and it was always sparkling and yes, it was so clean that you could eat off the kitchen floor! She cleaned in every sense of the word and as far back as I can remember, she was either baking, cooking, cleaning, doing laundry, decorating, painting, canning, gardening, or sewing.

My mothers favorite past time was knitting or crocheting and she always had a project on the go. She created sweaters and jackets for her children and several baby outfits and blankets for many new arrivals. However, her first concern was towards the wellbeing of her children. I'll never know how she found the energy to take care of all of us and everything else too. Every so often, she was either rearranging furniture or painting a room in the house, even though, none of the rooms needed painting because this was a new home. My mom was the best at whatever she did and there was absolutely nothing that she couldn't do.

One day when I was five years old and she was on the phone, I went into the refrigerator and I started touching the eggs. She looked at me and told me to stop. I picked up an egg and as I did, it fell out of my hands onto her shiny kitchen floor. "YIKES!" She looked at me and said, that I was going to get it when she got off the phone. I knew enough to know, that she meant what she said and I was in big trouble.

Since I was somewhat adventurous, I spent the next hour or so dodging her inside and outside our house without her seeing me. I heard her asking our next door neighbor, if he had noticed me anywhere at all? Little did she know, that I was standing underneath the sundeck as she was standing on top of it, calling out to me. I felt awful for not answering her whenever she called out my name. I finally got tired of our hide and seek game and, even though, I was scared to go back into our house, I did. I went upstairs into her ensuite and as I heard her approaching the doorway, I hid behind a towel that was hanging on the towel bar. I guess that I wasn't as smart as I thought I was. She had at last found me and she held true to her word.

My siblings and I were held accountable for a large share of the work load. We helped out in many different ways and as we got older, there was rarely any time to be idle. We cleaned, dusted, vacuumed, raked, swept, gardened, washed, and waxed the cars, and stacked large loads of wood. And as the girls got older, we baked, cooked, sewed, ironed, waxed floors, polished silver, brass, chrome, did the laundry, painted, and so much more.

During the autumn I didn't like having to go outside each day after school to rake any leaves which had fallen onto our lawn. I can still remember how cold it was. And I often said to any sibling who was also out there with me, "Let's just knock all of the leaves off the trees so we don't have to do this again tomorrow!"

My mom insisted that we do this everyday, along with sweeping the long curb which began in front of our house and wrapped around the sides. It took forever since we had a huge corner lot which was the same width as that of two large homes. Besides, how fast can a child sweep?

I absolutely hated it when my mother wanted all of her children to work on the outside of the house for hours on end. We had to weed the massive area of lawn which covered the entire front section of our house and extended right around to the side. We also tended to the never ending flower beds and helped weed her small vegetable garden, while one of my brothers mowed the grass. Our yard was so big and there was so much to do, even though, it looked great when it was all done.

Our bedrooms had hardwood floors and when we got older, we helped out by hand waxing the flooring in these big rooms, and than buffing them with the electric polisher. The large hallway, kitchen, and bathroom floors also had to be waxed and all of these rooms took so much time to do. When my mom decided that the wall to wall drapes in each of the rooms had to be dry cleaned, we helped out by taking the drapes down. And after they were done, we put the curtain hooks back on and re-hung them straighter then ever. This took a long time since a couple of the rooms had two wall to wall windows. If we were ever idle for a moment, she always found some work for us to do. I was even folding diapers at the tender age of five. As I got older, every month or so I had to take all of the items out of the kitchen cupboards. And then use "Old Dutch" cleanser to wipe the shelves and drawers out because they just might have gotten dirty. HOW, I DON'T KNOW!

Nothing in our home had a chance to get grimy or dusty including the people that lived there. I wasn't sure, what the heck we were in training for, but any army would have gladly welcomed us. As well, I have no doubt that we could have taught them a thing or two. This was our life and there were no other options available.

Our mother wouldn't tolerate nonsense from anyone, let alone, any of her children and quite often, she'd be chasing one of us with a wooden spoon to keep us in line. Now and then, I would gather up all of her ammunition and hide it under the china cabinet in the dining room or underneath one of the living room sofas. However, she eventually found my stash whenever she was rearranging the furniture. When she discovered her utensils, she always laughed while saying, "I wondered where all my spoons went?"

She no sooner put them back into the kitchen drawer, when I hid them again.

When we were younger, each morning before school my mother combed our hair and this was never a very nice time for any of us. I especially dreaded these moments as she splashed our faces with soap and water and then saturated our hair with coconut oil or "VO5." As well, I use to cringe at the thought of it because I frequently received a slap or more whenever I resisted her grooming attempts. I quite often left the bathroom in tears, as I tried to wipe some of the shiny and smelly ointment off of my throbbing head. I spent most of the morning in my classes trying to get the oil out of my hair, but that wasn't a good thing because it transferred from my hands onto my snack for recess time. And eating a nectarine with coconut oil on it was not a very pleasant thing, but it probably accounts for my silky locks now!

I enjoyed my life as much as I could and, even though, my mom was very strict, it was always easier being one of the youngest children in our family. Quite often when we got home from school, my mom had the radio blasting away with the latest tunes from the station that we listened to. She also made it a point to exercise daily with "Jack O' Lane" and as we got older, she joined the health spa.

My dad was a handsome man and he was always well dressed. He was quite often mistaken for being Caucasian since his coloring was very fair and he had blue eyes. He bought the best of everything, whether it was his clothes, cars, or the furniture in our home. He was a generous man and he quite often helped out a friend, gave donations to our temple, and he also sent money to India from time to time. As I was growing up, I noticed that he was always giving someone's child money as a treat, as we were leaving their home from having been there for dinner.

He was a very proud and severely demanding person and he never wanted any of us to challenge his authority. My father was so controlling to the extent that he surpassed the power of any other man that I had ever known. And his strength equaled that of some domineering men in history. He left for work at about seven thirty a.m. and was back home by 6:00 p.m. My daily life was pretty good until he came home because whenever he was around, we had to be on our best behavior and to always be very alert to whatever his needs might be. Once my dad walked through the door, everyone was as quiet as could be and he expected his every whim to be catered to. He was sometimes scary and I did my best to always stay out of his way.

Each morning before leaving for work, he would call one of us to bring him a clean handkerchief and a pair of his socks. I had a problem with this because whenever he asked me to get him his socks, he always said the color in Punjabi. I didn't know our language very well, let alone the names of any colors. Consequently I went back and forth bringing out different pairs of socks for him, while really hoping that I got it right. He became impatient, so I eventually took him one of each color to pick from.

On Saturdays he quite often went to the horse races and he was always dressed up in one of his three piece suits, one of his felt hats, and a pair of his many shoes. He always called one of us girls to put his cufflinks on for him and I can remember doing this many a time.

On the other hand, my mother took some of us children every Saturday and dropped us off at the library at the Oakridge shopping center, while she ran some errands. Since I loved books so much I felt that it was such a treat to be set free at this nice and new large institution, and I always gathered up as many as I could. We had to dress very nicely or we couldn't go at all. And if we helped with the grocery shopping, we each got a ten cent bag of popcorn from Welch's candy store on the way to the car.

My parents had many friends and their families over for dinner and we also went to their homes, but as we got older this socializing slowed down considerably.

I remember spending many weekends at our church and as young children, we always had a great time meeting other kids. We played together and sneaked off to the corner store for candy. The women were always the major contributing factor in getting everything ready for our three day services, celebrations, and weddings. They handled all of the buying, preparation, cooking, and the cleaning up after meals which was quite often for a couple hundred people at one a time. There were always children around to help out and I can remember sweeping, vacuuming, drying the dishes, wiping off tables, and buttering the tops of many rotis. Quite often my mother would go to church at 6:00 a.m. to help out and one of my sisters and I would go with her. There was rarely a male in sight to offer a hand, even though, everything took place on the weekends.

When our services began, everyone proceeded upstairs. There was a separate entrance for the females and one for the males. And before anyone entered the sacred prayer area, they were required to remove their shoes. Once inside, one walked down the long aisle towards the altar and gave a small amount of money. They then knelt down and touched their forehead to the carpet and as they stood up, they showed their respect by bowing with their hands clasped together as if in prayer. One then proceeded to sit down on the carpeted area. The females sat on the right side and the males on the left, as the priest sits cross legged at the altar facing the congregation.

When the two to three hour service was concluded, the priests gave everyone a sacred sweet offering which was prepared by them. It consisted of cooked flour, butter, and sugar and it was always absolutely delicious. A few of the men helped to serve this confectionary treat and when I was growing up, I always noticed that they served all of the males first and then the females. However, today they serve both the female and the male members at the same time. We always received an orange also.

Sunday was always considered a family day. If we were not at church, we went to White Rock beach, Stanley Park, Little Mountain, or just out for a drive and then to "Kings" for a cheeseburger. Sometimes we stopped at Chinatown and my dad would pick out a couple of live chickens and we waited for them to be slaughtered and cleaned. There were chickens clucking away everywhere and I didn't like this frightening place at all. And I was especially quiet, just in case I was next. While we were waiting for our soon to be curry dinner, we drove to another eerie lane and my dad parked at a restaurant window. He ordered two boxes of chow mein and we all shared it in the car together.

I began my school life at a brand new school named Dr. Annie B. Jamieson Elementary. It had just been built and I was amongst one of the first grade one students to attend it. What I remember the most was that everything was new and shining and the air was filled with an overpowering smell of floor wax. The floors were always buffed and gleaming, and on rainy days some of the boys loved to slide across the hallways in their socks. It always reminded me of our home.

My first grade teacher was an older looking woman who was tall, spry, and mean. She was very scary unless she was smiling and this was a very rare occurrence and even then, one was not entirely sure of its authenticity. Her face and hands were very wrinkled and she sported light tawny colored freckles everywhere. She also had a few dancing curls amongst her thinning patches of reddish brown hair.

Whenever I went up to her desk to ask for help with a math problem and I didn't know the answer, she pinched the skin at the back of my upper thigh over and over again, while smiling at me. It hurt a lot and I didn't know what to do about it. I backed away a bit, but I never considered telling her to stop, let alone, telling anyone else about it or even screaming out loud. As well, I certainly didn't consider telling our principal. It was unbelievable that this was even happening to me, and equally as bad that someone in a position of authority with such young children was actually abusing them. If I had told my mother about it, I thought that I would have been blamed for the situation, so I learnt to keep my pain a secret within me as I had already been doing for years.

One day when I was in grade three, our school was going to have a fair at lunchtime. I couldn't get up the courage to ask either of my parents for any money, even though, my siblings had. Therefore, when the craft fair started I went up to my classroom and I stared out of the window with tears in my eyes. About ten minutes later, a friend of mine named Kim, came into the room and said, "Let's go to the fair."

I tried to stall her by taking her attention off of the subject.

She continuously kept on saying, "Let's go together."

I just couldn't tell her that I didn't have any money, but after five minutes of this, she must have figured that out because she offered me half of her thirty five cents.

I said to her, "No, that's okay," but she insisted on sharing her money.

She wouldn't take "No" for an answer. We went to the fair together and I was so grateful to her. Over the years as I looked back on the incident, I found it amazing that someone so young was so in tuned and kind. I'll never forget her.

There were two horrible neighborhood girls that were older than I was, and whenever they saw me walking to or from school they called out "Racial

Slurs" all the way home. I always dreaded meeting up with them and one day when I was in grade five, they were walking behind me on the way to school. I could see the silhouette of their shadows on the sunny sidewalk as they imitated me as I walked along. They were bigger than I was, but I had enough of these bullies for the past years so I took a chance and I turned around. I told them that I could see what they were doing.

They continued to make fun of me, so I told them, "To Go To Hell!"

They burst out laughing, but as I proceeded to tell them to "F... Off," their shocked expressions showed on their faces. After this incident, they never really bothered me again. I'll never forget their names either, but for a different reason… they were mean and racist. I know what type of upbringing that they must have had, but which parent did they learn it from, their father or their mother, or both?

I was happy enough in elementary school and I played with friends almost daily. In addition, I always participated on sports teams and loved competing against other schools and baseball was my all time favorite. If there were no friends to play with after school, I'd always make myself happy by roller skating on the long sidewalk at the back of our home. I didn't draw any needless attention to myself, so my mom wouldn't have any reason to seek me out for after school chores.

One day a friend and I wanted to make some money so we could buy some candy at "Freemans" corner store. Hence I took our shoe polishing kit from my home and we went to another part of our neighborhood. And we asked at each residence, if anyone wanted their shoes shined for fifty cents. We earned money at each place that we went to. Later when I went home, I found out that one of my sisters had told my dad what I was doing and he was quite perturbed about it. I'm sure that you can well imagine, what I thought my dad would say to me regarding this venture. Oddly enough by the time that he spoke to me about it, I was quite surprised to find out that he wasn't upset at all.

He looked embarrassed and said to me, "You don't need to be doing things like that, if you want any money ask me for it."

If I had absolutely nothing to do at all, I'd rearrange our basement area for my mom and then I'd show her what I had done. She'd always smiled and said that it looked good. It's strange though, because whenever I was down there all alone, I always felt the presence of someone else in the room with me, even though, I never saw anyone in there. I was a bit afraid at times so I sang out loudly, so the room wasn't absolutely quiet just in case whatever it was said something to me.

I liked taking electronic things apart and then trying to put them back together again. I wanted to see how it all worked together, but sometimes I couldn't get all of the pieces back into its original state.

One of my sisters frequently said to me, "You break everything!"

I always believed that I could repair anything if I just moved a few wires around. Whenever the television wasn't working properly, I was the only one that my dad called to adjust it. He wouldn't let anyone else touch it and each and every time I got it working perfectly to his satisfaction.

All of the children in our family took activities at the Marpole Community Center. My twin brother and I went to gymnastics and we also took craft classes. On Saturday afternoons most of my siblings went to public roller skating in the gym, where there was always loud music blaring away. It was co-ed and it certainly was a lot of fun skating to the "Beatles" greatest hits. My sisters and I also went to a sewing class during the week while my older brothers took karate and judo classes. And my younger sister took tap dancing and baton. We were always involved in one activity or another and many of us were on school teams or other sports out of school. My mother always drove us and our friends to our games and then back home again.

One day my dad bought a big blue bike for my two older sisters to share and each one of my brothers had a bike of their own. My younger sister always had a new bike and I was the only child that was left out. I can still remember being six years old and watching my twin ride his new red bicycle up and down our street. I never asked him if I could use it because I felt that I really wasn't allowed to. It was bought for him and no one said that I could borrow it, so quite often I stood on our lawn and looked on, as I wished that I had one of my own.

Sometimes on the night before sports day, he and my younger sister came home with a new outfit that they couldn't wait to show me. I remember watching them as they decorated their bicycles for a contest, in which the students paraded their adorned showpieces around the school field. On the day of the main event, my two siblings rode their bikes to school and I ran alongside trying to keep up. This is what my life was truly like, but I kept smiling. I didn't let my true feelings show and I certainly didn't say anything to anyone about how I felt, even though, I was hurt at times. In the great scheme of things, I just didn't seem to matter, so I did whatever I wanted to do whenever I wanted to do it.

When I got a bit older, I taught myself how to ride my older sister's bike. It was much too big for me, but one day I dragged it out of our basement and up the twelve steps to the outside ground level. It took some time to master the huge hunk of metal and I even cut my knee as I ran into the city street pole. "OUCH" did that ever hurt, but I kept at it until I could ride it well. After that I loved bicycling everywhere. Sometimes one of my sisters said to me, that I couldn't ride their bike, but I didn't care what they said. I quietly took it to the front of our house and rode on my merry way without looking back at our house. I felt free pedaling away as fast as I could, while riding in neighborhoods that were a little too far away from home.

When I was in grade six, I sometimes went ice skating with my brother and some of our friends at the Kerrisdale skating rink. A couple of months later on Christmas day, we both received identical large white boxes. He opened his box and pulled out a nice new pair of ice skates which sent him beaming from ear to ear. He smiled at me as I started opening mine. I had no doubt in my mind that I was getting a pair of skates also, but when I lifted the lid off the box I didn't know how to react. I was very disappointed because I had received an ugly pair of white rubber boots for Christmas. OH HOW I HATED THEM! When my siblings saw my gift they laughed and I laughed a bit too, so I could hide my disappointment, even though, I truly wanted to cry.

However, the best Christmas that I ever had was the year that I received a Barbie dream house with furniture. I absolutely loved it and I still have my Barbie and some of the furniture.

I shared a bedroom with my twin brother until we were in grade four. We each had our own new twin bed and when he moved out of our room, he got a new bunk bed set just to himself. I was left with our beds. It was a bit painful to have to separate and the only good thing that came out of it was, that he also got our cowboy bedspreads. Gosh, they were UGLY!

I then shared my bedroom with my younger sister and this wasn't a very pretty situation. I absolutely detested having to do this! I'm sure that you've heard of the odd couple. Well that was us! We were completely opposite types of people. I had to have everything in its place and she didn't give a darn where anything was. I remember my half of the bedroom closet was as neat as a pin and she had everything thrown on the floor on her half including her clothes. If anything of hers landed on my side of the closet, I picked it up with two fingers and threw it back on her heap. She was so spoilt and with being the baby of the family she received whatever she wanted.

Sometimes when I came home from school at lunchtime, I discovered that my mom had reorganized my bedroom. And she had even thrown some of my stuff out that had gathered dust on them. One day I found an ornamental doll and some other things outside on top of the incinerator that we had in the lane. I never had a doll and this one was given to me as a birthday gift from a friend, so I brought it back in and cleaned it off and put my things back into my bedroom. On other occasions as soon as I walked into the house, I could see that my mom had rearranged the living room and den furniture, but I didn't really like how it looked. While I still had my coat on, I moved everything back the way that I thought it looked the best.

My mom would tell me to stop and come into the kitchen to have my lunch, but I just answered her by saying "Okay."

I continued until everything was all arranged back to the way that it was when she had started. She had spent all morning on these rooms and it was her home, but I thought that my decorating ideas were better then hers. Quite often I'd also put away certain things which she put out on display, especially unflattering pictures of myself.

Frequently when I was tired of playing outside, I'd go inside and reorganize my bedroom by moving the furniture around. I went searching through the house for unusual knickknacks and hunted through the linen closets for a different bedspread to put on my bed.

One day my mom and my eldest sister painted our bedroom a soft pink color and wallpapered the walls in a coordinated flowered paper. My sister painted our furniture white with a pink trim on it. I moved a desk and matching chair from the hallway into a corner of our bedroom. I painted it white and pink and I wallpapered the seat of the chair so it would match the walls. It all looked very pretty and now I finally felt like I had a girl's room. I always had a need to have everything in its place and to always be matching.

During the summertime our family went to Lake Cowichan and spent ten days or so with our cousins and their family. It was the greatest time for all of us and we had a lot of freedom. Why I don't know, but my cousin and I did whatever we wanted to during the day in their neighborhood. Other times throughout the year, they'd come to stay with us, but it was definitely more fun to be at their place.

We also went to Portland the weekend before school started. I remember getting a new outfit for the first day of school and a brown pair of penny loafers with a shiny new penny in them.

Both of my parent's mothers were the only grandparents who were still living. My father's mother came for a visit from India when I was a baby, but she didn't like living in Canada so she went back to live there. My other grandmother was the only grandparent that I have ever known and she only spoke Punjabi. This was hard for me to understand because of our language differences. We called her "Gramma" and whenever she visited us at our home, she always came with my uncle in his pale yellow convertible car. What a cool grandmother, eh! She was always dressed in western clothes and at all times, she wore a nice dress with a white silk scarf draped over her head.

I'll always remember that she had a twinkle in her eyes and she was forever smiling. She still lived on the same farm that my grandfather had bought years earlier. And whenever we had dinner at her place, all of the curry dishes were too hot for me. In her living room, she had a huge dark brown wooden rocking chair that I loved to rock in and I can still remember her black old fashioned telephone on the wall. In the main area of her house, there was only one bedroom, but the room was so big that it had four double beds side by side. In her bathroom there was a large hole in one of the walls above her bathtub. And when I went in to use the facilities, I had to hurry because I thought something might come jumping out at me. She also had an upstairs with a living room, two to three more bedrooms, a huge hallway, a big bathroom, and many pictures hanging on the walls. We weren't allowed to go upstairs, but sometimes when we went up there to snoop around, a bird would fly through from the attic.

Whenever we were playing in her backyard, I could never quite relax and enjoy myself because there were roosters and chickens running around everywhere. I was afraid of the creatures and it wasn't very pleasant trying to avoid them for hours. Quite often when we opened her back door, one or two of them would run inside of her kitchen and this always added a lot of excitement to our visits. It was always an adventure visiting at my gramma's place.

Every summer my mother took my siblings and I to the Pacific National Exhibition, and we always found my grandmother sitting on a bench facing the band shell. When we went over to say "Hi" she gave each of us children five dollars to spend.

Our gramma had diabetes and whenever she came over to visit, I can still remember her yellow insulin kit. I'd watch her on the sly as she gave herself an injection. If at that very moment she saw you looking at her, she'd start laughing out loud. One time when she was over for our birthday, she brought a pair of pink corduroy pants for my brother and a miniature toy pink fridge for me. And for once, I received the nicer gift!

My father always joked and said that my grandmother thought that he was such a great catch. Moreover, she was not about to let him slip away from her and that's, how he ended up marrying my mother.

Our grandmother had twenty-four grandchildren and in the summer of 1964, she passed on. My parents had already planned a three month trip to India with three of my siblings. However once this happened, they were going to postpone their trip, but my father had already shipped his new shiny Chrysler over there. I was in grade four and I'll never forget the day that they left. My mom was very upset and we didn't even say goodbye to each other. I missed her a lot when they were away especially since no one in our family had ever been apart, let alone, for that long. When they returned from their trip, the four children who had stayed at home had all gained weight because we were constantly having late night snacks.

My dad was not impressed when he noticed this and he said, "What happened to my kids?"

The parents of a neighborhood friend offered to have my sister and me, stay with them during the time my family was going to be away. My parents thanked them and said that they wanted to keep all of us together at our home, so an aunt and a cousin came to stay with us. Our friend's father was a really nice man and throughout the summer months, he quite often took us out to "Peter's Ice Cream." I remember that he always sang along with the radio while he was driving us there. Years later, he became the Chief Justice of the B.C. Supreme Court and afterwards, the Chief Justice of the B.C.

Court of Appeal. I send him the best of wishes in all of his endeavors.

My dad had promised the four children who had stayed at home, that when they returned from their trip, he would buy a piano for the girls and a pool table for the boys. Hell, they probably would have left me at home anyway!

Seriously though, I never wanted to go to India and the thought of it really frightened me. I had an upsetting vision of myself walking up the stairs to get onto an airplane. And as I was about to enter it, I started screaming to get off as I held onto the door trying not to go in any further. Furthermore from a young age, I had no desire to ever visit that country and as I got older, I thought that my feelings must have reflected a fear from another lifetime. I wondered, what the hell had happened, for me to still feel such terror over it now?

When they got back from their trip, we all received some great things. I got a charm bracelet from the New York World's Fair and a tambourine from India. One of the nicest gifts was a transistor radio that my twin and I were to share. Over time it became just mine and yes… I took it apart one day when it wasn't working properly.

My sister took private piano lessons at our home and I took mine through the school. My brothers received a really nice pool table and my twin also got an electric guitar with an amplifier. And of course, he also had private lessons. The girls were not allowed to ever play pool because it wasn't ladylike, but whenever my parents went out, we rushed into the recreation room and played until they got home.

My brother and I had co-ed birthday parties all the way up to grade seven and it was always a lot of fun. He invited all the boys and I invited the girls. Everyone liked coming to it because we were the only children who had mixed parties. One year my mom took all of our presents away except one, and locked them in her cedar trunk. Later that year in July, when she was going through the trunk I took out one of my presents and I said, "I am keeping this one because I passed into the next grade."

It was a box of paper cutout clothes for prince charming and his princess.

I still have my Nancy Drew books, my recorder, and instruction book from grade five. And all of my piano books and my large fifty story book that I use to read on Sunday mornings when my family was still sleeping. However, the most telling of all, I still have my write-up that I did on some of the Suffragettes movements (Women fighting for their rights.) and my article titled, "Comparing A Man to A Woman," from my English 10 class. I, along with several others had won a oratorical contest and I still have my certificate. The theme of females without equal rights to males had angered and plagued me for years.

We had a lot of friends who were Jewish, and in grade seven we went to their Bar Mitzvah services and then onto parties afterwards. After one of these events, one of the parents had even rented a bus and we were driven to a country club for a dinner and dance. These were the last days of my co-ed social life for quite a few years.

In high school I went to Sir Winston Churchill Secondary school for grades eight through to twelve, while my two older sisters went to York House private school. I didn't have to go to private school because I didn't pose a threat to my dad regarding boys, and he also didn't want to pay another large tuition fee since it had increased a lot. Besides, it was only for me! I always felt sorry for my sisters because they had to go there and even wear uniforms, not to mention, they were not allowed to get their hair cut. Their hair was so long that they could sit on it. It was not until the last couple of years of high school, that they were able to have it cut and styled. I sure couldn't have lived within that restriction.

I'll always remember the first day that I wore pants to school, even though, in that day and age girls weren't allowed to. However, one day about fifteen girls wore slacks to class. Our principal was angry about it and he gathered all of us together for a meeting in one of the classrooms. He said that he didn't want us to wear pants again, but he really couldn't stop us. And if any of us ever needed help in any way from the school, we should not expect to get it. I had a bit of a rebellious streak anyway and it didn't matter to me what he said, because for girls to be able to wear pants to school was a great thing to happen. As a result, from that day forward there were no further problems in this area.

Friends at school fell by the wayside because I couldn't do any of the normal things that teenagers do. I never shared with anyone just how controlled and rigid my upbringing truly was. I always made up excuses whenever there was anything going on, by saying that I was already busy doing something else. My sisters and I were not allowed to socialize, date, or get a job and I know that the more I tried to fit in, the more that I knew that I didn't. Our brothers were not permitted to date or socialize either.

Sometimes when I was walking alone in the stairwell of the school, there was a male student who always made a racial comment to me, while referring to a certain part of my body. He called me the "N" word, while saying the most appalling thing that I'd ever heard. I felt so terrible about it and I never told anyone about it until last year. He was considered a suck-up and I still remember the jerks name and that he walked on the tips of his toes. He was such a dud! Now I realize that I should have spoken to my school counselor about this incident, for she would have surely put a stop to tippy toes bigoted remarks. Over the years whenever I thought about him, I was very certain about what type of environment he had been raised in as a child. I certainly hope that Rodger is kinder to females of different nationalities now, and that he is no longer abusive, but truly, what are the odds of that?

Even though high school was a bit of a lonely time, there was a bright spot outside of school because there was someone who I thought was special. We only saw each other whenever our families got together, and every so often we spoke on the phone. Throughout the years I sent him birthday, Valentine, and Christmas cards and I must say, that just the thought of him made me smile.

All throughout high school if I ever wanted to go Oakridge shopping center alone, I simply told my mom as I was walking out of the front door. She looked at me with a shocked expression on her face, but she never stopped me. I was usually back home within an hour and a half and my mom knew that I was a pretty safe bet anyway. One day after I had graduated I really wanted to go see the movie, "The Way We Were." Hence I told my oldest sister who was married to meet me in front of the house at a certain time. Once again, I told my mom as I was going out the front door. She never really said, "No" to me about anything. We had come to a point that if I ever wanted to go out with my older sister, it was okay as long as it was during the day.

All of my siblings got along pretty well and we were a close knit family. My mother always liked my eldest brother and my twin the best. She was forever saying that, "He just had to bring me along with him," when he was born.

I felt uncomfortable whenever she said this, but I always smiled. It was as if, she didn't really want me and I was just along for the ride. One day when we were at a ladies tea party, my mother said to the group of ladies, that she would have preferred to have twins that were the same gender. I felt awful when she said this because I knew that the gender that she was referring to was not female.

There was a kind lady at the party who winked at me and said, "If I had twins, I would like it, if I had one girl and one boy."

I looked at her and shyly smiled. In fact, she was the mother of the guy who told me to stop crying on my wedding day.

In other moments, my dad singled me out and said, "Look at the chance baby now!"

You see, I turned out to be the stronger and healthier twin and quite often if my dad ever commented on anything at all, it was usually at my expense.

When you throw a child into the water without a paddle, they either sink or swim, and I chose to swim. I had a tendency to not let anyone get away with anything and my inner and outer self was extremely strong.

I also had a strong role model who I highly regarded since I was in grade three and she was Jacqueline Kennedy. She had style, grace, dignity, and so much strength. And I noticed that whatever happened to her within her life, she held her head up and kept right on going. She was a courageous woman who I greatly admired and I constantly read the magazines which I had on her family's life. I loved to look at any pictures of her and I still have the publications today. As I got older, I sometimes styled my hair the same as hers. Mrs. Kennedy's classic sense of style for herself and her children would greatly influence my style and dress code for myself, and many years later, with my children when they were younger.

I also followed the life, speeches, and campaign trail of Robert Kennedy. He was the first male public figure that I really took an interest in. His words of wisdom and actions towards human and equal rights for all, was something that I could relate to and I fully supported him. I still remember that I was mopping the kitchen floor before school, when I heard on the radio at 8:20 a.m., that he had been shot and later died. It angered me and I hated the injustices of our world and the man who did this to him and his family! Also I still have my copy of a "Look" magazine on his life that I bought with my allowance, way back when I was in grade 7 which was forty years ago.

Thus far my story only contains a part of my childhood, but there were other facets which were very different than that of our neighbors. The daughters in our family were born into a family and a culture who deeply believed in inequality between the genders. However difficult that was for us to accept and live within, we were expected to never question the role that we had been born into.

I was treated differently because I was born a female.
I fought hard to rise above any negativity which was aimed at me.
I was rarely accepted for the person that I became, because I seldom
went along with our way of life, and the viewpoint of our culture.
However, I have always had my own belief system and the strength
and determination to never give up, for whatever I believed in.
No matter how badly you are treated, don't let others carry your spirit away,
fight to keep your power, and continue on your path to freedom.

– BONNY BILLAN –

A Childhood Entwined Within a Culture

Chapter 4

My ethnic upbringing consisted of being part of a family and a culture that believed in male superiority and discriminated against the female gender. We were raised with the concept that males within our society and especially in our home were considered to be more important. And their needs came before that of all others. Most of the adults in my world only wanted females to see to their own requirements, after the males were taken care of. I absolutely despised living within this subservient role which my fate had destined me to be a part of, even though, my soul never allowed me to surrender to it in any way.

When I was younger all of the children in our family had dinner together, but as we grew older and certainly whenever my father was around, my sisters and I were separated as much as possible from our brothers. We were brought up to completely cater to our father and one day we began with some of the needs of our brothers too. It was at this point that my parents and male siblings began having their dinner in the living room or den, while my sisters and I ate our meals in the kitchen. Once again, it had been made very clear to us, that we were not equal to the males in our home.

It seemed like we were only living and breathing, so we could look after the wishes of our elders and we were treated as such at all times. I often referred to my sisters and I, as being their maids because that was what we were considered to be. I honestly felt like I was the hired help, especially whenever I took them their dinner on trays. My parents were served their meal and when they were finished, one of us would pick-up their dishes. We returned with their tea and dessert and then went back again for those dishes, when they were done. It didn't matter if any of us were still having our dinner, for whenever my dad called out his needs were met immediately. My sisters and I cleaned the entire kitchen and not one of us could do anything else until it was spotless. We did this for many years and I completely hated every second of it.

I suppose that my other siblings accepted this way of life, but I couldn't be silent and once I began high school, I found it difficult to tolerate. Quite often I'd be bitching away in the kitchen as the males and my mom ate their meals while watching the television. Furthermore, I was quite often furious as I said out loud to my sisters, "WE ARE SLAVES!"

My father knew that I never agreed with his way of thinking and he was mean to me much of the time, as he did his utmost to try and shatter my strength. It seemed like neither of us liked each other and at times it was very apparent that he could barely tolerate me. I felt so stifled and as I got older, the only thing that I looked forward to was the day, that I could escape this way of living.

One day when I was in grade eight, my parents had just finished eating their evening meal and my father bellowed for me to come and get their empty plates.

I wanted to scream out loudly as he called out, "Bona, come and get these dishes!"

I went and picked them up, but I was so angry that I couldn't hide my disgust. I absolutely detested my submissive role from within every part of my being, and when I went back with his dessert, my annoyance showed on my face.

As I placed his tea on the table, he shouted out to me, "Watch it, before it spills!"

I said to him, "If it spills, it spills" and I turned to leave.

I had never spoken to him in this manner before, but this time I just couldn't keep it in.

My dad followed me back into the kitchen and it was quite clear that he was livid as he approached me. He flung his arm out to me and began slapping me repeatedly quite uncontrollably. This cruelty went on for what seemed like an eternity and at one point, all I could see was blackness. I even had ringing in my ears. It felt like he was using all of his might and I suppose that all of our years together had finally taken its toll on him.

When he finally stopped, there was even hair from my head on the floor and both of my pierced earrings were no longer in my ears. And I couldn't even find one of them. He told my older sister to take me upstairs and help me wash my face. I guess that my gasping for air to breathe, somehow bothered him.

This was the only time that something like this had ever happened to any of the children in our home. My dad never had any cause to strike us, especially since no one ever did anything out of line. Oh yea... except me!

In my father's great desire to always keep the genders segregated, he not only kept our brothers away from us, but he also didn't want them to even speak to us. If any of them were in our company for longer than a few minutes, they were told to get away. My dad didn't want any of us to receive any phone calls and the girls never answered the phone if my dad was anywhere around. Life at times was not very pretty

I loved joking around and whenever I was laughing especially when we were having dinner, my dad always called out from wherever he was, for me to stop. And this went on for years. I always had the feeling that he thought that I was making jokes at his expense and some of the time, I was. My mother always asked me what I had to laugh about all the time and this continued throughout my adulthood. It seemed like someone was always trying to stifle my spirit, but I never really paid much attention to whatever they were saying to me.

In high school I remember how much I wanted to get a job especially since many of the students at school were working, but this was not a possibility for me. However, once a month my dad gave my sisters and I, twenty dollars each as an allowance. He also had opened a savings account for each of his children which we would receive when we married.

One year around Christmas time, the girls in our family went shopping with our parents at Oakridge shopping center. My dad asked me, what I wanted for a gift. I truly wanted a cassette player for $49.99. After hesitating, I told him and he bought it for me without so much as a blink of his eye. It was my absolute savior because music had always made me happy and listening to it made my life so much more bearable. I use to record music off of our stereo and I always taped the top one hundred music hits of each year. I had so many years of enjoyment with it and I still have my player and all of my cassette tapes.

One day when we were all teenagers, my mom had a casserole dish in the oven and the glass lid cracked and some of the pieces fell into the food. My mother was horrified as she said "What if any of the boys had eaten some of this?"

I looked at her and said, "WHAT! What if any of the girls had eaten some of it?"

By this age these comments didn't hurt me anymore or so I thought. I didn't realize it at the time, but my heart, mind, and body had taken in every negative and positive word and action that had ever taken place for me. One day, together with my soul they would all rise up, rebel, and completely explode.

Our strict upbringing didn't allow us the opportunity to express our wishes and whenever I attempted to do so, it was quite often met negatively. We were to have no opinions and we had few rights. We were brought up in such a constrained manner and we were expected to do everything we were told to do and to never think for ourselves.

I had to suppress my desires and life was never very easy, even though, my father was a wealthy man. Far too much was expected from the females in our family and everyday living became extremely tough especially during our teenage years. Life wasn't exactly smooth flowing for our brothers either, but it seemed like they had it so much easier, for at least they were able to get out to go to work or to the gym and one of them had a car.

I had battled a lifetime of struggling through my cultures restrictions as the echoing pleas of my voice were seldom heard. And I deeply resented even the implication that males were superior to females, let alone, living in the thick of that thought daily. I found myself fighting this concept wherever my culture took me, and it would continue to lay the ground work for my anger towards it. This way of thinking was something, that I just couldn't accept and I never did in a very quiet manner.

I knew of no other father that was as severely harsh as ours, and because my family was well known within our society, many people living in Vancouver and Victoria knew how strict he was. Quite often other parents referred to the children in our family as examples for their children to follow. It was commonly known that our life was extremely rigid and that we weren't allowed to socialize freely with others.

It was also a well known fact that my mother had raised her daughters in a very traditional manner, and that we knew how to manage a home very well. When I was in grade twelve, I made a blazer every few days for a couple of weeks just to keep busy. I always wanted to be working on some sort of project and once I finished high school, I told my mom that I was going to decorate our house and I wanted to be paid for it. She agreed and I guess that I thought of this as my job, since I wasn't able to go outside of our home to do anything else. You know what they say, a mind is a terrible thing to waste. I started refinishing some bedroom furniture sets and wallpapering every wall that I could in our home. I also bought matching accessories to compliment each décor and I spent many hours at this undertaking since I really enjoyed this activity immensely.

A huge part of my childhood memories include constantly being shown that my parents didn't think of me as an equal to my siblings, and it was confirmed to me often enough. How could I ever feel, that I was cared for and loved as much as the rest of our family especially, when I was sometimes left behind when they went away? My mom said that it was because it was too hard for her to take care of two babies and I was always the happier one. I can respect and understand that, but if our behaviors were reversed, they never would have left my twin behind. I'm sure that this is what started my feelings of not really belonging to my family. My mother frequently teased me as she said, that our housekeeper was my godmother. How was I to know if this was true or not, or even, what the heck a godmother was? I hated being singled out all of the time and I soon came to truly feel and know, that I was very different from the rest of my siblings in every which way imaginable.

When the time came for me to learn how to drive a car, my mother said that my twin could teach me, even though, both of my older sisters had taken driving lessons. It really didn't bother me because I didn't want to be driving with some strange guy anyway. Besides, he was a good teacher since he and I were the only two children in the family who had passed our road test the first time around. However, I was consistently being shown that I wasn't good enough to have the same as my sisters and brothers.

Since there were no opportunities for the girls in our family to further themselves after high school, it was recognized that marriage was the inevitable next step within our lives. Also in view of the fact that we weren't allowed to date, it was a given that within a couple of years after graduation, the children in our family would have an arranged marriage. As such, our daily tasks were in preparation for this major event. Once I graduated, my mother wanted me to take full responsibility for making dinner each night, but I told her that I wasn't going to do it, until I was engaged. I was already doing so much of the housework and I wasn't going to do everything! My character was strong enough that she never really questioned what I said, she simply agreed with me.

Most of the young adults in our society were also following the same path as we were in having an arranged union, for it had become the next stage for the majority of them also. They too had fully understood at a very young age, that this was going to take place since many of them were not allowed to socialize with the opposite sex either. Several young males dated females outside of our culture without their parent's knowledge, and then dropped them and went on to marry young women in our culture.

An arranged marriage seemed to be accepted by most of the interested parties since many of them didn't have much of a life outside of their families. And this was the only suitable means of beginning to have one of their own. Many young adults simply agreed with their parents on the issue of an arranged marriage, just as they had agreed with them on other matters throughout their childhood. One was lucky if they were able to continue their education because this usually delayed a marital union for at least four years.

Marriages are arranged in our culture because it was a traditional mindset that was passed down from one generation to the next. Young adults were customarily not allowed the freedom to choose their spouses, and parents felt that they knew best what to do considering their children's future. During the sixties and the seventies approximately ninety per cent of the marriages were arranged without the bride or groom knowing one another. A parent or a friend of the family would consider who would be best suited for one another, and quite often they came up with the suggestion of which female should marry which male. They then represented the female's side and approached the male's parents with the question, "Would your son be interested in marrying so and so?"

This was always officially done through a middle person because it was unheard of to do so without one and it wasn't good manners. Our culture looked at marriage as the joining of two families, not just the union of two people. Arranged marriages still have a place in our society today, but with updated modifications.

When I was eighteen and nearing the age of marriage, I tried to keep busy and stay out of my dad's way whenever he was home. I didn't want to give him the opportunity to bother me just yet, about the soon to be explosive subject.

Three of my older siblings had arranged marriages, but this was not an option for me. I had never accepted my upbringing and the very thought of marrying a stranger or someone that I didn't really know, let alone, barely have the chance to communicate with, was not something that I was going to participate in. I can still remember how outraged I felt at the very mention of the fact that I was going to marry someone of their choosing, but at the same time I felt a bit helpless. My dad was a powerhouse and a force to reckon with and I would have to endure hell, if I chose not to be married off in this fashion. I wasn't looking forward to any of it.

I really couldn't understand how I was just expected to hand over my future to my parents in such a major decision, even though my life had not been my own so far. It was just too hard for me to grasp and I had decided that if the situation warranted it, I was prepared to run away to avoid this from happening. It was difficult for me to fathom, how my dad could give his daughters to some guy, who he really didn't know much about. Especially since he had taken every precaution to safeguard us while we were growing up. He had gone to the greatest measures ever imaginable in protecting us and then one day pouf... we were to marry some stranger.

My dad often said, that once his daughters were married we were in another family and we were no longer his responsibility, for we would then be a part of our husband's family. It hurt to think that we were being discarded and no longer a part of our original family. However, as time went on, something else hurt even more. And this was, that whenever any of the females in our family had any children, my father only thought of them in terms of being related to our husband's clan. It was their congratulations and not his. I guess because someone else's son had fathered this child. In reality, none of his daughter's children were actually considered to be his grandchildren, even though, we all had the same blood racing throughout our veins.

My parents carried this out by showing their immense love, care, and attention for the children of their sons and they would do anything to accommodate them. Their families received numerous larger gifts than their daughter's children did. Consequently it seemed that the inequality was not just reserved for the daughters in our family, it also extended to all of our children whether they were male or female. This was my parent's belief and I suppose that this was how they were raised. It was painful enough when we weren't considered equal to our brothers, but it completely stung when this inequality was extended to our off-spring. Everyone has feelings and when females are shown repeatedly since their births, that they simply are not good enough to be considered equivalent to any male, it infringes on their self esteem and implants deep rooted scars trapped within their souls.

My spirit could never accept the idea of discrimination between the genders or the segregation that took place in our home, our church, and in our society. And all of this set the stage for my refusal to embrace my culture. My feelings on this subject were constantly being fueled as I stumbled over these beliefs everywhere that I went. This was the reality of my life, but equality and freedom was something that my heart longed for.

Even though my childhood was not an easy one, I came out of it a reasonably happy person looking forward to a life with someone that I loved and I hoped loved me too. I most certainly wanted him be someone who was kind and caring, especially since I had already experienced much oppression and harshness. However in reality, what did the word "love" really signify to me? Did I even know what love and respect were?

If one has been shown small amounts of it, how do they know what love truly feels like, let alone, allow themselves to believe that they deserve it or are worthy to be treated better than they have been?

What about all of the gender unfairness and dominance that had taken place in my years? Had I completely escaped the negative effects which this had on my soul?

I had fought against the injustice within my world for years and it was deeply embedded within me. Would I have to continue in my battle all alone, without ever having someone special who truly understood my hurts and beliefs? Perhaps my destined pathway would shine upon me and draw me to a man, who knew how to treat his wife with respect, and possibly we would live happily ever after.

Only time would tell me, just where my karmic ties lay, who they were connected to, and what affect my past influences truly had upon my heart and rebellious soul.

One never knows, who they are going to meet,
or what is truly destined to absolutely be.
However, one must remember, all that their soul
has experienced and believes.
For it's easy for another to take advantage of you,
when you are young, naïve, and life is rather blue.

– BONNY BILLAN –

A Fateful Meeting

Chapter 5

One day when I was in grade eight, I asked my mom if I could go with her to attend a wedding that our family was invited to in Victoria. After a lot of coaxing, she allowed me and my younger sister to accompany her.

We arrived early at the Tsawassen Ferry Terminal to catch the 7:00 a.m. ferry and after a two hour crossing we docked at Swartz Bay. Once we were there, we went to the Sikh Temple on Topaz Street and joined numerous guests at a traditional East Indian wedding. After the ceremony, everyone carried on to the reception which took place at the Cedar Hill Recreation Center.

My mom didn't really want to go the reception, but we convinced her to go for at least a little while. There were a lot of strange faces there and as I glanced around the room, I noticed a couple of older looking teenagers staring at us. And one of them was smiling. I looked a few years older than I actually was and since my younger sister was only in grade four, I guessed that this guy was smiling at me. Though, my sister insisted that he was checking her out. One of them was cuter than the other and the one who had been smiling at me was still trying to get my attention, when we left the reception a short time later. He gave me a bit of a creepy feeling and I was glad that my mom was near so he wouldn't approach me. I was quite happy to leave for the ferry.

A couple of weeks later, a guy called our home and one of my sisters answered the call. He didn't know who to ask for, but he said that he had been at a reception in Victoria and he would like to speak to the girl who was wearing the white dress.

It was very fortunate that my sister had taken the call and that my parents and my brothers weren't at home or I would have been in big trouble. I later found out that my caller had been warned by his uncle to stay away from me because my dad was so strict, but he chose not to listen to him.

I spoke with him on the phone for a bit and he asked me what grade I was in. I told him that I was in grade eight.

He said that he thought I was in grade twelve which was the same grade that he was in. We spoke for awhile and he wanted to meet with me. This type of situation was an absolute first so I asked my sisters what I should do. They said to tell him to call back twenty minutes later, so in the meantime we could figure out what to do.

When he called back, we agreed to meet the next day at Mr. Macs at 3:00 p.m., but I certainly had no intention of going alone. Besides, I needed my older sister to drive me there and this seemed to be a good time, since my parents usually went out for a Sunday drive together.

The following day at 2:15 p.m. my parents were still sitting around the house and there was no indication that they were going to go out anywhere. I started praying and about twenty-five minutes later, my dad said to my mom, "Do you want to go for a drive?"

While she was making up her mind, I urged her on by saying, "It would be nice to get out."

She finally agreed, but I had never seen two people take so long to get ready. They finally left the house at 3:25 p.m. Whew! My sister then ran swiftly to get my mother's bronze colored Lincoln out of the garage. She parked it in front of the house and just as we were about to drive off, you can't imagine what happened?

One of my brothers who knew nothing of my rendezvous ran outside to the car and jumped into the back seat while the engine was being revved up. My sister and I just sat there in horror! We asked him what he wanted and he said, that he was going to buy the latest sports magazine.

Oh great! I wasn't sure what to do now! If I decided to go, how was I going to be able to speak with the guy that I was meeting with my brother there? I only had a few seconds to decide, but I thought that I'd go and see how things were going to play out.

My sister drove to our destination and as soon as she stopped the car, my brother jumped out in a flash. I slowly got out of the car as I was repeating to her, "What am I going to do now?"

My insides were flipping cartwheels and just as I was leaning down to the car window to get my sister's advice, someone from behind me said, "Hi Bonny."

I turned around and I felt sick. It was the guy who was smiling at me at the reception and it wasn't the cute one! I started thinking, "How do I get out of this now?"

I said "Hi" to him.

He replied by saying, that he went up to my brother and asked him, "Where is Bonny?"

This guy wasn't the brightest one that I had ever met because I told him repeatedly how strict my family was. He never should have asked my sibling where I was and he was not only careless, but he was selfish too. I felt such an uneasy feeling in the pit of my stomach which must have been my warning to me. I didn't listen to it, but I really didn't know how to handle this situation. Guess I was being hasty too!

We were standing on one of the busiest streets in our area and I knew a lot of people that lived and shopped around here. And within two minutes of us standing there, a friend of mine drove past and honked. I began wondering how many other people had driven past that knew me. I didn't have to contemplate for long because by this point, our extra passenger was back at the car staring at us.

Once again, you have to understand that this scenario was totally new to me and if my parents had seen or had heard about this meeting, I would have been in a tremendous amount of difficulty. Also having a conference with my father was about the last thing on earth that I ever wanted to have to deal with.

We all stood there not knowing what to say, and then the stranger said, "Let's go somewhere to talk."

I really didn't want to go anywhere with him and besides an alarming look flashed in my sibling's eyes and on their faces. Therefore we decided to meet across the street at the Oakridge shopping center since the mall was closed on Sundays.

Once we arrived there, we both stood by one of the stores and conversed for about half an hour while my bodyguards looked on from the car. I was wondering how I was going to get myself out of this situation, but eventually my sister started the car. I told him that I had to go. I can't quite remember how we left it, but he called my house again.

He came to my school the next day and we spoke together for about half an hour. I still remember that I had the absolute sickest feeling in the pit of my stomach and I had never experienced this awful sensation before. It was almost to the point that I thought that I was going to get sick. He certainly wasn't anyone that I was attracted to and he had long hair and there was sweat forming on his face as he spoke. I just wanted to run away as fast as I could. What's more, he wanted to begin writing one another and I didn't want to hurt his feelings so I said okay, even though, my insides were screaming.

I just didn't know how to say, "No," even though, he was a total stranger. And remember, I was only twelve or thirteen years old with no experience in this at all.

I said goodbye to him with no intention of carrying it any further. However, I wrote him one letter saying, I had a special friend and if things changed I would get in touch with him. I let him down nicely and besides, there was already someone else that I was attracted to. This was the only time that I corresponded with him and once I sent the letter off, I felt very relieved. Also, why would he want to be with someone who was so much younger than himself?

About a month later my brother asked me, "Is anything going on with that guy?"

I said "No."

As I walked away I turned and said, "I just know that I am going to end up marrying him."

I don't know what made me say those words. They just came out without me even thinking about it. It wasn't anything that I ever wanted to happen.

I would like to say to anyone who finds themselves in a similar situation such as mine, if you are asked by someone to be cautious because of the strictness of their family, please listen to their warning. You have no idea what the consequences would be for them because you refused to listen to their request.

I didn't hear anything more about him until four years later, when one of my sister's had married and moved to Vancouver Island. She had met him and his family and she really liked them. As well, whenever I spoke to her, she would continually speak about how nice he was. And, that whenever she and her husband would visit them, he would take their coats and get them a drink.

She insisted repeatedly that I just had to meet him again! Also if we liked each other and things worked out, maybe we could get married. And then she and I, would be living close together. My sister had it all, figured out!

Yes, I would have liked to live near to her and even though, I told her that I was not attracted him, she never let up on us getting together. She hounded me every time that we spoke to each other and she just... wouldn't ever STOP!

I think there was a bit of scheming going on between his mother and my sister. And I was about to get caught in the middle of the whole frigging thing! They had a plan... and that was for me to meet him in the near future in Victoria.

I was now seventeen years old and he was twenty-one and our age difference didn't seem to matter much anymore, plus I had always been mature for my age.

A few months later in April of 1974, we went to Victoria for a church service honoring "Basaki" which is the birth of Sikhism. This is a celebration which is held on April 13th or 14th, and it represents the birth of the Khalsa order. Services are held in our temples and athletic games are organized. Today it has grown into huge celebrations with parades and the sharing of our ethnic food with every nationality.

When I was growing up, this day was commonly referred to as Basaki, but now it is often called Vaisakhi also. The Khalsa is when a Sikh chooses to be baptized into the Khalsa brotherhood by living a life based on wearing the traditional five Ks at all times and reciting five prayers. The five items are Kesh which is uncut hair, Kanga which is a small comb, Kara which is a small circular bracelet, Kirpan which is a small sword and Kacha which are shorts. The tenth Guru, Guru Gobind Singh, ordered that the five Ks be worn so that a Sikh could use them to make a difference into their own spirituality and to that of others.

After church the matchmaking plans began and were set into motion as his mother invited us to come over for a visit. Since there were so many other people visiting her also, her son and I had a chance to spend some time talking with one another. He seemed like a nice guy, but I had no idea what I was getting myself into. I had been so sheltered and I was very foolish to even consider what all of this involved. I was so darn naïve. Actually, there was a guy at his house that I was attracted to and I would have rather preferred to meet him!

On my second meeting with him, he said to me, "Everyone knows that you girls are the best in all of Vancouver and Victoria."

His comment didn't mean much to me. Our family always received a lot of compliments and my father had worked hard to earn a reputation that held him and his family in a high regard. We were considered a good looking family, but there were only two of my siblings who really thought they were the absolute cat's meow. And I wasn't one of them. He also told me that he had a girlfriend for quite a few years and she wasn't East Indian. And he was practically engaged to her since they had been going out for a long time, so I wondered, what he was doing here with me.

We began writing back and forth to one another, but there were at least three things that were bothering me about him and the feeling never went away. Both of our family's backgrounds were at opposite ends of the spectrum and we had been raised so very differently on each and every other level. We both had different places in our families stepping order and I could feel that we weren't exactly on the same wavelength. He was the eldest of three children in his family and I was the sixth out of the seven children in ours. He was the first grandchild born to the eldest son in his family. His father's father was still living and since his birth, he had spent a considerable amount of time with this grandparent. This had to have had a major influence on the shaping of his traits. Needless to say, his world was filled with much attention from others and he had become quite accustom to getting his own way.

I was also use to getting my own way too because that's what I insisted upon, but it was only within my own needs and never at the expense of someone else. I had a certain standard of living that I was accustomed to and I was fairly particular about cleanliness. I would only use a certain type of shampoo or whatever, but I was always kind and considerate to others.

I had a sister and a sister-in-law that both had babies two months apart, and they had both come to stay with us for a few weeks after their babies were born. They slept in my room and we each had our own double bed to ourselves, but their babies were also with us. During the night whenever their infant cried, I got up and helped out by heating up the baby's bottle. And I sat with them until the baby was done and back to sleep again. After both of them went back to their own homes, I was so worn out that I became sick.

I also helped out a different sister-in-law when she came to live with us, after she and one of my brothers had married in India. Every morning I asked her what she was going to be wearing that day and then I ironed her clothes for her. I did whatever I could to make her stay as enjoyable as possible. When they moved out of our house and into theirs, I painted their entire home with my mother and helped set up and organize all of it to her satisfaction.

We continued corresponding with our letter writing and we spoke on the phone. And four months later when I opened one of my letters, it said that he loved me. I was shocked that he felt this way because most of our contact had been through our phone calls. At this stage, I just liked him and I didn't know if I was ever going to feel anything more than that. If he was being manipulative, I really wouldn't have known it because I didn't have much experience dealing with males other than my family members. I was young, innocent, and feeling very bold. And I suppose that being a part of something which you really were not allowed to partake in, just adds to the excitement of it all. In hindsight this situation was thrilling, but could it have been because it was so very much forbidden?

On December 30, 1974 we had lunch at the Quarry house restaurant at Little Mountain. I was almost twenty years old and we had known each other for a couple of years. After lunch we went to the Hyatt for a drink and it was there, that he asked me to marry him. I was happy about it and I said, "Yes."

Now the hardest part of all would begin. I had to tell my dad that this was the guy that I wanted to marry. When I told him, a major battle began and continued over a painful period of ten months in which so much turmoil ensued. In fact, a war erupted between my father and I. This was not because I wanted to marry someone of my own choosing, but because my dad didn't want me to marry him or marry into his family. I was now living in PURE HELL!

My dad thought of Victoria as quite a forward city compared to Vancouver. He felt that many people in our culture who lived there, were living a life which was quite the opposite of how I was raised. He added that, this guy's family's lifestyle was "Much freer than ours" and there was intermarriage within their family. He went on to say that they were "More like working people because his mother had a job" outside of their home and that this was completely unheard of in our family.

I could understand where my dad was coming from because he wanted his girls to marry into families of wealth, and into surroundings which we were accustomed to living within. Of course, if he was going to look at everything he wanted a guy who didn't have long hair and who had a good job, so he could support his family. My dad never wanted his daughters to have to go out and work and all of this was non-negotiable.

My choice for a husband was in his third year at university and he had high ambitions which were great, but it didn't impress my dad. Each night before my dad came home I began to feel a bit anxious. I didn't know what frame of mind he was going to be in or what would transpire throughout the course of the evening.

When my dad first began this entire marriage process, I gave him the name of someone who I really liked, but my dad said, "No" to the suggestion. Therefore I moved on, and now my dad was trying to rack his brain as to who would be better suited for me to marry.

He quite often asked me the question, "Who do you want to marry?"

I kept saying the same name and he became absolutely furious. Suffice to say, that it wasn't very pretty over at our house and I was now very desperate to leave my prison.

One night in early October 1975, I listened for the sound of the garage door closing as a signal to tell me that my dad was on his way to the front door. Since the subject of marriage had come up, his arrival home each night had become something of a gut wrenching roller coaster ride for me. I didn't know it yet, but I was about to experience one of the most frightening nights of my life.

On this evening he was in a very foul mood and he gave angry looks to anyone who was within his line of sight. His eyes were searching for me and as his gaze met mine, he began slinging insults at me, even though, he had never done this before. I suppose that he was feeling rather frustrated and frantic about the entire situation. Within minutes, matters were rapidly becoming worse and a commotion began. It looked like I'd have to rely on myself against this man who was now very livid.

There was only my mom, my younger sister, and I, who were inside of the house with him. I knew that my safe keeping might be an issue, so I didn't wait around to see what was going to happen next. Therefore I quickly ran up into my sister's bedroom with her and I locked the door. I pushed her large dresser in front of it and as an added precaution, I pressed my 120 pound body frame against the dresser. And I didn't move for hours.

My father immediately bolted up to her room and repeatedly asked me to open the door because he just wanted to talk to me. He said that he wouldn't hurt me, but I knew better. This was the first time that I had openly refused to listen to him and his pleading went on for quite some time. After awhile it finally stopped. I thought that he had gone to bed, but I was not completely sure. From time to time, I wondered if I could hear the sound of my parents breathing on the other side of the door, but I wasn't going to take any chances by opening it. I was frightened and I didn't sleep at all that night. And I couldn't believe that my life had come to this point. I debated running away because there were no other options left and I prayed to God for help throughout the night.

The next morning my dad left the house to go to the health spa and I didn't come out of my bedroom until he was gone. When he returned home, my older brother came over to our house. He came into my bedroom and he said, that he had a message for me from my dad.

He said, "If you want to marry him... fine, but we will never speak to you again."

I said, "Okay" as I was thinking... "This is too easy."

My brother went to tell my dad and within seconds my parent came storming into my room with his eyes bulging out of its sockets.

My dad was furious as he said to me, "Do you mean to say that I raised you all of these years and now, you are not going to talk to us?"

I just looked at him for I had nothing more to say. I had been through enough torment and my life had become horrifying and I just wanted the agony to stop. My father knew that this whole situation had turned really ugly and it was all beginning to have its effect on him also. He told me that he was so upset that he had accidentally flushed his dental bridge down the toilet.

Then he said to me, "You can only marry him if you have a home of your own to live in and then, I will give you a car like I gave your sister when she married."

Now, it seemed like he would only allow the marriage to go ahead if the groom's parents provided a new home for us to move into when we married. And the home's title would have to be put into both of our names.

He left my bedroom and I thought, "How am I ever going to be able to tell them this?"

Later that day I phoned the person that I wanted to marry because I needed to tell him what the latest demands were. I was very embarrassed as I stated what my dad's request was. He listened to what I said and he replied, "Okay" and said something to the effect of, he was already having a house built.

In order to make everything official, there was a middle person involved who spoke with his mother regarding our proposal of marriage. After that, my older brother became the middle person with them. He and my dad went to Victoria to see the house in its building stage. And to make sure that the title was in both of our names before our engagement could ever take place. Even though it all went according to my dad's wishes, he was still unhappy and I thought that he would eventually get over it, but I was wrong.

In all fairness to my dad, he had provided a new home for my two older brothers when they married. He also insisted, that when my eldest sister married, that she had a new home with her groom too and that the title was in both of their names also. This was one of his stipulations for his children's marriages and he had plenty of respect and clout to receive it.

We got engaged within two weeks and our wedding date was set for December 13, 1975. I told my dad that I didn't want to get married on the 13th, but he was still very angry and at this point he just wanted to get it over with. He definitely didn't care what I had to say regarding anything to do with my wedding.

The first part of our engagement began on October 25, 1975 and this took place with my father, male relatives, and friends going over to Victoria to my fiancée's parent's home. My dad gave him some confectionary treats, a gold watch, and $101.00 and all of the guests in attendance also gave him sums of money.

On November 8th his family came over to our house for dinner and I received my engagement ring and one or two outfits. My fiancée and I managed to sneak out of the house after dinner for a quick kiss on our special night. And aside from my parents, most of the household knew that we were outside.

Once our engagement was over, my dad asked me a few more times "What do you see in this guy because I just don't see it?"

I didn't have an answer for him because I wasn't so sure myself. I was just hoping to get through everything till my wedding day. In hindsight as I look back on those events, I now realize how smart and intuitive my dad truly was.

My mother wouldn't allow me to select my wedding invitations. And when they were delivered, I noticed a spelling mistake on them, but she refused to take them back to get corrected. I wanted everything to be as perfect as possible, but things were turning out to be quite the opposite as I had little control over this situation. I wasn't permitted to pick out the color of my bridesmaid's dresses either, but I was happy that I was able to get the wedding dress, veil, wedding cake, flowers, and trousseau that I wanted.

On the night before our wedding, Vancouver had a huge snow storm and it ended up virtually paralyzing the whole city. My dad arrived home at midnight from my pre-wedding festivities. He looked at the snow that was still falling outside and he shook his head with quite a look of concern on his face.

He looked at me, and he said, "I will give you ANYTHING, if you call off this wedding!"

I looked at him in shock, not quite knowing what to say. It was hard to believe that he was still fighting it at this late date. My eldest sister was there also and she immediately said to him, "No daddy, it's too late now."

He paused as he looked at her and said, "It is. Okay."

Many situations of the past year displayed to what extent my dad went to as he tried to discourage me from marrying this person. I had suffered through so much misery to marry him and who knows, maybe in the end, my dad would be proven to be right.

I felt that I loved my fiancé deeply and that he loved me, but what did I really know about him or true love? How much of that, did I experience?

We didn't get a chance to see how each of us lived in our daily lives and that is absolutely something that one must consider before marrying anyone. I had led such a protected life and our values were so truly opposite from each other. How did I even know what I wanted? Also within the era that I wed, having an arranged marriage was the only option open to many of us. And at least, I had known him for the past couple of years. What I didn't realize, but I would very soon find out, was that I was about to marry a stranger anyway, even though, I thought that I knew who he was.

He was allowed every bit of freedom in regard to dating and everything else. And he didn't have to take the same route as me because his family was very modern. Why did he tolerate all that he had to go through with my dad? Did he really love me or was he just looking for the best looking woman that he could find that would marry him? Did he even know what love was? How much love had he experienced in his life? Was it warm and welcoming or was it cold and aloof? In his early beginnings when he had spent a considerable amount of time with his grandfather, I wonder given the era, could this have been quite a distant relationship? It would explain a lot of what was to come over the years.

In retrospect, I had major second thoughts about marrying him because there were more matters that concerned me about him, than what I actually liked about him. About ten days before our wedding as I was packing up my bedroom, I got an uncomfortable feeling in the pit of my stomach. I absolutely knew what it was... it was my warning that I shouldn't marry this person. It was such a strong reaction. And as I stood in front of my doubled mirrored dresser, I avoided lifting up my head, so I couldn't see my eyes.

It was too hard to face what they were saying to me. Every so often, I would glance into the mirror, but only for a few seconds and than I would quickly divert my eyes away, before they told me too much.

When I finally looked into my eyes, I knew what I was being told to do. I received the message within me, "Why are you marrying him? What are you doing?"

My forewarning came in loud and clear, but I didn't give it an answer. I swiftly went back to packing my trunk and I heard a voice say, "How attracted are you to him?"

Now I stopped in my tracks. I already had some turmoil within me and I had been in conflict with myself for the past while, regarding my up and coming marriage. On some level, I had already been receiving gut feelings to reconsider my decision because I knew it was the wrong move for me! I thought about everything that had led me up to this moment, as I considered the past year which had been a complete hell to live through.

Did I want to do that again with another guy... one that my dad and I could not agree on again?

No! I told myself that everything would be all right and things would work out. I continued with this positive attitude or rather foolish one, as I finished my task.

In all honesty, did I truly care for him or was I just so desperate to leave my home life that I would risk it all and throw all caution to the wind? Was he just a way out of a very awful situation? Was he my ticket to FREEDOM?

I didn't know it at the time, but my SOUL had reached out from the interior of my very being, bellowing at me, "STOP, DON'T MARRY HIM!"

I had no idea that the sick feeling which I had in my stomach so many years earlier was also my soul's way of cautioning me to discontinue. It appeared that my soul had not failed me. I had just failed to listen to my soul! However, I chose to disregard it because I guess... I was that desperate.

If I had been allowed to openly date, I never would have married him. He had not truly won my entire heart because of the reservations that I had within me about him. And he had certainly not been my first choice for a partner.

Many of the young adults within our culture were forced to marry, so we did. No one really knew how wonderful or how strange the person that they were marrying truly was, until they were living with one another. Several young women married so they could simply escape their family life, and begin living as a normal person or so they thought. However, what was normal? Who really was normal... the males, the females? None of us were!

Most of us had come from a similar type of upbringing and to some degree, we as females were silenced, stifled, and thought of as servants to male members of our families. This also continued for some of the young married women because of the attitudes of their husbands and the families that they had wed into.

How many of us had been raised with parents that truly honored and respected our feelings, wants, thoughts, and desires?

It takes an exceptional man to look at his pampered upbringing and break out of old traditional roles. And begin a new way of thinking and living with his wife and children in today's day and age. A woman was extremely fortunate if she was lucky enough to marry a special man who grew to truly love, respect, and appreciate her. I noticed that not many of these types of relationships had actually been created.

The past couple of years had not been very pretty, but I was looking forward to beginning a new life with my partner and further down the road, fulfilling my hopes of having a loving family of our own. We had discussions about having children and if my fiancée was not in sync with the idea, he never mentioned it to me. He knew how important having children was to me, especially since I had come from such a large family and I enjoyed my two little nieces so much.

All of the young adults in our generation were much too young and inexperienced in life to marry anybody. One never really knew their true selves or what they wanted out of their life at that age, let alone, marrying just for the sake of it. Over the years as every couple matured or not, and life changed, so did many of our needs and wishes. Some of us grew academically, some grew spiritually, and some never grew at all, while others remained as deadly and selfish as they were at the beginning of their marriages.

In today's world, whatever way we raise our children and whatever we subject them to positively or negatively, will be the situations which will influence them in their adulthood. If they know from a young age that their education comes first, their livelihood second, and marriage if at all in third place, then the vision of their future will have a different outlook and outcome then many of ours had.

In the end, would the love that I thought I felt for him survive throughout our impending marriage? Would we each add positively to one another's life's and give a chance for each others souls to lovingly learn its lessons and grow? Would the character traits that we didn't know about each other, nurture and prosper us within our destined time together, or would they eventually splinter and sever our souls to the very core of our entire beings? In any event, I made the choice to marry this man, and whatever our future held for us positively or negatively, I would deal with it. And I sincerely hoped that our union together would be great.

I thought that I loved him, yes I did,
but what did I know of love, since I was a kid?
I was shown that females were never considered as good as the rest,
and I resisted and rebelled against anyone, who put me to this test.
This was my battle in life, and I fought this concept with all my might.

– BONNY BILLAN –

It's Time To Get Married!

Chapter 6

I woke up after three hours of sleep and I quickly looked outside. It had continued snowing throughout the entire night and there were huge mounds of the white stuff everywhere. I was happy enough, but I didn't forget that the date was December 13, and deep down I didn't want to get married on this day. The one day that was truly mine had betrayed me with the weather and not only had my soul told me not to wed him, but the Gods in heaven were also telling me the same thing. However, my head and heart were full of love and I was still not listening to the forewarnings and the loud grumblings of my soul.

The wedding photographer came to our home and took pictures of my family and I, in my last moments of being single. My dad was still unhappy and very quiet. When it was time to leave for my ceremony, I rode with him in his white Lincoln to the temple where my marriage was going to take place. The ride was very uncomfortable and neither one of us said a word to each other as I sat in the back seat alone. He was angry as he was mumbling something under his breathe about the snow. I was just hoping that we wouldn't get stuck anywhere because I felt he was going to use that as the next excuse for my nuptials to not take place.

When we arrived at the church it was a bit disappointing because the weather had stopped many of our guests from attending our wedding. The groom's side made it over quite easily from Victoria, since his mother had rented a bus to get many of their clan over to the mainland. It looked like my vision of a perfect wedding wasn't going to happen on any level.

Didn't the universe know, that this was to be one of the best days of my life?

I didn't know if I should smile or not as my dad walked me down the aisle because he had such a solemn expression on his face. It was quite evident that he was giving me away to someone who he absolutely didn't like. Once we arrived at the altar, my dad helped me to sit down on a large white cushion which my groom was already sitting on. This extra padding makes it a bit nicer for every couple's comfort level as they sit throughout their lengthy service.

There's not really much for the bride and groom to take part in throughout their two to three hour ceremony. And throughout this ancient ritual, not one word is uttered between the couple. Our ceremonies are in Punjabi and I didn't really understand anything which was being said. At one point my groom and I, very quietly said a few words to each other. My mom noticed, and told one of my bridesmaids to tell us to stop talking. Near the end of our service, we each received an equal amount of money from our parents and some of our guests. My dad gave $20.00 to my spouse and me, even though he had given all of my siblings and their spouses $100.00 each. We exchanged wedding rings and were both given one end of a long white scarf to hold by my dad, to signify that we now married to one another. Once we signed the church registry the legalities were complete.

Our wedding party then went to Little Mountain at Queen Elizabeth Park to get some pictures taken. There was so much snow that our cars couldn't get up the hill, so my groom and I slowly walked up the snowy trail and the photographer got some breathtaking shots. The bridesmaids and ushers thought we were crazy. They refused to venture out of the car to join us, so we all continued onto the portrait studio for some group shots. Normally a couple returns back to the church for lunch, but because of the weather conditions we carried onto my home. After our cake cutting, I changed out of my dress so we could depart for Victoria with my husband's family. While I was getting ready, some of our female guests sang a sad song about me leaving my family. My groom sat on a chair in the middle of the living room and he once again received money from our relatives and friends.

After I said my tearful goodbyes to my family, my groom and I walked to our wedding car. I was upset that I was leaving all of them behind me. And with the way that everything had transpired with my parents, I was feeling very uncomfortable and sad. As we got into the car, I noticed that the "Best Man" was sitting in the driver's seat and a male friend of his was on the passenger side. This friend looked at me and sternly said, "STOP CRYING!"

I don't know what business it was of his, if I was crying? I had just said goodbye to everyone that I had ever loved. And as I looked back to the front porch of my home, I saw the tear stained faces of my family and it was heartbreaking. I was leaving behind the only life that I had ever known and I was now newly married and moving to a city filled with complete strangers. Little did I realize, that there would be a few weird and mean young men there also and two very strange women. I had left my old world behind me as I descended upon... some very sinister vultures.

I no sooner sat in the back seat when my husband said to me, "Give me your money."

I was so shocked by what he said and I hesitated as I decided what to do. Everyone in the car had heard him and even though, I didn't want to give him my money, I did.

He didn't pay any attention to the fact that I was crying, let alone, try to comfort me. We had only married a few hours earlier and now this supposedly "love of my life," was sitting beside me counting my money. I felt embarrassed for him, that he was so insensitive and uncouth. And I thought, "This guy has no class!" Over the years this would be confirmed to me repeatedly.

I wasn't exactly sure, how he had been raised, but I knew that our monetary backgrounds were different. The small fortune which I had given to him, included that which I had just received from my family. My first mistake was in handing it to him and my second mistake was in not speaking up about it. I sat there in shock, as tears were still streaming down my face. I should have said something to my rude groom, but I was raised to be respectful. First and foremost we were always told to be polite and I was ill prepared to go out into the world with anyone.

I had an awful feeling in my stomach. This was the first warning sign which I would receive and there would be two more to follow within the next seventy-two hours. In those moments of discomfort I knew for sure that I had made the biggest mistake of my life. And I realized that it was too late, for my karmic fate was playing out and it was now sealed.

Once we arrived in Victoria we went to his parent's home and then we proceeded onto a small reception at his aunt's home in the Broadmead area. Everyone was very nice, but I didn't know any of them. I kept waiting for my sister who lived on this side of the ocean to arrive. However, she never made it to our party and I still remember how terribly uncomfortable I felt. Our large wedding reception was going to be in January, but that was six weeks away and at this precise moment, I only knew one person in the entire city.

And it was becoming apparent that I didn't even really know him!

We spent our wedding night at the Oak Bay Beach hotel and it was nice. The next night we spent in our new home and we slept on the carpet because the bedroom suite from my parents had not been delivered yet. A couple of times I said to my new husband, that "it was hard to sleep on the carpet," but he didn't care to hear what I had to say. He had become a different person.

All he said to me was, "What do you want me to do about it?"

He was so cold, as he turned over to go to sleep and this was only the second night of our marriage! I thought that he would have wanted to at least cuddle, not to mention anything else, but he didn't. I had already begun to feel uncomfortable and I started to regret my decision to marry him. Something felt so wrong and where had his kindness gone? What about the love that he had pledged to me? He sure lost that loving feeling quickly. Why was this guy so unfeeling and distant? I didn't realize it just then, but my history of being unloved, disrespected, and treated cruelly was about to be repeated.

The next day we went grocery shopping at Safeway and even though we needed a lot of groceries, he really didn't want to buy anything. Our bill only amounted to $25.00 because he refused to spend any more and most of the food that he bought was for his work lunches. I objected, but he didn't care and by this time the feeling that I had in the pit of my stomach was very unsettling. I felt awful as I walked around the store thinking, that he had portrayed himself to be someone who he really wasn't.

He was very domineering for a child of our generation and he didn't even take a second to consider any of my wishes. Also he had not only shown me that he lacked any compassion towards his new wife, but he was also very CHEAP! It was suffice to say, that he had hidden these traits quite well and he had changed within three hours of us getting married. I guess that he didn't need to hide, who he was anymore and it looked like my days of the Hyatt and Quarry house were over. Now that he had finally shown his true colors, deep down I didn't really like him and I was seriously considering, how I could escape from my marriage!

All of us have a guidance system that alerts us regarding different people, situations, and sometimes even impending disasters. It may come through a message or a little voice in your mind or you may experience a sick feeling in your gut. Otherwise, you might just simply know within yourself of someone or something to avoid. These are all little gifts that God gave to us to help us through life and we need to pay attention to these warnings before it is too late. I had my warnings also, but I had chosen to not listen to them by tossing them aside because I was so frantic to begin a new life. Also because I was young and lacking any outside life experiences, I didn't have the true understanding and insight to really see what was happening in my world. It was clouded over, even though, my soul had tried to protect me when it told me, "Not to marry him." When I looked into my eyes and felt what was truly within my body, there really was no more that needed to be said. If my family living had not been so disciplined and smothering to endure, my life choices would have been different and my life would have been also.

Now that I had gone from my parent's home to that of my husband's, I started out content enough, but what did I know of happiness. What was happiness? All that I had to compare it to was the stifling life of my past.

My new world was going to be a big adjustment and this was not only due to the fact that I was now married, but also to the fact that I was somewhat free. However... was my soul truly free? It seemed like my spouse was not much different than my previous years were, and he was just another overbearing and controlling male from my culture. Would I ever escape the deep demons of my history and live with whatever demons he was carrying deep within the confines of his soul? I was now, so concerned about, how all of this was going to work itself out.

We had moved into a beautiful new home in a nice area of town and it was quite close to Arbutus school and the University of Victoria. Our wedding gifts provided us with much of everything that we needed to set up our home completely. I didn't get the car that my dad had promised me, but he bought a very nice king size bedroom suite. And a crushed velvet sofa and chair set that complimented our living room carpet perfectly. We were also given all of our appliances, a washer, dryer, a kitchen table set, a large television, and even a deep freezer as gifts from family members. Also we received enough money to buy a dining room suite, and I was even given a sewing machine because I liked to sew so much. The only things that we needed to buy were two end tables for the living room and two lamps. We went to an exclusive store to buy them and the two tables that I wanted to buy were $169.00 each, and the color of the wood on them matched the wood on our sofa set exactly. However, my spouse wasn't interested in what I had to say about it. He went ahead and bought two different shaped tables in a different color while I was still protesting. One of them was put in front of the sofa and the other one was put on the side of it. I truly disliked both of them and I wasn't too crazy about him either. It was becoming apparent that he wasn't about to consider or listen to any of my wishes.

With some of our wedding gift money his mother said, that we had to buy a dining room set from the department store where she worked at that time. She gave us the choice of two different sets, but I didn't like either of them. I would have preferred a light cream color set, but again, no one cared what I had to say. His mother made sure that it was delivered in time for the weekend of our reception, so her friends could see our home was fully furnished. The day after the reception, our home was filled end to end with their guests. And as soon as they started arriving, my family left immediately to go back to Vancouver. If my mother-in-law didn't invite all of these people over, I could have visited with my family much longer, but now I was alone once again with all of these strangers. The night before was a very late night and I was exhausted. And the last thing that I wanted to do was to entertain anyone. Our lifestyles had been so different in that I came from quite a quiet home life and he came from a home filled with much socializing. Consequently whether I liked it or not, it seemed that this was now my lifestyle too.

Our home was very nice, but I was only able to pick out three of the carpet colors. My mother-in-law and her son had picked out everything else. It really would have been satisfying for me to pick out something that I liked in the way of any furniture.

One day as I opened the front door I was quite surprised! My spouse and a friend of his were about to bring in his parents old dilapidated bedroom suite from when they first married. She wanted him to put it, in one of our spare bedrooms. No one asked or told me anything about this matter, and I certainly didn't want anyone's old stained mattress and smelly, decayed furniture in our new home. His mother knew no boundaries whatsoever in any part of our lives, and her son simply followed along with almost everything she said.

When we went to my parent's home to open our wedding gifts, my father told other members of my family that they could also open our gifts at the same time. Though, he had never done this to any of my siblings. As soon as I asked them, what they were doing, my dad said, "Do you mind if I see what my friends gave?"

My dad was being very mean. When it came time to go to bed, he made my spouse sleep downstairs because he didn't want him upstairs since my younger sister's room was beside ours. I went to bed in tears and I got up early so we could take our leave as soon as possible. We had rented a small mini van to take my trunk of clothes and gifts back to Victoria, but my dad only wanted us to take what we absolutely needed and to leave the rest. Fortunately my eldest brother was over and he helped us load my belongings into the van, and he packed most of our gifts into it too. I felt awful and I guess that my dad was going to follow through on what he said, about having nothing to do with me, if I married who I did. As we pulled away from the curb, my eyes filled with tears. On one hand, I was leaving my family once again and the last forty-eight hours had not been very enjoyable. On the other hand, look who I was leaving with. Life was somewhat unpleasant… anywhere I turned.

My in-laws were very modern people in every which way possible and they were more up to date then I was. They were big hearted people who were kind and always very generous and they enjoyed entertaining people from every age group in their home. In the beginning of our marriage, it was quite a huge change for me because they often had quite a crowd at their house. If there was ever a main event in town, everyone visited them and their home was absolutely jam-packed. One could rarely get any peace when at their home and a quiet one on one conversation with anyone very seldomly happened. I never cared for the large gatherings.

My father-in-law was a quiet sort of man who never caused anyone any grief and he was always kind to me. My mother-in-law was nice to me also, but she pushed herself into every facet of our existence. Her strength was overwhelming as she also tried to force her beliefs onto me. I wasn't a weak person, but I was quiet as I was trying to get to know these people. I certainly didn't want her telling me what I should be doing. I was polite and I followed along out of respect for her, but I wanted to live my life on my own terms.

She found it hard to mind her own business and she voiced her opinions on everything, as she cut into any conversation that I was having with another. When we first married, she moved things around in our home whenever she visited us. I felt very uneasy about this matter, but out of respect I never said anything to her regarding it. Yet I looked at her with a stunned expression on my face, but she never noticed and after she left I moved the items back into their original places.

When my mother-in-law first saw our wedding pictures, she said that they weren't very nice and we needed to have them retaken. She didn't even want one of her son and me from the day of our wedding, but I gave her one anyway. Quite surprisingly, she wasn't thrilled about it and didn't try to hide her dislike for it.

A year later on the day that her daughter was getting married, we had our wedding pictures retaken because she insisted upon it. We were also in the wedding party and three hours before the ceremony was about to begin, we met her daughter's photographer at Government House. I had to buy another bouquet and get back into my wedding dress and my husband wore his wedding suit, even though, it wasn't what he wore to our wedding. Actually her daughter was ready to get married long before we were, but she was told that she had to wait until we were wed. She was marrying a guy outside of our culture, and her mother knew that if my dad had discovered this, our marriage would never take place. Consequently, she and her fiancée had to abide by this decision.

My spouse's mother didn't give a second thought to inviting people over to our place for a visit and this went on for many years, regardless of whether I wanted company or not. This is what my life was like with her and she did whatever she wanted to do without ever checking, if it was okay to do so. I never enjoyed living in Victoria and I would have preferred to be living back in Vancouver anytime.

A few months after our marriage, my dad came to Victoria for a friend's wedding and he asked me, "How are things going?"

I burst out crying in front of everyone.

He was in shock, as was my mother-in-law. My dad took me aside to ask if everything was okay, but I didn't tell him the truth. I couldn't explain to him that I made a mistake because I knew that there was no turning back in my situation.

I said, "Everything is fine."

My dad asked me once again, "Are you sure?"

I said, "Yes."

If I had ever received any sort of loving support from my dad, I never would have stayed with my spouse and I would have left immediately without ever looking back!

Within our marriage, my everyday living went along well enough, but if I ever bought anything at all, my spouse became terribly upset no matter what the item cost. If I spent five or ten dollars, let alone, twenty, he would have a fit and wanted me to return the item immediately. He was in his last year of university working towards his Bachelor of Arts degree and I was working full time.

Every time that I went back to visit my family, my dad always gave me money as I was leaving to come back home. I told my spouse that this is what I used to buy whatever I did. This part of my life was absolutely awful and it deeply worsened to past dreadful as the years went by.

I kept an immaculate home and I expected him to do the same, but he was sloppy. And on the weekends he never cleaned himself up, unless he was going out somewhere. I decorated our home the way that I wanted to and he never cared to get involved, let alone, offer any help. We really didn't have much in common with one another.

Life improved as we got to know each other and I was somewhat happy, except in the moments when I missed my family and I truly missed them a lot. My spouse was considerate when it was my birthday. We always went out for dinner. And earlier in the day, he often went to the restaurant which we were going to be dining at that evening, and left a birthday cake there for me. After dinner, the staff came out with the lit birthday cake and sang happy birthday. It was special and very kind of him to do this, and quite often he also had flowers delivered for my birthdays and Valentine's Days. We showed a lot of affection for each other and we enjoyed a great loving relationship.

In the beginning, my spouse was fairly nice and somewhat giving, but he always put his needs first. He also had a mean streak within him and if he ever got angry, it could last for quite some time. And no matter what I said or did, he was frigid and unemotional. In those moments, whatever way I turned, I couldn't win.

We had now been married for two and half years and the only item which we didn't have for our home were drapes for our bedroom window.

Consequently, there was a bed sheet covering our large wall to wall windowpane. I had wanted to get curtains to replace it, but he never agreed with me and let's face it, he was damm cheap! Every other part of our home was decorated with great care except this window and every morning, I took the sheet down and put it back up at night. He thought that it was quite funny and he joked about it to his friends, but I didn't find the humor in it. His mocking only added fuel to my frenzy over it. and I was so very embarrassed about it. By this point, there was even mould growing on the sheet.

We were about to begin a family and I knew that if I didn't get the drapes now, we probably never would. I had some extra money from a cheque that I had received from my work sooooooooo, I went with his mother and ordered full length wall to wall drapes and a matching bedspread for our bed. Oh YES, I did!

OKAY... I admit, that I went way overboard. The items didn't need to be full length or velvet. Anyway, you can well imagine what his reaction was when he saw the bedroom in its entire splendor. He had a complete fit and he wanted me to take it all back, but it was a custom order so that wasn't a possibility. As a result, he didn't speak to me for an entire month.

What effect do you think that this would have on your spirit, if your partner didn't speak to you for this amount of time?

My whole marriage was like this and he questioned me about every purchase that I ever made. He went to the bank every Saturday to get a print out of our chequing account and then he came back home to interrogate me about it. Later on in our marriage, he began to call me a sponge... and a leech... for leeching off of him.

When we went out for a special celebration dinner to a nice restaurant, we could never eat at a reasonable hour because my spouse wanted to have cocktails for awhile. He didn't want to have any alcoholic beverages after he ate his dinner, so instead we rarely had our meal before 11:00 p.m. or later. When we finally placed our orders, the kitchen was often out of whatever we wanted. After our dinners came, he gobbled his up so fast and then he started eating mine. We always had another couple with us, so I never said anything to him about it because I didn't want to embarrass him. However, he was certainly lacking in social graces.

One day he had a label maker and he was making labels for some of his files. He thought that it would be funny to make labels with my weight stamped on them, and then I could arrange my clothes under these categories in my closet. His began with a sticker for ninety pounds, even though, I had never been lower than one hundred and twelve pounds. The next ones were for ninety-five, one hundred, one hundred and five, etc., all the way up to one hundred and thirty pounds. He thought that this was pretty funny and of course, he proudly told his friends about it.

93

Quite often when we were entertaining, he made it a point to tell a joke with me as the brunt of it. I asked him, why he did this and he said that he was just kidding. I'm certainly not saying, that I never said anything about him. Hell... there was so much material to work with, but there was something very bizarre about him. He did his utmost to be condescending to me, but why? Did it make him feel superior to me?

On a couple of different occasions I told his mom how mean he was, but she never said a word back to me, she just stared. It was the first time that she was ever speechless! Some years into our marriage, I told his father that I would never stay married to him and his father laughingly said to me, "You'll never leave him."

I said to him, "Yes, I will." I knew at that point, that I wasn't going to stay with him for the rest of my life.

When one of his grandparents passed on, my spouse said that I didn't need to ride in the family car because I wasn't a part of their family. One of his aunts shouted out to him, "She is so!"

I now had parents that didn't consider me a part of their family and I was married to an idiot, who felt much the same way.

Whenever anyone in my family came to visit me, my mother-in-law invited herself over to our home or told all of us to come over to her place. I rarely had a private visit with them and over the years I couldn't stand it. When we did get together, we had to do it in secrecy or we had a time limit. I could never quite relax. It was an awful way to live. She was so INTRUSIVE in every which way.

Whatever way his mother wanted things to be, that was the way they were. We both had strong personalities and even though our relationship started out well enough, over time our feelings for one another became obvious because we rarely agreed with one another. She wanted people to think that everything was fine, but we never truly bonded and we grew to just tolerate each other. I doubt that she ever enjoyed my company either and from the moment that I married, she always raved and commented about how much she just loved one of my sisters. She repeatedly said, that she'd always be her favorite and she considered her to be her pet. And she continually voiced this to me throughout the years. It wasn't exactly the right way to endear a new daughter-in-law to one and I didn't have the heart to tell her, that I also preferred one of her sisters to her.

I didn't need her help for anything because I had been brought up with so much knowledge regarding the house and home. I could entertain, decorate, bake, cook, wallpaper, paint, garden, sew, crochet, knit, and needlepoint. In addition, I also knew a lot about childcare since I already had nieces and nephews. I think that she considered me to be her rival. She needed to show me that she knew better, but my mother had already taught me how to do so many things, and anything that I didn't know, I learnt it on my own. This woman eventually tried to erode my self esteem as best as she could. I never received any praise from her, but she was very quick to point out anything which she regarded as a flaw. I now had her and her son as the bane of my existence.

One day matters became even worse. Whenever we were over at her home especially when she had any company, she served appetizers to everyone in the room, but me. At first I thought that I was mistaken, but it happened repeatedly. I felt kind of sick about it, but I never confronted her about it. I wasn't sure who had the worst attitude, she or her son, but one thing was for certain, I was definitely lacking kind relatives in my life, at least on this side of the ocean! When life became too much to handle, I went to Vancouver for a visit. And as I was driving off the ferry over there, I felt like I was home and I could breathe and smile easily.

I also had a sibling who was living in Victoria for a time and our relationship went along well enough. However at some point in time, I couldn't understand why it seemed that whenever I was out at a function with a certain group of people, some of them were not as friendly to me as they once were. One of them wouldn't even speak to me and in fact, he was the same male who had told me to stop crying on my wedding day. I always minded my own business, I had never been a gossip, and I rarely saw any of these people, so I wondered what the heck was going on. It wasn't until years later that I found out from one of them, that my sibling had told a lot of people, that I was saying negative things about them.

I was shocked as I said to this person, "I didn't even know you, how could I say anything about you? I was always at home raising my children."

She replied, "Well I didn't know and she was so convincing!"

I now had another person I needed to be wary of. I had a triple threat and I hadn't even realized it. Years down the road I asked my sibling, "Why she did this to me, since I always treated her in a decent way?"

She replied that she wasn't in the best state at those times and I had everything... a husband, children, and a nice home. Another woman who had divorced and had a young child said to me, that I had such a nice family as she looked at me with disappointment about her life. I don't think that either of them realized, how very hard I worked and persevered at keeping our lives all together and smooth flowing. And I rarely veered off track. Also I had children to consider and the need to truly concentrate on myself had never been a major part of who I was. We were all different types of women and as I dedicated much of my time to my children, they had given their moments to themselves which were filled with many self indulged pleasures.

Much of my social life was also touched by my mother-in-law. She pushed herself onto many younger people. And since she opened her heart and her home to them, she and her husband were invited to every function and party that we were ever at. One day she and I, were both at a pre-wedding stag for a young friend and there was a male stripper there for entertainment. How was I able to truly enjoy the spirit of that event with her there? When was I ever able to really let loose? I suppose it was my problem if I couldn't.

Can you imagine how you would feel if you rarely had a private life of your own?

My life had become challenging for me many times since I moved to Vancouver Island. Every new bride finds out very quickly what adjustments and sacrifices that she is expected to make on behalf of her husband's family. And since she is the new one going in, her struggles are imminent. I don't know of any woman who has had it easy. However, if they have a caring, unselfish, and supportive husband at their side, then they have won three quarters of their upcoming battles and they are truly very fortunate.

I had already experienced much domination and rejection in my childhood and now there were others, who were adding to the insecurity of my spirit. And their negativity was having an adverse effect on my happiness and sense of well being.

To be a mom, that's what I want,
I truly do, oh so much.
The gift of holding my babies in my arms,
and to always keep them safe from any harm.

– BONNY BILLAN –

Gifts From Heaven

Chapter 7

We had now been married for three years and my husband had graduated from university and he had a great job. Our life was going along quite well and I was ready to start our family. My desire at that time was to have two children spaced a couple of years apart, and to be well done before I was anywhere near thirty years old. He wanted to wait, but I was twenty-three years old and I wished to begin in order to stay on my course, it was after all, my body.

I was working at the Memorial Arena at the time and as I was about to leave for work one morning, my stomach started feeling a bit unsettled. I took two "Rolaid pills" to try and calm it and this continued for three days. At the end of each day the thought of having dinner made me feel queasy.

On the third day as I was driving along on Shelbourne Street at 4:42 p.m., it finally dawned on me, that I must be pregnant. I had planned to go off of my birth control pill for three months before we even tried conceiving, so my body would have a chance to return to its normal state. Also, even though, we had taken other precautions for the past two months, it seemed like God and Mother Nature had other ideas for me.

I had been wearing an expensive gold amethyst ring which had turned

97

the skin on one of my fingers a dark blue color. Therefore I already knew, that something different was going on in my body, but what could it be? Nothing like this had ever happened before, even though, I had been wearing this ring for six years. I called my doctor's office to tell them that I thought that I was expecting a baby, and they suggested that I wait another month before I went in for a blood test. After the results came back, it was confirmed that I was indeed pregnant.

Our first child was due on June 30, 1979 and I was happily awaiting the new arrival into our life, but that date came and left with no sign of a baby. Six days later, I began having labor pains and at 5:55 p.m. we arrived at the Jubilee Hospital here in Victoria. Over the next few hours my labor was becoming increasingly difficult to handle, and my spasms were so close together that I couldn't even speak. I had decided to have a natural Lamaze delivery, so I had no medication at all. I didn't want any drugs which was given to me, to be transferred to my baby. Now years later, I surely have second thoughts about denying myself any of this help, but that ship has already sailed. What on earth was I thinking? It was such a tormenting condition to be in and I was in a great deal of agony without any medicinal help! I must have been out of my mind to even consider this option!

A specialist was called in at 10:00 p.m. for a consultation because my doctor wasn't sure if I needed to have a cesarean delivery or not, since the head of the baby was not working its way down. I was in so much anguish that I couldn't even get the words out of my mouth to tell the doctors, that this was the last thing that I ever wanted. The specialist said that he thought that I would be able to deliver the baby naturally, so at midnight I was wheeled into the delivery room.

It had the biggest, brightest lights that I have ever seen. I began pushing for a while, but my baby's head was just not crowning, so the doctor said that he was going to do a forceps delivery. I opened my eyes and I saw a gigantic set of metal tongs coming at me. I closed my eyes fast because I just couldn't watch. The pain was excruciating as the doctor inserted the tongs into me and I was frantically wondering where I could get any drugs fast! He put the tongs around the babies head and pulled the infant out.

Our healthy baby boy was born on July 7, at12:59 a.m. and he weighed eight pounds and two ounces. He had so much hair that whenever anyone looked into the nursery window, I could always hear them saying, "Look at that baby with all the hair!"

It was such a special feeling to hold my baby and to be granted such a wonderful and miraculous gift. My spouse left quickly afterwards because he said that he was tired, but he returned around noon with a beautiful bouquet of yellow roses for me.

On the day of our home coming, my husband didn't want to take a few hours off from working at a summer job at the parks department, so his mother came to take us home. As we were driving along, I remembered that I didn't have a house key so we went to his place of work to get one.

My spouse was on his lunch break and we waited in the sweltering heat in the car with a baby who wanted his bottle very badly. Thirty-five minutes later he drove into the lot and he gave me the key. There was no reason why he couldn't take us home himself, other than, he just didn't want to. I was disappointed in him. I treated him well and we deserved better, but he had an arrogant attitude that could be seen in every area of our marriage.

His Mother was understandably very excited about her first grandchild and once we got home, she told me not to do anything. She said, that she would get the baby's bottles ready for his formula by rinsing them under hot water and filling them up with milk. I told her that I wanted to sterilize the bottles and she said that I didn't need to do that. This is where my struggles began with her in regards to the care of my children.

I said to her, "I am sterilizing them."

She went to rinse the bottles out before putting them into the sterilizer and I took them out and started re-rinsing them. She asked me, why I was rinsing them out again?

I showed her the bottles which were still filled with suds and after that moment, she didn't have anything to say and she moved out of my way.

Her answer to everything to do with cleanliness was that it was good enough for her kids, and dirt never hurt anyone and they turned out all right. What she didn't realize was, that this was my child and I would do things the way that I wanted to. Whatever she did, she did in the quickest way possible, and I did everything to the best of my ability with the high standard of living that I was raised with. This whole episode could have been avoided, if my spouse had just taken the time to drive us home. It seemed like the moments in my life that I wanted to cherish the most were often overshadowed by someone else's negativity.

When I first became pregnant my mother-in-law said to me, you sure can tell that you've gained weight.

I told her, "I am three months along and I've only gained three pounds."

She answered me by saying, "It's all on your face."

His mother often had something to say in a judgmental manner. And since I was a self-sufficient person and I never needed her for anything, she couldn't wait to get her digs into me whenever she could. Throughout my pregnancy she said, to me, "Don't think that I'm staying at home to baby-sit your baby."

I was so worried throughout this time thinking about this and often wondered, "Why couldn't she just be a regular mother-in-law?"

Sometime after the birth of my first child my in-laws were away for six weeks and I started exercising everyday. And by the time they got back, I had lost 20 lbs. I now weighed 125. I thought for sure, she would say something positive about my weight loss. I even had her face in my mind whenever I did my daily one hundred sit-ups. However, she never said one word to me about it, even though, a lot of people were commenting on the weight that I had released.

One of my sisters even said to her, "Doesn't Bonny look great?"

My mother-in-law looked at her and said, "It was about time she lost it."

I knew right then and there, that I would never be able to please her no matter what I did, and it seemed that our relationship had turned into a competition of sorts.

From the time that I had my first child, whenever my husband came home from work each day, he picked up the mail and the newspaper and he sat down. After a week of this I asked him, "Aren't you going to see the baby?" He slowly started changing this routine. I guess that it's hard for some men to relate to babies.

Whenever we were out in public, our friend's husbands always ran over to see our son in his carriage, no matter what age he was. I always wanted a very attentive father for my children and with the way that we married; I didn't have the opportunity to meet someone better suited to my desires.

I was very happy being a mother and my infant quickly won over a lot of my affection which I felt for my husband. My son became number one in my life and I discovered that I loved my child more than I did him.

One day when I was washing my hair in the shower, I had a strong sudden urge to go and check my sleeping baby in his crib. The feeling was overwhelming, so I wrapped a towel around myself and with my hair dripping, I went into the nursery and looked into his crib. My son was lying on his stomach awake and he had vomited, but luckily he had his head raised away from it. He had never gotten sick before and I quickly picked him up and changed him and his sheets. I don't know where this warning came from, but I was very grateful for it. On another occasion while I was showering, I thought that I should make sure that he was all right and when I did, he was sleeping peacefully.

Our son never cried during the first year of his life and if he did, it was just one little cry for his milk bottle. He was very special and this was especially so on my husband's side of the family, since he was the first grandchild born. As the weeks went by and his personality emerged, his father became a very loving and good father. On Sunday mornings he always woke up earlier than me and feed him his breakfast, so I could sleep in. Later in the day, we always went out to do something special with our little guy.

Since the birth of our son, I never really missed my husband whenever I went to Vancouver to visit my family. I was with the one person who I loved completely and who gave me my greatest joy in life. When I was near him the happiness that I saw on his face warmed my heart and told me, that what I was doing was so much more than just worthwhile. There were no strings attached to his love and my life was great.

One day in the month of September 1981 I wasn't feeling very well, so I went to see my doctor. I discovered that I was expecting our second child and I was already ten weeks along in my pregnancy. This was quite a shock since I had just stopped taking my birth control pill. We were going to use another method of contraception, but we never had the chance to. My plan was to once again stop using it for at least 3 months, but apparently all I have to do is think about this state and it happens.

On the evening of September 23 I was totally exhausted and not feeling very well. I had spent a full day taking care of our very active two year old son and doing my daily household tasks to maintain our spotless home. After I made dinner and cleaned up the kitchen I was so drained of energy, that I just really wanted to lie down and rest.

I told my spouse how awful I was feeling and that I wasn't going to go with him and our son to kindergym. However, he didn't agree with my decision and he started to harass me. He knew that I was expecting and yet he had no compassion within him whatsoever, so I decided to go only for our son's sake. We proceeded to the gym at Henderson Center which was about seven minutes away from our home.

Once we were there, I sat down on the hard gym bench with nothing, but the cold yellow cement wall to lean against. It was uncomfortable, but at least it was support because by this time, I was beginning to feel worse. I watched my son run happily from toy to toy and I managed a smile for him whenever he looked in my direction. I stayed in the gym for only ten minutes before I got up to go to the restroom because I felt like something wasn't quite right. I sensed that an event was going to happen to me and as I stood in the bathroom thinking, I didn't know what it could possibly be. I paced back and forth trying to figure it out. I really just wanted to be at home in my bed!

Why didn't I just do that? Oh... I remember now. I didn't because I had been bullied into going, so instead of disappointing anyone else I would be the one to pay the high price for that decision.

I went back into the gym and I sat there for about fifteen minutes, when all of a sudden I had a strong feeling that I should go home right away. Our son was having so much fun and I hated to ask him to leave, but I suddenly jumped up and said "We have to leave now, RIGHT NOW!"

My spouse stared at me, but he didn't argue about it and our son came without a complaint too. He drove home and as soon as he stopped the car in our driveway, I quickly snatched the keys out of the ignition and hurried to our front door. I had a strange feeling within me and after I ran up the stairs to our hallway, I very quickly continued to my en-suite bathroom.

I sat down on the toilet and that's when it happened. Something rushed out of me and it was awfully big, but what could it be? I was afraid to look!

I started to shiver a little and I knew that I had to get up to see what had just happened. After a few minutes, I stood up and as I looked down into the porcelain bowl my stomach felt sick. I had never seen whatever that was, ever before.

I knelt down on the bathroom carpeting so I could peer inside to get a closer look and the image that I saw will be etched in my mind for the remaining days of my life. I knew that I hadn't been feeling very well, but what was I looking at?

Could it be the child that was growing inside of me?

How was I going to tell if it was? I really didn't want to pick it up. I started praying that it was something else, but on some level I knew what it was. I sensed deep down, that I miscarried my baby!

What was I going to do now? I had lost my child!

The one who I had only known about for the past few days, but the one, who my soul had already begun loving, nourishing, and taking care of for quite some time. It was a part of me, and how was I going to continue my pregnancy without it inside of me? How was I going to get it back within me, so that everything would be all right. And life would be the same as it had been that morning when I had first woken up? How could I turn back the hands of time?

I simply couldn't believe what had taken place and I was shocked as I stared in complete utter horror! Things like this just didn't happen to me! Oh God... WHY?

I phoned my doctor to see what I should do next. He suggested that I didn't have a miscarriage. And that I should remove whatever it was and put it into a jar filled with rubbing alcohol. Once that was done, he wanted it taken to a lab in the morning for testing. After I spoke to my doctor, I was somewhat relieved and I thought that perhaps I had a second chance, but I once again felt a sense of horror. I was mortified at what the doctor was asking me to do! I certainly didn't want to follow his instructions, but I knew that I had to. I asked my husband to bring me something so I could pick up the mass. He brought me two forks.

I was a bit frantic as I said to him, "Am I suppose to stab it out of the toilet? Get me two large spoons!"

Once I had them, I proceeded to pick up the bundle and put it into a jar and I covered it with the alcohol. I left the container on my bathroom countertop and throughout the night I stared in disbelief at the jar's contents. I was cold, shaken, and very numb. My body was drained of human life and I felt as if all of my energy had suddenly been sucked out of me.

Earlier I had asked my husband to call his mother to see if she could watch our son, just in case I had to go to the hospital. What a mistake that proved to be! She came over to our house and then she and her son argued non-stop outside my bedroom door because she insisted on seeing what was in the jar!

He kept saying "No," to her and she continued battling insisting with her demands.

This woman never knew when to stop intruding in anyone's business, let alone, what the meaning of the word "No," meant.

I just wanted them to stop arguing, so I yelled out, "LET HER SEE IT!"

A few days later, I went for an ultra sound scan and as I looked at the monitor, I could see that there was nothing inside my stomach. Hot tears trickled down my face as my heart felt the loss. I didn't need to have anyone tell me that I was no longer pregnant. I already knew.

My doctor told me that it was a complete miscarriage and that something went wrong at the very beginning. He added that there would have also been a problem with the baby had it been born and that, this was nature's way of taking care of an unborn fetus. And having a miscarriage is the reason, why there were not a lot more handicapped people around.

My husband stayed home for a few days to take care of our son while I was recuperating, but he wouldn't comfort or even speak to me. He never tried to console the part of me that ached. He didn't care about any pain that I was in emotionally, nor did he tell me that everything would be all right. And he didn't say to me, that we could try again. Most importantly, he never told me that he loved me. My deeply callous spouse didn't talk to me for at least three weeks and he never once mentioned the fact, that he bullied me into going out that night. This behavior was deplorable even for him and once again, I was reminded about my idiotic decision to marry him!

I thanked God that I had my two year old child to hold close and love at this awful time in my life. When my little son hugged me, I hid my eyes that were filled with my burning tears, pain, and sorrow. I will always be grateful to him, for he was the only one that I had to hold at this time in my life. He helped me greatly to get through a very painful period, even though, he never knew what he was doing. I was also thankful that this didn't happen while I was still in the gym, where there were many little children with their parents, grandparents, and instructors all about.

From the time that I miscarried, whenever I passed the baby department in any store I always stopped and looked at the matching baby outfits. I constantly said to myself, "If I had twins, a boy and a girl, I would buy this outfit for him and this matching outfit for her." This carried on for years and I just couldn't shake it each time that I went out shopping.

I waited three months and I became pregnant again. This baby was due on September 17, 1982. When I heard the good news, I phoned my spouse at his work place and told him about it. He was happy and so was I. Later that day, I received a plant of daisies from him and my son which included a card that said, "Congratulations, you mean a lot to us."

This time everything went along well, until one day when I was getting off of an escalator during my fifth month. I became dizzy and I fell down. As I was falling, I put my hands out to protect my stomach and after I had a checkup with my doctor, he said that I was fine. I hoped that he was right.

One day when I was eight months pregnant, my spouse and I were playing with our son on the carpet in the hallway. I don't know why I decided at that stage of my pregnancy to be on the ground, but there I was with them. My son was playing a game and he was hitting my husband lightly, but when I hit my spouse, he got mad at me within a split second. As a result, he got up and sat on my stomach and I couldn't even breathe. I JUST COULDN'T BREATHE OR SPEAK!

This JERK could not have cared less! He is over six feet tall and I am five feet and four inches tall, but this is how cruel he truly was at times. I still have my diary with this entry in it from 1982.

On another occasion, my spouse came home from having a haircut and he asked me what I thought of it, since he had it cut in a different way than he normally did. His hair meant the world to him and he always spent hours styling it. I didn't want to answer him, but he kept asking me, so I said I preferred his hair cut the other way, and that's all that I said. However, within a few seconds he became so angry that he picked up a frozen pound of bacon off of the counter, and hurled it through the kitchen window. There was now shattered glass spread all over the kitchen floor and on the sundeck outside. Thank goodness that our son was playing in another part of the kitchen area! I couldn't believe, what had just happened over his freaking hair! I told him to get the window fixed immediately and I didn't care what it took to do it, especially since it was the weekend. He called a family friend who had a glass framing shop and he came to put a new window in. My spouse told him that our son had thrown a toy through the glass. Most of the time my husband was a very controlled and mild mannered person so these couple of incidences were out of place for him. It didn't quit match who he was or what he portrayed himself to be. He even shocked me!

I had fulfilled my role by being a good wife to him. I helped him in his career especially whenever he needed anything done such as typing his documents. I had prepared his resume and made one hundred copies of it, but nothing I did was good enough for him. He also returned every gift that I ever gave to him unless it was gold. Many years later, he said to me that it was good that I ironed his clothes because it gave him a head start in the morning, when he re-ironed the same item. This was the moment that I stopped ironing his clothes for good.

When we first got married, he wouldn't wear his wedding ring and I kept asking him where it was? He repeatedly said that it was in his glove compartment and weeks later when I checked in there, it wasn't anywhere to be seen. There was no sign of it in our home and I wondered if he had just thrown it out? I guessed that he didn't want to wear it because my Dad had picked it out for him, so on our first anniversary I bought him a gold one with a little diamond in it. He wore this one. I'm sure that when my father rejected him so deeply, it just added to whatever he truly believed about himself from his upbringing. However, I was honestly trying to love him devotedly, but his mistreatment towards me was constant and very overpowering and it had begun to override my feelings for him.

Furthermore, the universe seemed to be sending me some sort of message because quite often on our anniversary something strange happened. The first year my hair started sizzling from a candle which was on the table, as I leaned over to give him a kiss. The next year I lost a stone from my wedding ring set and I can't remember what happened the third year. However, I was a bit concerned over all of the odd occurrences on this day each year.

Our second child was now five days overdue and my labor started in the evening of September 22. My spouse was at a wine and cheese party which was at a hall, and he never called home to see how I was. My cramps continued throughout the evening and into the wee hours of the morning. When he arrived home at 1:10 a.m. I told him that I was in labor. He had had a lot to drink and he just conked out on the bed. And even at the best of times, he could only handle a couple of drinks at a time. Throughout the night as I was timing the intervals of my labor pains, I was becoming more and more anxious because my labor coach was still passed out. At this point, my contractions were beginning to get very close and I kept trying to wake him up, but he wasn't budging. I actually waited until 6:00 a.m. so he could get some more sleep and then I TOLD him, that he had to get up. He was angry about it and after ten minutes he got up. It takes him at least 1 ½ hours to get himself ready everyday.

His mother came and got our son and told me not to worry about him. And before I knew it, she had dropped him off at her other son's place who had just had some sort of surgery. She then went off to work.

My spouse was ready at 7:30 a.m. all dressed with every hair in place and after he walked into the kitchen, he went to the cupboard and took out a frying pan.

I asked him, "What are you doing?"

He said, "I am making myself an egg."

I yelled out, "Oh no, you aren't! I have to GO TO THE HOSPITAL NOW!"

He didn't listen to me, as he put the kettle on and waited for the water to boil. After he made himself a cup of coffee, he asked me, "Can you walk down the driveway or DO YOU WANT ME TO BRING THE CAR IN FRONT OF THE HOUSE?"

His car was parked at the end of our long driveway so I told him, "THIS TIME I WANT THE CAR IN FRONT OF THE HOUSE!"

He looked at me in a disrespectful manner as he sipped on his coffee and went to get the car. On the way to the hospital he put on his right hand turn signal, but we still had quite a distance to go until we were at our destination. It was all straight forward driving at this point and I wondered, what he was up to now?

I asked him, "Where are you going?"

He answered, "To McDonalds... I need something to eat."

I said to him through my contractions, "Drop me off at the hospital and then go and get something to eat!"

We arrived at the hospital at 8:04 a.m. and when the nurse examined me, she said that I wouldn't be delivering until that afternoon. Hence my spouse, my partner, my labor coach, left the hospital immediately and went across the street to "Mr. Mike's, so he could satisfy his selfish cravings.

My contractions were two minutes apart and I needed to go to the bathroom which was at the far end of a very long hallway. As well, my labor pains were so bad that as I inched my way along the passageway, I had to stop and lean against the walls until some of it subsided. I was so hot and I needed a cold compress or something, but there was not a medical person in sight. I managed to get to the washroom and I was in there for at least twenty minutes or more, and then I slowly made my way back to my room. As I sat on the bed, I had three sharp contractions and I had to go the bathroom again. I somehow made my way down the long corridor and as I sat down on the toilet, I felt like pushing. I stood up, but I couldn't stop myself from pushing. There was blood dripping away onto the floor and as I reached down to check myself, I could feel the baby's head with my finger. I was in so much pain and as I flicked on the emergency buzzer, the dud had made his way back from his breakfast.

He could hear me groaning through the bathroom door and he asked me, "Are you okay?"

I screamed out, "NOOOOOOOOO!"

All of a sudden, the empty ghost like hallway filled up with five medical personnel who came running out of nowhere. And as they dragged me to the delivery room, I left a trail of blood behind me.

They quickly put my feet into the stirrups and two seconds later, our second son was born at 10:11 a.m. After his birth, he didn't make a sound for quite some time and I was so worried that something was terribly wrong. He needed oxygen to help him breathe, but after a time he was all right without it. The staff watched him closely for the rest of the day. I thanked God for his safe arrival and good health.

Our second son was born on September 23 and he weighed seven pounds and four ounces. I was blessed with his arrival which was one year to the day of my miscarriage a year earlier. He didn't have much hair, but he had the longest eyelashes that I had ever seen on a newborn baby.

He was the sweetest natured and happiest child that one could even hope to meet and as he smiled at everyone, one couldn't help but being drawn to him. My children were the best part of my life and I loved being a mother. I always thanked God for them, their good health, and safety.

I was a mother who preferred to stay at home and raise my children myself rather then having someone else care for them. On the other hand, I am not putting anyone down for having a job outside of the home, but it simply wasn't an option for me. I chose to go without extras in our life and I was fortunate that it all worked out, though my spouse always wanted me to get a job. However, with everything that I was already doing around the home and taking complete care of our children, I thought I'd have to be crazy to have another job outside the home. Year after year, I said "No" to him as he tried to get me to work anywhere, besides I already had a big job at home.

My in-laws were very generous and with all of the gifts of clothing that the boys received for their birthdays and for Christmas, they had plenty to get them through. I am especially grateful to them for the use of their camcorder for without it, I would never have had all of the lasting memories that I do of my children. It was also very kind of my mother-in-law to bring over dinner each night for the entire week after the birth of each of my babies.

My spouse spent a lot of time at his job and I understood that. He was a very hard worker and he sometimes worked at an extra job during the summer when he had two months vacation time. At one point, he decided to get his master's degree so he did this over the span of a couple of summers. Needless to say, I rarely had any time away from the children and their father never seemed to be around to help out much. I seldom identified with any of our friends who had vacation time or had the summer months off because I never had any time off at all… ever!

One morning I was leaving our home with our two sons to drive the eldest one to Campus View School for his kindergarten class. As I drove along I was thinking about an argument which I had with their father, and I was very deep in thought as I turned onto Edgelow Street. When I looked up from the steering wheel, I was horrified to see that we were headed towards a small pick-up truck, that was parked on the left side of the side street.

We were almost right in front of it and as I woke up from my daze, I slowly turned the steering wheel to the right. Just then something quite amazing happened! Some sort of STRONG FORCE took hold of the steering wheel and turned it so sharply to the right, that we avoided a head on crash!

EXCEPT that FORCE wasn't me!

It was like someone grabbed the wheel out of my hands and took control! Thus only a small side part of the back fender scraped the side of the truck. I couldn't even explain to the police officer that I phoned, how I ended up on the other side of the road.

It was mind boggling and yet there was something miraculous about it all at the same time. I knew that something else was going on here, and we were being taken care of.

I have always felt that I had a great heavenly force protecting me and God wouldn't let anything really bad happen to me. When I had my miscarriage it was quite a shock that it even took place. However, I knew that it could have been worse for as situations go, I was very fortunate the way that it had happened.

Have you heard the saying, "That everything happens for a reason?"

Well… it does. However, I wouldn't know the real purpose of these two incidences, for many more years to come. Later on in life, I often wondered what I did, and who I truly was, to be worthy of so much protection.

For many years I had a great wish to have a daughter, but I really wasn't sure about having another child. While I was still debating whether to let this ship sail or not, I came across an interesting article in a magazine while I was waiting for a doctor's appointment. It was a step by step guide on "How to have a girl or a boy." This was the first time that I had heard about this so I asked my doctor about it. He didn't see any problems with me trying it, so I asked his receptionist to please photocopy it for me.

I spoke with my spouse and he said that since I was the one who would be raising the child it was up to me. Hence I thought about it for another month and then I decided to go for it. I followed the information which I had received and charted out my temperature for a couple of months. When the moment for conception was at its best, I did one other procedure on two different occasions and I became pregnant immediately.

Many people that we knew, heard that more than ever, I wanted a daughter. One of my friends from my culture said to me, "You are the only one that I have ever known, that has ever wanted a girl, everyone always wants a boy!"

I thought that this was odd of her to say considering, I already had two boys. Did she think that I wanted a whole team of them?

It had been four years since my last child was born and I had put all my faith into God that he would grant me my heart's desire. This baby was due on June 17 1987, but that date came and left without me delivering. When I had given my information to my doctor eight months earlier, I told him that the due date was near the end of July, but he thought that it was in June. However, I knew better since one of my ring fingers had told me as much, when it changed color once again. I had a scan done and sure enough, the babies due date was now given as July 17.

My contractions began on the evening of July 21 while a friend who was a police officer was over visiting me. No… my spouse was not home yet, but I had other people in place to help out, especially since I had my two other children to consider. The night was quiet and my mother-in-law came to get the boys at 8:00 a.m. We arrived at the newly built Victoria General hospital at 10:00 a.m. and once we entered through the doorway, my contractions completely stopped. And as I was sitting in bed thinking, "I came here too early," my husband was reading the newspaper. He didn't make any effort to converse with me, much less be supportive.

Once again he had the summer off for holidays and we had been building a new home which had put an even further strain on our relationship. My partner couldn't stand to look at me today, as I was walking down the hallway with him trying to get my labor started again. It felt like we were indeed strangers and I realized, that he was not the best person to be with me at this time. He had no love, understanding, or compassion to offer me. I don't even think that he liked me at this point.

An intern broke my water bag at 1:05 p.m. and this action began my contractions again. They were so intense that I asked for medication and I was told that it was too late. Half an hour later, my third child was born at 1:35 p.m. It was a GIRL and she looked so identical to my first child that she could have been his twin. I was so very happy. God had given me another healthy baby and I was very grateful for her arrival. The date was July 22, and she weighed eight pounds and one ounce... ouch! It was the best delivery ever and I only had one stitch.

I had a private room at the hospital and I had packed a picnic basket of goodies and drinks for when our sons came to visit. My spouse's attention was rarely into taking great care with the children, so I had them stay with me at the hospital for most of every day. In this way I knew that they were safe and sound. Also since my daughter was in my room all day, my sons had a lot of time to bond with her. It was a good decision for all of us.

I thanked God for my healthy daughter. She added much joy to all our lives especially with her sparkling character. Everyday I enjoyed dressing her up in her little frilly dresses. And one day when we were out shopping, I heard a woman saying to another woman, "Look, there's that baby who's always dressed up!"

Our daughter has always been a very lively, strong minded, and independent child. When she was two months old, school had begun again for the boys and each morning as I dropped them off, it was also time for her to have a bottle of milk for breakfast. Thus I put her in the front seat of my car in her car seat, and she held her bottle with her own hands and fed herself as I drove. Our home was only four minutes away from the school and it was quite amazing to see that such a young baby could do this. When my mother came over and saw her holding her own bottle, she was quite astonished as she said, "LOOK at her feeding herself!"

My life had become hectic and each day I also went to check on our new home in its different building stages. I wanted to make certain that everything was done according to the way that I had envisioned it, and since our life was busy she grew up very fast.

My babies gave me so much enjoyment and I savored my time with them as much as I could. I made most of their baby food and I did my utmost for them. There were no other people who I felt closer to or who were a bigger part of my world. The love which I felt in caring, nurturing, teaching, and keeping them safe has always been my absolute driving force in life. This part of my existence was the most rewarding so far.

And though at times my spouse and I had stopped being a loving couple to one another, we always had three blessed bundles of love and hope which we had created. We had given each other... the greatest gift that we ever could have, and they were with us throughout every second of our marriage since their beginnings.

I will always be grateful to God for granting me three beautiful children for they have been the finest and happiest moments of my life.

My Wedding Day at the Sikh Temple - Dec. 1975

My Dad - Gurdave Singh Billan - 67 years old

My 2nd Son — 2 years old Dec. 1984

My Daughter - 3 years old - July 1990

I often feel an energy around me,
especially when I am alone.
Who is there... I'd truly like to know?
Yes... your world intrigues me greatly so,
but you must sense I am fearful, and I'm sure it shows.
Why do we need to actually connect?
How will our meeting, truly be of benefit?

– BONNY BILLAN –

Love From Beyond

Chapter 8

*I*t was the last days of the summer in 1988 and my husband had been on vacation from his job since the end of June. I could hardly wait for him to get back to work because having him around was twice as hard, as taking care of all three of our children and the home. The boys were now nine and six years old and my precious daughter was fourteen months old. We had moved into this home last October when our daughter was only three months old.

A couple of years earlier, we had been debating whether to add onto our present home or move to a different one, when one day I discovered this area merely by fate. Our eldest son had a baseball practice at a nearby school field and there was some sort of mix-up and two teams ended up at the same place. After that game, his coach moved their playing time to a different spot. If this hadn't happened, I never would have found this neighborhood. However, whatever is meant to be, will be, and as soon as I saw it, I loved it.

I insisted upon my husband inquiring into buying a lot nearby. The only vacant one happened to be on the outskirts of a forested area of the school field. I knew that it would be a perfect set up because our children would have a safe area to play at the schoolyard, ride their bikes through the trails, and a whole lot more. There was even a view of the ocean from the grass field, so you can well imagine what views the surrounding homes had. It was all very enticing to me.

However, when we checked into the availability of the only empty lot on the joining street to the school pathway, we found out that it was already sold.

I had a great feeling for this area and I sensed that it would be great for my children and I, since we all spent a lot of time together. I foresaw us at the schoolyard a lot of the time. As well, I wouldn't have to drive the children to school any longer because they could walk safely by themselves. It seemed to be the perfect solution to many things especially since I had a baby on the way.

My spouse wasn't that enthusiastic about the whole thing at first and he refused to give our name to the owners, so I stopped speaking to him for a few days. He had received a big promotion and he was never home very much and this move would make my life much easier regarding the children. He finally agreed.

We asked the owners of the property, if they could please keep us in mind if they ever considered selling it. I guess that it was truly meant for us to live there because the owners of the property called us about eight months later, to see if we were still interested in buying their lot.

Now a year later, I was continuing to keep our home in complete order and still tending to all of the handyman jobs which included wallpapering and painting. I often worked at these tasks into the wee hours of the night because it was much easier to do these things when everyone was out of the way.

On one occasion I wallpapered till 3:00 a.m. and in the morning when I asked my spouse what he thought of my job, he replied, "It's not my style."

I remember thinking, was it so hard for him to say that it looked good? Everyone needs love and encouragement from someone, and if you can't get that from your spouse, then what sort of bond do you really have together?

Our children were a reflection of my upbringing in more ways than not. They were always dressed well and their bedrooms were well organized, immaculate, and decorated in whatever theme that they wished. I read them bedtime stories, I helped them with their homework, and whatever else they needed. I taught my two younger children how to ride their bikes and how to throw a baseball. They had their friends over almost daily, and I always had a hot baked goodie coming out of the oven when they arrived home from school. My eldest son use to say, that he could smell it as soon as he opened the door of his school to come home. Our children were thriving and doing well living here.

My life in itself was very busy and I had more than enough to deal with daily. I received very little help from my spouse and I had to often plead with him to lend a hand with the children, and to do any yard work that needed to be done. When he did do any, he would do the minimum that he could get away with. He took great care with the front of our home, but this was only through the summer months when he had a large amount of holidays.

I told him, "Life can't wait until your summer break because there are things to do here all year around."

He also cut the backyard lawn, but he said that he wasn't going to do anything else regarding the shrubs and so forth, and if I wanted to take care of this area to go ahead. Our home was beside a school pathway and many parents walked past our yard, so he knew that I would take great care to have everything looking its best. I tended to the edging of the plant borders, the weeding of the shrub areas, the planting, care, and watering of all of the flowers, and flower boxes in our front and backyard.

During the summer months I sometimes worked outside on the yard until 11:00 p.m. and I always ended up with an aching back. By the time that I was finished I was out of breathe and I couldn't stand up straight. My spouse rarely asked me if I ever needed any help in any way, shape, or form inside or outside of our home. And in a lot of ways, I actually had my mother's life!

I had slowly become accustomed to a less than mediocre marriage whereby parts of it had become very heartbreaking and had especially contributed to the onset of our problems. At some point in time after I had my miscarriage, whenever we had a major argument my spouse began to call me the most horrible name imaginable.

He screamed out to me in his loudest voice, "YOU ARE A MURDERER!"

I was stunned when he first said these horrendous words to me, that I just stared at him in shock! After its meaning sunk into my psyche, it felt as if he had taken a dagger and plunged it into my heart. How could the man that I married, the one that I made love with, the one whose children I bore, ever say something so horrific to me?

Sometimes when I wanted to stop these hateful words from coming out of his mouth, I lunged at him as I screamed out, "I AM NOT!"

Consequently the more that he repeated these poisonous words to me, the more that I started believing in them, year after heart wrenching year. I had experienced great amounts of unkindness at various times in my marriage, but these toxic gut punching words were leading me down a very deadly path. I had entered into a passageway which was further overshadowing my sense of self-worth, darkening my joy of living, and permanently destroying my spirit. As this was happening, my soul was slowly plummeting into a deep hole of despair. One day his spine tingling brutality would finally make its way and penetrate into my heart, and seep down to the very core of my soul. Over the years, it was as if he had taken a chisel and chipped away little by little, at who I was, what I stood for, and who I was once so proud to be. I had allowed this man to murder my soul.

I never told any others about my ordeal because it was too awful to share with anyone, so I kept it to myself for another seven years. This was the cruelest, most heartless, and brutal thing that he had ever said to me and in these times, I hated him to the core of his very dark soul!

Shortly after I married, they were also three male relatives on my spouse's side and one female, who were not very nice to me. I disliked being around any of them My spouse had been the first one to marry out of his group of friends and young relatives, and some of them just couldn't handle the fact that all of their lives were different now. As a result, they acted very childish towards me and as their jealousy grew over time, three of them took their frustration and anger out on me. I couldn't escape from one of them because he was closely related to my spouse and quite often, he was where we happened to be. However, he was the absolute worst one and he made my life so uncomfortable. It wasn't until some time later, that it was discovered he had a major problem, so I don't know if he ever realized what he had done. I'm sure some people resented the fact that we had a new home which was fully furnished and so on and so forth, but I grew to hate living in Victoria and being anywhere near any of these strange people.

I was beginning to wonder, what on earth I had ever done in my past lifetime to have created such an awful one this time around, especially with the masculine gender. Why did God want me to endure so much hate from malicious males and why was my pain never ending with these self-centered and slimy snakes? Who the hell did these men think they were anyway… some great gift to women? None of them were a gift to anyone!

Now getting back to the beginning of my story, on this particular day my spouse had decided to go to Vancouver for a baseball tournament with his family. It was hosted by acquaintances and there would be other children there also, so I insisted that he take our two boys along or not go at all. After an argument he agreed to take them, but he was not happy about it. I had never been adamant about him ever taking the boys out of town before, but by the end of every summer I was utterly drained and I needed a break from it all. Also I knew that they would be safe since his parents were going to be there too.

Once they left the house I opened the sliding doors to the living room. And as I stood in front of the window, I stared up at the blue sky as tears of loneliness streamed down my face. I was so exhausted as I recalled various times in my life and I realized how very unhappy I was with myself and with whom I had married.

My spouse had become totally selfish and this was not, how my life was supposed to turn out. I had envisioned a fun, loving, and caring husband, who I truly loved and who loved being with his family. Instead I had quite the opposite. I did everything that I could for him, our children, and our home. And I put myself on the bottom of every list, that is, if I was even on it.

My life had become one of complete dedication to my family, but I also needed to do something for myself. This is the reason, why I spent so much time decorating because it always happily revitalized me, and gave me an endless supply of energy at any time of the day or night.

My spouse never considered the role of motherhood as being very important, let alone being a stay at home mom. All he ever really wanted was for me to be working outside of the home. He was very condescending to me as he considered himself to be above my status, especially as he succeeded in his work.

Yes, I was a woman who strived for perfection and this showed in everything that I did. I didn't realize at that time in my life that nobody was perfect, but this is what had been expected of me since I was a young child. And I carried it on. I always tried to be the best wife and mother that I could, but I was hugely missing the kindness and affection of a partner. One, who respected me, and who I reciprocated back with loving feelings and respect for him. I had everything and I had so much to be grateful for, but how did it all go so wrong between us?

We had nothing in common except our offspring and even then, we were rarely all together with one another, and our ways of raising them were so very different. He was very hard core with little compassion and his tough love stance wasn't how I dealt with our children. It was as if he had been raised somewhere in a very cold and unfeeling world, since he lacked ordinary human kindness and was so devoid of simply feeling.

My family meant the world to me and the thought of getting a divorce was never anything that I ever wanted to do. I had married and I always planned to stay that way, but I was being horribly disrespected. He was actually slaughtering my soul piece by piece and I had nothing to halt the spikes, that this bastard was brutally injecting into my entire being!

Today as I was feeling very alone and thinking very deeply about my life, I had a message for God. I said, "I'm not doing anyone here any good and they would all be better off without me."

I then walked into the kitchen and as I did, I opened the sliding door that separated the kitchen from the dining room. This was a bit strange for me to do, since I always kept both of these doors closed unless we had company. I started washing the dishes and as I did, I felt that someone was standing behind me. I kept turning around to look over my left shoulder, but when I did there was no sign of anyone, even though, I could feel that I wasn't

117

alone!

After a few minutes of wondering, who was there and exactly what the heck was going on, I washed a glass and I placed it on the counter. As I did, it slid across the top about six inches and then it stopped. Nothing like this had ever happened to me before, even though, I had put the dishes there everyday.

I sensed that something spiritual was going on, so I picked up the glass and placed it down near the same spot as I had before. Oddly enough, the glass moved along the surface again. I wasn't really sure that this was actually happening, so I picked up the glass and I tried it for a third time. Sure enough, the glass glided along on its own. I was a bit scared now as I screamed out in my mind, "YIKES!"

I quickly dried the glass and after I finished the dishes, I ran out of the kitchen to go upstairs. What's more, I didn't want to stay home because I was a bit overwhelmed by what had just transpired and I didn't know what was going to occur next. I woke my daughter up from her nap and quickly fed her in her room and we went downtown to the Bay. We arrived at the department store and as I got to the house wares section, a petite elderly woman walked towards us and approached me.

I had no doubt within my mind as to who she was, as something within me automatically understood, just where she had traveled from. She was from another time and place, and I recognized this as surely as I knew my own name.

As soon as I looked at her, I said to myself, "She's from heaven."

I thought that she must be my spouse's grandmother in spirit, since she had never seen our daughter because she passed on while I was expecting her.

This extremely small woman was friendly and pleasant and there was nothing scary about her at all. In fact, I had the impression and feeling that I already knew her and I could feel the energy around her was pleasing. She was dressed in a floor length thick black dress with a long black cloak over it and she had on a big ruffled hat that was tied under the chin. Her clothes were definitely out of place by about a hundred years. It was an outfit similar to what an older woman might have worn on a cowboy television show of long ago.

My daughter was sitting very quietly in her stroller as she kept looking up at this woman. It seemed like she couldn't take her eyes off of her and she never made a sound as she stared up at her.

Our visitor kept saying to me, "You have a really beautiful baby."

I smiled and I kept replying, "Thank you."

After a few minutes of this, I was starting to feel that we had made enough contact so I wheeled my daughter over to another section. We no sooner got there, when our new found friend was right beside us yet again.

Once more she commented, about how nice my baby was and she said, that she would touch her, but her hands were dirty. As I looked at her hands, I noticed that they were tucked deeply into her pockets.

Just then, she touched my shoulder with her hand and while looking straight at me, she said, "You are a nice lady and your daughter would be very lucky to be like you."

She then said, "I am her Great, great, great grandmother," and as quick as could be, she turned and walked away.

By the time that her words had sunk into my mind, I turned to look at her as she was just turning a corner. We rushed over to where she was and it only took me a few seconds, but she had truly disappeared into thin air. I stared at the spot where she once stood with a look of shock and amazement on my face, while my eyes were bugging out trying to comprehend what had just happened.

I didn't quite realize the miracle of the whole situation at that time. However incredibly, my Guardian Angel had reached out from heaven to let me know, that I was truly not alone and to not give up! And, I suppose that since she commented on my baby, she wanted me to remember, how blessed I was there, too.

God had instantly heard my painful plea and within seconds sent me an angelic messenger to show me, that there was someone who supported me and understood my pain. God had sent me the greatest comfort and help that could be sent at that time, as my Angel was permitted to descend upon my world to touch my heart and soul. I can still feel her loving touch.

This was the start of a long line of miracles which began to make its way into my life to awaken me. And show me, my true connection with God and eventually confirm to me, that we were all much more, then mere human beings.

Also during the late eighties and nineties, I discovered two gentlemen who helped me to change my perception about myself and others. The first person was Dr. Wayne Dyer and his introduction of viewpoints regarding how one perceives things, expanding one's thoughts, changing their beliefs and life, began a new process into my perspective and everyday living.

The second person was Dr. Deepak Chopra and he initiated a completely new thought development to me with the mind and body connection. I was fascinated to hear his words of wisdom, and his knowledge on this subject was so very different from anyone, that I had ever come across.

I understood, related to, and appreciated, what both of these men were introducing to our world. I bought their books and cassette tapes and I also video taped them whenever they were speaking on different programs. Both of these innovative men were positive role models for me, and helped create new belief guides into my philosophy. And, they were a big part of my path towards my increasing growth, healing, and enlightenment.

One day when I was feeling lost,
my guardian angel reached out.
She wanted to let me know, that I was not alone.
I didn't realize, how truly blessed I was
or the miracle which had taken place for me.
Except in my heart, I knew that God had sent me an Angel
and I can still feel her touch.
Have you felt your Angel's touch in your life yet?

– BONNY BILLAN –

Somebody...
Please Help Me!

Chapter 9

The subject of the "Other Side" had been of interest to me since I was quite young. I always enjoyed watching any scary show or movie that didn't have anything in common with the standard way of looking at things.

My fascination only grew as I got older and my connection with the paranormal also increased. I loved to discover whatever I could about myself within this captivating subject. I had never been a person who just went along with the natural flow of everyday living anyway and I rarely accepted my life the way that it was. I was always pushing things a bit further then others who were around me, and if they thought that I was strange it didn't bother me.

However, at this point in my life, I had actual spiritual occurrences that were happening to me. And although I thought that it was incredible, I was also a bit frightened by it.

In the past I would often seek out an intuitive person who gave readings so I could learn more about, who I truly was deep down inside me. Except now my life had taken a new turn and I was no longer just watching a television show or having a reading. I was quite literally being encircled by the unknown. What's more, I needed to urgently discuss my concerns with one, who could explain this new world which was coming to me and help me make sense of it all. I truly desired to discover and understand, why it was occurring and what it all meant.

I spoke to a gentleman who I had been having intuitive readings with for the past year or so. My mother-in-law initially had him to her home and that's where I first met him. The following is a conversation which took place between us on September 14, 1988 regarding the different situations which I had been experiencing.

Bonny   "I would like to know, if you see any people around me? I asked you about this last time, but none of it recorded on my cassette tape."

John   "OH!"

Bonny   "I don't know why. I thought, gee that's strange... and it was all of the good parts. (Laughing) So I would like to know, if you feel anyone around me?"

John   "I am getting three people around you actually... one man and two ladies. The man is very distinguished, very tall, a great bearing to him. I think we would call him a prince actually... that sort of a bearing of a very noble sort of a person. I guess that would be the way to put it. He definitely gives orders. This is where you get your take over... you know, the way you make things happen. You don't take too much nonsense from most people... that sort of a thing. Yea, this is where your confidence has come from... this man. He has helped you, to build that up as well.

His name is Andrium. He is a very distinguished man, very kind, very sort of a smiley man. And there is very much peace around this man, very much so.

There is also a day to day lady. She is a little older of a person and when she passed away she was in her fifties. A tiny sort of lady... very much your guardian. She is very aware of what you do, and how you do it, and looking after you, quite often here okay?

The thing that she is saying, is that if you want my name, it is a very common East Indian woman's name that begins with the letter "J." It would almost be like "Mary" in England, say for instance."

Bonny "Not Jager or Jagit?"

John "What would Jamal mean? Is that a ladies name?"

Bonny "That's not an East Indian name."

John "I am getting that it is a very common East Indian name."

Bonny "Jarnail?"

John "Jarnail... okay. Yea.
I think that I would go back to a great, great, great grandmother."

Bonny "Okay. (Laughing) Can you please go to the third person and then I have something else to ask you. OH GEEZZZZ!"

John "Okay. The third person is a very regal lady is the way that I want to describe her. She has very dark skin almost like a Negro colored skin... very, very dark. This lady gives you understanding, she gives you knowledge. She is imparting things like... all of a sudden you just know."

Bonny "Oh yes... yea, yea."

John "Like they sort of just pop in. Okay? You just know this. You do not have to be convinced. Yea... I know how to do this and I can do it! This type of thing which you have evolved into your own self confidence as well and you feel good when you have done something like this.
I want to say that her name is Analisa, but it's Aneluzha."

Bonny "When these people are around me, how do they help me?

John "In many ways... it depends on what you are doing at the present time or what needs helping. Okay?"

Bonny "Okay. So... they come through in your... mind?"

John "Yea. And sometimes you can visually see them. Some people do… they visualize their own guides."

Bonny "Okay. I ahhhh… ran into this lady… the other day… at the Bay.
Is she one of the people that are around me? She was an older lady, dressed in black and she said to me, that she was my daughter's great, great, great, great grandma."

John "Okay. Uh huh… yea… yea that's the little one there. That's her."

Bonny "YOU'RE KIDDING!"

John "Yea, yea. They sometimes appear at the strangest times believe me. I was in the middle of a massage when one of mine showed up."

Bonny "My husband and boys went to Vancouver and I was home with the baby. And I opened my living room doors and all of a sudden I wasn't by myself anymore."

John "You had someone with you?"

Bonny "I kept looking over my shoulder while I was doing the dishes and then a glass moved across the counter three different times. So I picked it up, wiped it, and put it away, so it wouldn't move again!" (Laughing)

John (Laughing) "Actually, what she was trying to do, was make you aware that she was there. She has to do something sort of physical."

Bonny "I was afraid."

John "Don't be."

Bonny "I was so scared."

John "No, that's understandable. It'll happen again. Okay?"

Bonny "Ohhhhhhhhhh." (Groan)

John   "What they will do is something physical to make you aware that they are there. Okay?"

Bonny   "What will happen?"

John   "Like the moving of a glass."

Bonny   "OH GEEZZZZ!"

John   "Or this sort of a thing like the opening and shutting of a door.
                What she is trying to do perhaps, is to just talk to you, so just sit down and RELAX."

Bonny   "What happened when I opened the living room door? It was the living room and dining room French doors that are always kept closed. I really had this feeling since …"

John   "It was time to open the door."

Bonny   "We… yea. We had a priest over at our house for my daughter's blessing and since then I've kept those doors closed in the living room for some reason. I really can't explain it. Is that just me being weird or…?"

John   "NO! Not necessarily."

Bonny   "When I opened it, I KNEW, at that very second, that someone was there. I even looked over my shoulder while I was washing the dishes about ten or twelve times."

John   "Yea. BUT, she is no HARM! She is there as, as a GUARDIAN."

Bonny   "But I'm just so scared."

John   "No, I can understand that."

Bonny   "She came up to me twice and she said, "You have a really beautiful baby."
                She said that she didn't want to touch her because her hands were dirty. Her hands were in her coat pocket and she

was all dressed in black. And I kept thinking that she was my husband's grandmother who has never seen my baby.

She touched me and said, "Your daughter would be very lucky to be like you. I am her great, great, great grandma."

Or rather, I don't know how many greats she said and she left. When she left, I noticed that she no purse, no bags, or anything and she was gone."

John   "She was there just to touch you and to let you know that she was there. She's there to look after you and to look, after the child.

THIS IS… THIS IS A WONDERFUL THING!"

Bonny   "What would have happened if… oh geezzzz!"

John   "Do you WANT, to communicate with her?"

Bonny   "I don't know." (Laughing)

John   (Laughing) "When you do, YOU WILL KNOW! Okay?"

Bonny   "It's so scary. I have been going to psychics for nine years now and each time, I find out more and more about my past and I have been thinking more and more, about it. I just knew that this was the next stage."

John   "Uh huh. Obviously, you are suppose to know."

Bonny   "I just KNEW, that this was coming!"

John   (Laughing) "That's fine.
And with a child like that, with a younger child, they are so close, to the other side. Okay?
That these people come through them sometimes when they are there, when they are around, and that is understandable."

Bonny   "Why would you say that her hands were dirty?"

John   "Pause… I think that if she had tried to touch your child, that you would have freaked."

Bonny   "Oh I see."

John   "Okay?
             So she was just sort of saying in her own way, I am NOT
             going to touch your child… no need for you to panic."

Bonny   "When she first came, I immediately thought of my
             husband's grandmother right away, although this lady was not
             East Indian."

John   "Yea, uh huh. That doesn't matter because when they get over
             there, they can change to whatever they want to be. (Laughing)
             Okay."

Bonny   "Yea, yea.
             I started thinking about it all and how she had come up to
             me twice. It wasn't until I told my sister and she said to me,"
             "Aren't you scared?"
             Then I thought about it again and a few days later it dawned
             on me, that I knew that, she was somebody who was around
             me."

John   "Uh huh. Very much so. And that's fine. Sometimes, they
             are a stronger presence than other times. It depends on what we
             are going through in our life. Okay?
             If you need a hand with something, they are just very much
             stronger there. If they feel it is something that you should deal
             with on your own, than they just sort of, let you get on with
             it."

Bonny   "If she came again… "

John   "Talk to her."

Bonny   "And, say WHAT!"

John   "Say HELLO! That's a good opener. (Laughing) Okay.
             And say, you know… "

Bonny   "Okay, she wouldn't come if she knew that I was afraid,
             would she?"

John   "No. I don't think that you are really afraid. What I think is
             happening here is a bunch of old beliefs and stuff that you are

sort of working out for yourself. I don't think that you are really afraid of HER!"

Bonny   "No. It's just different things that you see on television and stuff and that's how you… "

John   "You have been programmed into different aspects here and you think ohhhh it's this sort of a thing, but you are not afraid of her, because she wouldn't come TO YOU, if you were."

Bonny   "Oh no, she was… yea… oh I see."

John   "Okay? She wouldn't reach out to you, if she knew that you were afraid. She wouldn't want to frighten you. That is the last thing that she would want to do. But, she obviously would like perhaps, to communicate with you or maybe not. Maybe she is just making you aware that she is there."

Bonny   "She wouldn't ever hurt me or anything?"

John   "No. In no way, shape or form. She has no reason to… absolutely, no reason to at all."

Bonny   "I always feel that there is someone in my daughter's room."

John   "This is not unusual with a youngster. Okay?
How old is she now?"

Bonny   "She is going to be fourteen months."

John   "You see, they choose when they want to come in. Okay? When they are that young, they are so close still, to the other side where they came from. Quite often, there are still some people there with them. You know, a friend or something… they will bring them along. That is not unusual… children who see."

Bonny   "It wouldn't be harmful or anything?"

John   "NO! Heavens no, in no way."

Bonny   "Her bedroom door never stays open and it is a brand new house. Whenever I open her door, it creaks halfway closed every time, and it scares the hell out of me."

John   (Laughing) "Okay. The other thing that you can do there, is to sit quietly in the room and say," "You know, I'd like to communicate with you as well. Is there something that you need to tell me or why are you here?"
"This sort of thing. Just do that... they'll let you know."

Bonny   "And you see... to do that... I don't know if I could because I am so scared of the unknown."

John   "WELL, it's... see the thing is, the unknown, is what you don't know and when you get talking to this or get tuned into this, it's not unknown anymore. And there is nothing more to be scared of."

Bonny   "Okay. Say you are in a room right now, how would they appear?"

John   "Sometimes, there is a light. Sort of a greenish, sort of foggy looking light and sometimes, basically, you can see, that person standing there."

Bonny   "How would that lady... have... like..."

John   "She can manifest herself anywhere that she wants."

Bonny   "Oh."

John   "But don't forget, she is working on a mind expansion that, you and I probably would not even begin to comprehend. She can do anything that she wants to make you sort of see, the physical side of things, if necessary."

Bonny   "You see, I was really upset the day before they left and I was in tears and I was very upset. I had had it with a lot of things. And, a lot of times when I am upset, that's when I feel that I'm not by myself.
I guess, that's when you need them the most?"

John	"Yea. That's when they come in to comfort you. Basically, they are sitting there holding you."
Bonny	"I figured that out… I figured that they are coming to help me."
John	"But the other thing, UNDERSTAND SOMETHING, that there is no reason for them to come and HARM YOU! Okay?"
Bonny	(In a whisper.) "Yes."
John	"Quite often, they are trying to impart knowledge or make you get on doing something that perhaps, you should be doing. These types of things, okay?"
Bonny	"Yes."
John	"They never give you anything that you are not ready for. Okay?
	If they know that you are ready for it, they will present it to you. They are NOT there to harm. That is the last thing on their mind, if it is ever there at all.
	What I am going to suggest to you is perhaps a little reading. Okay?"
Bonny	"Yes."
John	"There is a book that is out and I picked it up quite a while ago and I just recently re-read it. Pick it up and read it. It deals basically with what we are dealing with. What it is, is that, this soul is supposedly passing a test by another sort of soul. Okay?
	He is living his past lives, his present life's, and his future life's, all simultaneously at one time. It's quite interesting and I think it will help you, to understand a bit more as to what is going on. In that, he sort of lays it out and it looks like it's going to be harmful and really it is not. It is just somebody taking another step forward or learning something about themselves or doing these sorts of things. It is quite an education about what goes on with guides and this type of thing. I think that it might put your mind, quite a bit more at ease."

Bonny	"Okay. I guess that everyone has people like this around them?"
John	"YES! Very much so! Oh YES!"
Bonny	"So our house is filled… and my spouses… like you know?" (Laughing)
John	"Oh yea. Souls all over the place! Oh very definitely! I have had as many as ten guides sometimes in my own life. They come and then go."
Bonny	"I guess, that they would appear too?"
John	"Some of them do and some of them don't. I just know that they are there. Some of them show up in a reading."
Bonny	"What makes the strong feeling, that you know, that they are there?"
John	"Just the sense of them for me. I know a calm feeling will come over me, with one of them. Another one, I know… okay, you are there. "Hi, how are you doing?" Certain things will happen and I know that somebody is guiding them along."
Bonny	"Do they only come in, when you are upset… is it stronger?"
John	"No. The more psychic that you allow yourself to be, the more that they will show up because the more questions you are asking. And the more things that you are looking into."
Bonny	"There have been a lot of spiritual things that have happened to me, and I have felt like this for quite a few years. And I am trying NOT, to think about it."
John	"Yea. (Laughing) Well, they are going to make YOU THINK about it, because IT IS TIME!"
Bonny	"Yea. But I'm really trying, not too."

John	"But let it go. Enjoy it. It's a... the East Indian people have been practicing this for centuries okay... like the meditations and the whole nine yards. North Americans are just getting into it. They haven't even begun to touch the surface on it. So, it is nothing to feel threatened about by any stretch of the imagination."
Bonny	"Do you sense my grandparents or anybody else around me?"
John	"Not particularly strong. No. No."
Bonny	"They don't show up at all... or a little girl?"
John	"No. The guides do change from time to time too, if they have something to do or whatever. They can't sometimes stick around forever. And as we develop, they bring in higher levels so, we understand them better."
Bonny	"I would just... I don't know. I don't think that it will ever come to the point where I could say, "Talk to me." (Laughing)
John	"Why not? (Laughing) You can have some great conversations, I'll tell you."
Bonny	"When I think about the lady at the store and she was right there, I just...."
John	"Well, do a bit of reading on it."
Bonny	"Is there anything else that... books to read that might...?"
John	"Yes, there are quite a number. What I can suggest is to just sort of go wandering on your own on what feels good. Okay? You will find that the book will literally just jump off the shelf at you, something that feels right. And also too, when you are reading a book sometimes, you'll get part way into it and all of a sudden it doesn't want to make sense anymore. Put it down with a bookmark in it and two weeks, two months or six months later, all of a sudden you'll say, where did I put that book? And when you open it up and start all over again, the whole thing will just fall into place. It'll start to make sense again. That's the only thing that I can suggest to you about

choosing books and you usually pick up the right one. I've very seldom seen that fail."

Bonny   "Okay.

            How am I going to drive home alone tonight?" (Laughing)

John   "With a lot of help." (Laughing) You'll make it just fine.

When John was speaking about guides, he was referring to spirits from the spiritual realm, who are around every human being to guide them within their lives. We each have more then one and as he said, they change from time to time depending on our progress and what we have to learn. Also, as we continue in our growth, higher guides who are further developed come in, to inspire us within our thoughts towards the higher growth of our soul. John also said, that they may do something physical to make you aware that they are there, "Like the opening and the shutting of a door."

Well about ten days later, when I was in my daughter's room I heard a door slam shut very loudly at the end of our long hallway. When I heard this noise I was completely petrified and I stood completely still in my tracks. My pulse began racing wildly and I was starting to perspire along my hairline. I was terrified to walk over to her doorway and look down the hall. I started praying greatly that whoever slammed the door wasn't about to come walking into the nursery. I was absolutely frightened!

Every day I had above all else, made sure that all the doors upstairs were kept closed so I could avoid this warning which I was given, but somehow it happened anyway.

"Yikes! How can a door open by itself and slam shut?"

I eventually very slowly inched my way towards my daughter's door and I gradually peeked out of the opening.

WHEW… no one was in sight.

I didn't want to stay home since I was still very scared, so my child and I went out to University Heights mall, until it was time for my sons to come home from school.

Over time, spiritual occurrences would continue to happen within the walls of our new home and my sensing and understanding of it would also continue to grow. I also began to have premonitions and simply know things about family members and sometimes even friends, without any of them ever telling me anything at all. I didn't need to be around them to know, what was going on in their lives. A part of me thought that the natural born detective in me was coming alive from reading too many of my "Nancy Drew" books, but on some level I knew it was more than that. My interests had always edged on mysterious unknown circumstances and something within me had created this knowing. And I didn't know how this was being done, but it was. My sixth sense was developing more and more and it had become a natural way of life for me. Although at times, it was very uncomfortable not having anyone else around me who was experiencing this same type of thing.

When my daughter was about a year and a half old, my father-in-law sometimes stopped by to visit with her in the middle of the day. He never called ahead of time to say that he was coming, so I never had any notice, at least not from him. However each and every time that he came to the front door, I had a forewarning about it about five to ten minutes before he arrived.

In the flash of a second, I could feel his energy in the Gordon Head area of where we lived. I guess that as he drove closer and closer to our house, the feeling got stronger and stronger until I could actually picture him walking up the three steps to our front door. I could see him in my mind's eye. And see him place his finger on the doorbell and at that precise second, the bell would ring. I opened the door and sure enough, there he was. Other times, I could feel his energy in the area and it came to a peak and the feeling stayed for a time, and then it went away. He also had a cousin who lived a few blocks away from us and I suppose that he was visiting with him or with someone else in the area.

This was a great warning system because it gave me a chance to make sure my lipstick was on, and my daughter was ready for his visit. Also if it was her mealtime it provided me with the time to get her food ready, so I could feed her while we were conversing. She was so happy to see her grandfather and they both enjoyed this time together a lot. Now and then, I'd take a picture of them together and you could see that they loved each other very much.

He was always smiling and friendly and all three of my children enjoyed his company greatly. My father-in-law told me, that he really liked the way that I took care of my children.

As I look back on my spiritual events and premonitions, I believe that they became stronger after the birth of my daughter.

Furthermore, on July 17, 1990 something quite unique happened. My daughter's third birthday was on Saturday the 22nd and at the beginning of the week, I said to my spouse, "Something is going to happen to ruin her party."

The next day I said to him, "Someone is going to die, and it's someone in your family."

He said nothing and he just stared at me blankly as he often did. After he left the house to do some of his errands, one of his aunts called to speak with him.

I told her that he was out and would she like to leave a message?

She answered me by saying, that one of his uncles had suddenly passed away and they didn't know, how or why it happened.

He was not ill and it was one of those strange things that no one could foresee happening to him. As well as, he was only in his forties and the youngest sibling in their family.

My daughter's party was of course affected because his parents and relatives couldn't attend her birthday. Also many friends of their family were also paying their last respects at his parent's home, so it would have been impossible for them to get away at all. Oddly enough, I never said another word to my spouse regarding my premonition and he never said anything to me about it, even after it came true.

This conversation took place on August 6, 1991.

John   "Any other questions?"

Bonny   "Just about any guides that are around me. I just... I thought that I met one the other day. I couldn't bring my eyes to look at them and I was glad, that they weren't looking at me. They were talking to my daughter actually."

John   "Okay. Someone who stopped and talked for awhile?"

Bonny   "I couldn't look at them."

John   "Okay. Was it your guide or hers?"

Bonny   "I don't know."

John   "I think that it was hers."

Bonny   "WAS IT?"

John   "Yea."

Bonny   "I was worried. I took for granted that it was a guide, but when I thought about it that night, I thought that maybe it was someone who was trying to pick her up in the store."

John   "No. I don't see danger around this encounter. I don't get a sense of danger around her with this person that was there."

Bonny   "Okay. She was about twenty five feet away from us when we walked by. I didn't notice her, but my daughter turned right around and her eyes went right to the lady.

So I said, "Come on" to my daughter and I noticed that this lady was staring right at her.

She walked up to us and said, "She's looking at me because she caught my eyes when she walked by. And, we both know how PRECIOUS she is, TO YOU!"

John   "It's kind of a weird comment, for someone to say."

Bonny   "Yea. It's kind of scary. It was!

I later thought that her purse was undone and I don't know... there are so many crazy things going on."

John   "Yea, there is. I don't get danger around it. I don't get danger around that encounter at all."

Bonny   "Do you think it was just someone..."

John   "I think so."

Bonny   "In the store or..."

John   "No. I think it was someone to do with her. Very much so.

She is very WELL looked after. I know that! You see, like there is magic all around her. Okay? (Laughing)

She can pretty much do anything and she gets away with it, that type of thing. No, it's one of hers."

Bonny   "Would she have a purse?"

John   "Sure. Oh God yes! I've seen them with books of matches."

Bonny   "Then, I thought this poor old lady... her purse was open. So, I tracked her down and I told her that her purse was undone."

She said, "Oh, oh. That's a good way to lose things, isn't it?"

"She was so friendly. Most people normally say, "Hi" to my daughter, but this woman was SO FRIENDLY! It was... I just couldn't shake the feeling that something was up."

John   "Yea. All she might have been doing was channeling through that person, through a body that your daughter wouldn't get upset about. Had it been someone approaching who looked angry, she would have cringed back. She has a natural instinct to do that. It might have just been a friendly old lady that looks a little batty." (Laughing)

Bonny   "No… She looked friendly enough. It was just what she said, "We both know how PRECIOUS she is, to you!"

John   "Yea. That is not a normal thing that somebody says. She might just have been channeling through her."

Is ones fate formed at the precise moment that they are born,
depending on the alignment of the stars and the planets at that time?
Perhaps ones destiny is created by their soul, before its birth,
as it decides, what challenges and obstacles it hopes to overcome.
Destiny...Fate or Choice?
Who Decides Yours?

– BONNY BILLAN –

An Era Ends and
Something New Begins

Chapter 10

On December 22, 1992 my father was a passenger in a car and as he was leaning down to put a tape into the cassette player, the driver of the car slammed on his brakes to avoid hitting a pedestrian. Consequently my dad hit his head on the dashboard and as a result of this event, he was rendered a quadriplegic.

My dad had always been quite a healthy man, even though, earlier that year he had a slight heart attack when he was out for his daily walk at the Langara golf course. He collapsed while he was alone in the men's washroom and within seconds of it happening, a gentleman walked in who had medical training. My father was revived and taken to the hospital. His doctor was quite surprised that, even though, he was seventy-four years old, his heart was like that of a fifty year old. His recovery was quick and he was home a very short time later. He had always been a very fortunate man and it seemed like things just fell into place for him.

However, today everything had taken place very quickly and our family was in a state of shock and deeply concerned over his terrible accident. I can't even imagine, how his friend who was driving the car was feeling. I felt numb and couldn't quite believe that this had possibly taken place and to him of all people. My dad was almost god like and he was always powerful enough to get through anything with his never-ending amount of strength.

I prayed to God for my dad's condition to be reversed, but this didn't seem to be happening. And I found it extremely hard to even comprehend, that his life was going to end this way. I believe that everything occurs for a reason, but I just couldn't understand the logic behind this event. I kept asking myself, "Why the hell did this happen?"

This situation led me to think about one's destiny and if pre-determined events could ever be changed. While I was growing up, the man who was driving the car had immigrated to Canada with his family and they had stayed at our home for a time. I wondered, if this accident could have been avoided had he not moved here?

Chances are that something else would have taken its place. Would it not? Perhaps this was already going to be a part of my dad's fate at this time in his life and his friends move had already been factored into the equation?

One day I was in my dad's hospital room with my mom and he asked her to help him into a chair. He was getting a bit restless over it all and he hadn't noticed that I was standing in the background. All of a sudden, he sensed my presence and he asked my mom, "Who else is in the room?"

She said, "It's Bonny."

I looked at him partly nervous, not knowing what his reaction was going to be. He just half smiled in my direction, but he never made any eye contact with me. I left his room to give him his privacy and I went to the chapel to pray. My dad was such an active man and I wondered how he was ever going to be able to accept this life altering tragedy? I put myself in his shoes and I thought about what I would have wanted to do, if I were in the same situation as he. I had an answer.

Sometimes when I was growing up and my dad wasn't very nice to my mom, I'd ask God to take him away... out of the anger that I felt towards him. This time when I spoke to God, I asked... out of the love and compassion that I felt for my dad in that moment of time.

Did I have the human right to do this? I don't truly know, but this was the last occasion that I saw my dad alive.

Two weeks later on January 18, 1993, I said to my husband, "My father is going to die and he is not going to go home."

He said, "He's all right and he's getting ready to go home this week."

I began crying uncontrollably as I said, "NO HE'S NOT! HE IS GOING TO DIE!"

My hysteria went on for two hours or more.

The next morning I received a phone call at 7:45 a.m. from one of my sisters. She said that our father had passed away sometime between 2:00 a.m. and 6:00 a.m. during the wee hours of the morning.

I had been sensing my dad's outcome for a week or so before it happened. When I finally told my sisters about my premonition, one of them asked me, "Why did you not tell us?"

I never ever thought about telling anyone else in the family about it and how was I to truly know that this was going to happen? They were already experiencing enough anguish over his horrible accident and I wasn't going to add to it.

My dad's funeral was huge and there were a lot of people who came to pay their last respects to him. He was a giant and now he was gone. I found it so hard to believe, that he was no more. It was too incredible to even fathom!

After his funeral we went back to my parent's home. It was filled with many friends and relatives and it was very nice to feel such warmth at this time. A short while later I began to feel nauseous so I went to lie down, and soon afterwards I began vomiting. It was all very strange because I was fine earlier and I had never been one to get nauseous, not even with my pregnancies. I didn't know it at the time, but my body was giving me another premonition.

Later on that evening, three of siblings created a needless and enormous commotion with one of my other siblings. When my mother asked, what the problem was, she was told very rudely to stay out of it!

I came to her rescue and I screamed out at the top of my lungs, "LEAVE MY MOTHER ALONE, SHE HAS JUST LOST HER HUSBAND!"

Everything turned horrible at this point and the biggest offender of the night turned his attention onto me. What ensued was a terrifying chaos that lasted for quite sometime, as he tried to hurt me for defending our mother. When this ordeal and explosive situation was over, another domineering sibling went over the edge as he now tried to assert himself with me too. His rage was over me and another sibling not visiting our parents enough throughout the years, even though, my parents only came to visit me once a year for a day or so.

In those frightening moments of time, the power and the dynamics of our whole family had changed hands. And everything that my father had worked so very hard to create had started its downward spiral plunge.

I suppose that our brothers felt that by asserting themselves, they were going to show their sisters who the heads of our family were now. However, they didn't need to act in such an undignified manner because everything was quite calm between them and the three elder female siblings. This was the one day that our mother truly needed all the love and comfort, that all of her children had to offer her, especially since she had given so much of

141

herself in devoting her entire soul to them. If the loss of my mom's partner wasn't enough for her pain filled heart to endure, she now had to contend with the deeply selfish antics of some of her children.

This was also the true defining moment which caused my world to actually collapse and crash down around me and I couldn't do a thing to stop it. I began crying that evening and even after I went back home, my tears would not cease. My spirit was in fact caving in and I was beyond the point of no return. I was extremely crushed in how I was treated by someone who had only shown me great amounts of kindness throughout my life, and his actions changed my soul forever. We had just lost our father and it seemed like now, we were going to be losing our brothers too. They had erupted like angry volcanoes filled with searing blackened ash, but why? Is this how some males show how strong they are? Had they actually shown us their strength or their weakness?

This was the beginning of the downfall of our family and the respect that I had for these males. I was thoroughly disgusted by what had taken place, what I had endured, and how every male in my world felt that whatever they did was completely acceptable. They didn't realize that if they wanted their sisters to continue to respect them, then they needed to carry on treating us like they had previously done for so many years before. What they couldn't foresee, was that in the coming months, the women in our family would undergo changes also. And we would prove to them, what we were made of too!

My dad had huge shoes to fill and I knew of no one else who could ever have taken his place. He was so young when he immigrated to this country and he had so much to be proud of. I respected him for what he had accomplished in his life, for our very nice home, and how distinguished he always looked. Also I was always grateful to my parents for the lifestyle they had provided for us, even though, equality between the genders was quite another matter. They had given us a way of living that many in our culture didn't have the opportunity to experience. My dad often said, "He was a lucky man and it was like Christmas everyday in his home because of the family that he had."

Since that fateful night my tears continued non-stop and my heart had at last broken. It had fragmented into many splintered pieces and fallen into the deepest depths of my soul. All of my years of turmoil had finally taken its toll and my everyday living with my spouse certainly hadn't become any better, as it began an even bigger downward turn. The many mistreatments since my birth, my husband, the affects of my miscarriage, my father's passing, and now my brothers had added to the shattering of my spirit. It felt as if I was breaking apart from the very core of my being. The rejection and suffering that I had been subjected to throughout my life had finally surfaced, and my deep heartache and sorrow could no longer be disguised, as it refused to go away. Each day after dinner I had an upset stomach and I could no longer deny what was happening within me. My soul had started its uprising simultaneously within every part of my being, and I had no one to put their arms around me and tell me that I was ever going to be okay again.

My heart, body, and soul had experienced such a lack of love, that they had at last all collided and disengaged from one another, as they slipped away from within my reach. I tried to grasp them in my hands, but they were drifting further and further away from me as my soul floated out to space. I no longer had a healthy body to house it. My laughter had finally been silenced.

A week later I went to see my family doctor and I poured my heart out to him. He was my life saver and he was so understanding and compassionate, as he told me that I was depressed. This happened to me because the left and the right side of my brain were not level and one part was lower than the other. And I needed to get them in back into line. He gave me a video to take home which explained my condition, so I could understand what was happening within me. I started taking a mild form of an anti-depressant and I only allowed myself to take half a pill every second day. It worked very well for me and I needed this extra assistance at this time in my life, so I could function properly for myself and my children.

Since my dads passing, I wanted to know what I ever could have done to not be worthy of his love. I needed to truly understand, why he never treated me the same as he did my siblings. I always sensed that he simply didn't care about me and over the years, even though, he became kinder, I never felt that he ever truthfully loved me.

My spouse and my dad had treated me in much of the same type of manner and they were heartless males who did their utmost to bring grief to me. My father never succeeded at least while he was living, but he had laid the ground work and now after decades of emotional, verbal, and mental abuse, my entire spirit had worn out and was truly drowning.

The moments with my father were over now and I would never get the answers to the questions which I required so badly. As each day went by, my anger towards him increased and I cursed at him wherever he was!

I screamed through my tears, "WHY?"

I repeatedly called him every name that I knew, as I demanded a response. I asked him day and night, "WHY WASN'T I GOOD ENOUGH?"

How on earth was I ever going to clear myself of my chaotic upheaval and absolute fury that I felt towards this man, when he was now gone?

Has anyone ever passed on, whom you had unanswered questions of and you just wanted to speak with them one more time? Just one more time, so you could ask them, "Why you were not deemed worthy enough to be loved by them."

A few months after my fathers passing, some of my siblings and I experienced many strange occurrences. Certain events kept duplicating themselves in one way or another. I wasn't exactly sure what was going on, but deep down within me, a part of me truly knew, exactly what it was. However, I needed some proof about what I was thinking.

One day I noticed that one of my folded hand towels which I always left out on my bathroom counter for display, was lying in disarray in my bathroom sink. This happened almost daily and if that wasn't strange enough, this same towel was sometimes thrown on my bathroom mat. All of this was very odd since I never touched that towel and I never threw anything, anywhere, or at anytime. I was the only one who used this room. And this door and my bedroom door were always kept closed, especially since it had slammed by itself a few years earlier. It even got to the point that when I was out with my children and once we returned home, one of them would go running to my bathroom to check if my towel was in the sink. And sometimes it was.

I had mentioned the towel experience to one of my sister-in-laws and she said to me, "Don't you remember, that your dad always threw the towel in the sink after he had finished drying his hands? He would do that whenever he came over to our house."

It was at this point that I remembered, when we were growing up, my dad always had a habit of throwing his shaving towel in the bathroom sink, after he was done with it every morning. Could my dad actually be reaching out to me in these moments and this was his sign to me, that it was him? It just couldn't be... could it?

Not only did I wonder, "Why was he around me," but "How was he able to move my towel repeatedly?"

I also had light switches which had magically turned on, when no one else was in the room. I would be upstairs and when I came down to the main level of our home, the laundry room light was quite often on. I also received phone calls at the same time of the day, but there was never anyone on the line when I picked it up. Whenever I spoke on the phone with my sister who also lived on the island, many times our phone connection would just go dead, especially when we were discussing my dad.

One day I made a joke to her about my dad and she said, "You better watch out, he's probably listening."

I replied, "OH, WHAT'S HE GOING TO DO ABOUT IT?"

The next morning I drove my children to school and I didn't have time to open the living room drapes before we left. When I returned home ten minutes later, the laundry room light was turned on and the living room drapes were open.

YIKES! HOW THE HELL DID THAT HAPPEN!

No one else could have been in our home because I had left the alarm on and it was still undisturbed when I got back. I was absolutely shocked and whoever did this was certainly trying to prove something to me. Twenty minutes later when I began vacuuming the living room I felt a tugging on the hose a few times.

I screamed out loudly.

I was a bit on edge by this occurrence and I was certain that my dad was close by… somewhere around me. Yes, he was very near.

He was such a determined man when he was living and now it appeared, that he was just as strong in his death. It seemed that I might get the answer to my question which I demanded of him after all, or could he possibly be here for another reason?

Apparently if a human being didn't have a chance to say, "Goodbye" before they passed over or if they would like something done or changed after their death, they make themselves known to someone here on earth. This may be achieved through playing with electricity which could involve using lights or the phone etcetera, or they may even move items around, make noises, or show a flash of color.

This new wave of unexplained phenomenon which I was experiencing was more than quenching my thirst regarding, "The Other Side." It was beginning to answer my long time question, of whether one could truly reach out from heaven to earth after they died? However, I wanted to know how I could stop this shocking path of the unknown from continuing towards me, because I had no idea of the intent or mischief that they could cause in my world. Besides, I already had enough going on in my life, but it appeared that this force wasn't going away and it seemed to be getting stronger.

The time has come to say goodbye,
at the end, all we could do was sit and sigh.
You lived a full life on your own terms,
though you left this world too soon by God's wishes.
Now you will reside, with much peace inside.
Take care, one day... we shall all meet again.

LOVE BONNY

Dad's Tribute

Gurdave Singh Billan
Husband – Father – Grandfather
1918 – 1993

It is with great sadness that we announce, that on January 19, 1993, Gurdave Singh Billan passed on at the age of 74. He was born in the village of Raipur Dabba in India on September 10, 1918.

He will be deeply missed by his dedicated wife Malchete (Mary) Kaur Billan of 46 years in marriage, his 4 daughters, 3 sons, and 18 grandchildren. We will never know another man like him. Our lives will be forever changed.

He became a successful businessman, whose generosity touched many and his dedication and financial support was evident throughout the East Indian society. He was passionately involved in cultural, political, and religious affiliations, and gave his time and assistance wherever it was needed.

Gurdave will be warmly remembered by his family, relatives, and friends whose lives he touched.

My Awakening

What on earth could it be,
that I am sensing all around me?
Is it a force, a presence, an angelic sort of being,
or could it be a SPIRIT,
who is trying to connect with me?

I need another to talk to,
and I'm really not sure where to go.
I know what I feel and even though I am afraid,
if it happens again, I hope it'll be during the day.

Where is that person, who will truly understand,
for I want someone to speak with, even a man?
I know that I am not imagining things,
and I truly believe in what I've seen.
Why is this even happening to me?
What oh what, does it all mean?
Oh God, why are you even doing this to me?

Bonny Billan

Strange things are happening around me,
and I'm not exactly sure, what it could be.
I know what I think, and if it is so,
my world is about to be truly shaken,
as my soul has starting to be awakened.
Now that it has actually begun, I have no way of halting it.
Can one truly reach out from heaven and touch those on earth?

– BONNY BILLAN –

The Awakening Of My Soul

Chapter 11

This is a conversation which I had with John on March 9, 1990.

John   "Do you work at all?"

Bonny   "No."

John   "Why not?"

Bonny   "Well… my daughter is only two and a half years old and I am waiting for her to begin school, but in the meantime I am a bit bored."

John	"I think that you better start looking for a job, dear. It doesn't have to be some big career thing, but you need to get out and be amongst people. You don't need the money… you need a job."
Bonny	"What do you see?"
John	"What would you like to do?"
Bonny	"The only thing that I am interested in is decorating."
John	"Uh huh… and you are good at it too. The other thing is that you need to work with people. You are a people person and that's what's happening here because you put restrictions or whatever. You put yourself in a shell and there are no people here. The same people keep revolving in and out of your life and you're going… ohhhhhhh if I hear that thing once more, I'm going to kill somebody."
Bonny	(Laughing)
John	(Laughing) You know, but it's time to do something like this. If it is decorating, GO and DO IT! Okay?"
Bonny	"Yea."
John	"That is something that you can start out of your home. And a year from now… oops my goodness… LOOK how it has grown. Oh my God, I didn't plan this and yet you are reveling in it. There are ways and means my dear. There are ways and means. Fair enough?"
Bonny	"Yes, there was a neighbor that asked me, if I was interested in decorating her house. She has been asking me for years and now she has moved into the neighborhood."
John	"THERE is your first contract. AND, YOU ARE GOOD AT IT! TAKE a look around at this place. It looks MARVELOUS!" Yea… you walk in here, it feels comfortable and it feels friendly. That's what most people want to achieve and there never can, when they decorate a house."

Bonny   "It's funny, I guess that I am just lacking the confidence. I know what I like and I know what to do, but when I look at someone else's place, I think, are they going to like how I do it?"

John   (Laughing) "Well, you know something, after you get talking to a person, they literally tell you what they want anyway. And then you adapt it to what they like so it looks right."

Bonny   "Yea."

John   "BUT, WHATEVER YOU DO, do something where you can eventually do it, on your own."

Bonny   "Yes."

John   "Having a BOSS... you DON'T NEED! You already have one at home, you don't need one when you go to work. Okay?"

Bonny   "Right."

John   "So, create that type of atmosphere around you! So take a look at it seriously for yourself, will you please."

Bonny   "Yes."

John   "NOW! How much do you know, about being psychic? You were thinking about your dad, SO IS HIS DAUGHTER!" (Laughing)

Bonny   (Laughing)

John   "How often, do you use it?"

Bonny   "NOT, often."

John   "No. Well, we talked a little earlier, about a little FEAR involved with being psychic. That's normal. Okay. The more you use it, the more you see, how well it works... the easier it becomes to do things because someone is saying do this, do that."

Bonny   "Yes."

John   "The more YOU CAN TRUST IT, TRUST IT! GO see that neighbor OKAY?

TRUST, what comes out of your mouth. Do not even edit it, don't think about it, JUST say it! The next thing you know, she'll be standing there saying is "How did you know, that's the way I wanted that done? How did you know, that I liked that color?"

Go see her about that decorating job, will you? BUT TRUST, that what you are getting, is what you are suppose to be saying, IT WORKS!

SOMEBODY HERE, is trying to help you very much! And, you are not letting them. Okay? Each of us, have GUIDES! Okay"

Bonny   "Yes.

Lately, I don't know if it is just me because I sort of feel like... am I going off of my rocker or whatever, because I think I am hearing voices."

John   "Uh huh... it's around the corner."

Bonny   "NOT, JUST IN MY MIND! I AM ACTUALLY HEARING THEM! And, I WILL SORT OF LOOK AROUND... AND IT IS GONE!"

John   (Laughing) "WHO SAID THAT!

The next time that you hear it, just calmly say, "Sorry, I didn't hear that. Will you say it again?" You, don't have to say it out loud. Say it, in here.

NOW, one of the ways of being psychic is to be clairaudient. Clairvoyance see pictures, clairsentience senses things... like I am. If, you are hearing voices, it doesn't matter if they are coming from there, or just whistling around in your head."

Bonny   "Yes."

John   "The point IS, SOMEBODY'S TALKING TO YOU! THEY HAVE SOMETHING, TO SAY TO YOU! LISTEN TO THEM! Okay? THERE, IS NO RISK, INVOLVED. There really isn't!"

Bonny	"It was just something like two or three words... I don't know, maybe to just start off with, so they could get my attention."
John	"Quite often, what happens sometimes, is that if they want to say something to you, THEY DON"T ALWAYS pick the most convenient time. They pick the time, when they can CATCH, YOUR ATTENTION! As you LEARN, TO RELAX and say, "Okay its fine anytime or please don't wake me up at 4:00 o'clock in the morning, I need my sleep. Then, they will adapt to you more. Okay?"
Bonny	"A couple of days ago, I was by myself in the hallway and my daughter was in her room for a nap and I thought that I heard something. But you know, like you say, the fear... so I just shut it off. I said to myself, "I didn't hear anything" and I kept walking." (Laughing.)
John	(Laughing) "You shut it off. Next time, stop and say, sorry what did you say? Okay? I am getting very strongly, that there is a NEED to communicate."
Bonny	"With this person?"
John	"Yea... or with this entity... whatever it is. And when you NEED the HELP the most, is when they come in the strongest. One of the examples I'll give you, if you are driving a car and you suddenly hit an icy patch... all of a sudden, you know what to do with that car, usually. And you know, you'll usually save yourself, if you don't panic. Okay? You've never hit an icy patch in your life, but at that moment, YOU KNOW EXACTLY WHAT TO DO! And it's not YOU, it's THEM keeping you out of a jam. That's what, makes it work."
Bonny	"Yes, well I had a close call, a couple of years ago. Actually, I just turned out of our cul-de-sac... it was so silly. I guess my mind... it was after the summer and I don't know where it was. I was driving along and before I knew it, I was on the other side

of the street. And there was a small pick-up truck almost in front of me. It was parked on the road.

NOW... I... THAT WAS A MIRACLE, cuz I was right in front of the truck."

John   "Yes."

Bonny   "The wheel went this way and the whole car managed to get away except the very back of the car which got banged a bit. BUT, I was right in front of that truck and I... couldn't have DONE THAT!

I DID NOT MOVE THAT CAR, OUT OF THE WAY!"

John   "That's RIGHT! They did it for you! Yea."

Bonny   "I KNOW THAT! I KNOW THAT! And both of the kids were in the back seat."

John   "All you got was bounced around a bit. Yea... OH IT'S AMAZING!

A very good friend of mine rolled a van and I looked at her and I said, "You are worried about a bad back? Do you remember, them moving your head?"

She said, "What do you mean?"

Then she said, "YES!"

I said to her, "I saw your head being crushed when you said to me, that you were in an accident. I said, SOMEBODY REACHED DOWN and MOVED YOUR HEAD! They couldn't move YOU because you were jammed in, but they MOVED YOUR HEAD!"

She said, "I FELT LIKE TWO HANDS WERE ON MY HEAD THAT MOVED ME!"

I said, "That's WHY YOU ARE ALIVE!" Because she was all upset at that point and she was ready to leave her husband... she figured that the accident was ALL BAD. And I said, "No dear, you weren't quite ready to leave your husband, that's all! But, THEY KEPT YOU ALIVE, didn't they?

THAT'S, HOW THEY WORK!"

Bonny   "Yes. Do you know who the person is that is trying to get in touch with me?"

John   "Give me your hands and let's find out if we can get a name for you?

Bonny   "I've got dry hands." (Laughing)

John   (Laughing) "The name that I am getting is Selwan. It's a very deep voice, but I don't think it is a man. I believe it's a lady. Say, "Selwan," the next time that you hear a voice and say, "What did you say, Selwan?"

Bonny   "You don't know what they are trying to say?"

John   "No, I have no idea at this point. I think basically, what I am getting, is that they are trying to help. Okay? Because they are feeling the pressure inside of you and it is going like this. And they are saying, "Hey, we've got to do something with this lady. We have to help her out here, a bit. But, you have to listen, in order, for them to get through. Okay? Give yourself half a chance. Give it a try. Okay?"

Bonny   "Yes."

John   "No… you are perceiving yourself at this point because everybody is putting you down. And you are saying, "I must be worthless?" That's not TRUE! DEFINITELY NOT TRUE! But it's like being a prisoner with somebody, eventually you begin to love the person who is keeping you in prison.

What is happening, is that this one is putting you down, that one is putting you down. The kids are getting to you, like kids do, and they are being very demanding. And you are thinking, "Oh my God I am not doing the right things there either. And this all begins to revolve and yea… you are heading towards a problem, if you want to allow it to be a problem.

I am suggesting that its time NOW, to say SCREW IT! I'M GOING TO DO THIS and turn a corner. Okay?"

Bonny   "Yes."

John   "And having a bit of a business going or something of that nature, IS A BIG STEP! You know, it's a good step, but it lets the world know, that what I am saying, is that "I want some freedom."

When you start creating a bit of it, it'll be hard for anybody to stop you from creating a whole lot. And the next thing you know, in a marriage, you have a husband coming home, you've being bubbling over and you've been doing all kinds of things all day… things get interesting. What is lacking is the spark. It's a two way street, but it works that way.

Don't take things so personally from the kids. You are taking things and keeping them all inside and you are going to create an illness, if you want one. Okay? You can do a humdinger of a job of it. You see, when you have a lot of intellect yourself, and you don't use it, then you turn it towards the negative and the negative then, HAS to come out in some form. It's going to come out in an illness, if you want it to. Okay?"

Bonny   "I see. Okay."

This is a conversation which I had with John on Feb. 17, 1993.

John   "Are you working yet?

Bonny   "No, not yet."

John   "What is the controversy against you not?"

Bonny   "My daughter is in kindergarten and she only goes for half a day. And I don't really want to leave her with someone else, so I am aiming for Sept."

John   "Okay, keep going. You'll do it… please."

Bonny   "Yes, well I thought that I have stuck it out this long."

John   "What's another few months. I agree, but you can start looking though, for the job. Okay. You might need a little training here, but it's nothing to get too excited about, maybe a little updating. It's not a big deal, okay."

Bonny   "Okay."

John   "Now… husbands. Well, he's happy with his work, but that is the only focus, the entire focus. There used to be a little glimmer on the side, but now it's just work. It's totally work."

Bonny   "I've told him, how I felt a lot of times and he just looks at me.

I ask him, how he feels and he just stares at me without saying a word."

John   "Yea… there's nothing. Well his whole focus is work so let him have it I guess. That's what he WANTS! He LOSES! The thing is, is that he does quite well. There is another contract coming up for him in "94"."

Bonny   "Yes. He was talking about a different job that he should apply for."

John   "WHY NOT! It's ALL that is in his life and he might as will go as high as he can. And make as much money as he can. I don't know WHAT, he is going to do in his old age… be lonely I suppose.

Is someone going away?"

Bonny   "I'd like to get away with the girls."

John   "It's not a bad idea.

It's quite okay to run away from home, you know. (Laughing.)

Why not go away if you can do it, the sooner the better.

Well, you know, you have learnt, pretense. Okay?

And you are doing it extremely well… to everybody concerned, everything is marvelous. Okay. Well, that's fine. You keep up that pretense, but start another one, GET A LIFE! If you can pull this one off, you can pull anything off.

Do you understand what I am saying? And why not set a pattern of occasionally taking sometime and going off somewhere. Set it up so it works for you. It's not perhaps the best way to live, but at this point it is your only solution."

Bonny   "Actually I have started discussing, how I feel about him with my sisters because I just can't keep it in any longer."

John	"No, I don't think that you can, because you are going to explode. There's just a point where…"
Bonny	"That's just how I feel."
John	"And I think that there is going to come a point where there won't be a marriage, but I think that that is a ways down the road. I think that is when the kids are old enough to accept it, whatever, okay. You are not at the point to say, I am out of here and upset everybody's lives. I just don't think that you are that type of person. I wish that you were, cuz it would be a lot easier. Okay. Because, you are also not a liar and you hate, living untruths and the whole thing, but that is what you are doing at this point.
Bonny	"Yes."
John	"I think that you are going to keep up the pretense for the sake of the kids. I don't know, you'll have to decide, whether that is right or wrong. Okay. You know, find the time to yourself. Find a life for yourself as well, cuz when those kids are gone and I'm talking five to eight years, then, what have you got. You need to have built something by then. So put the plans into motion."
Bonny	"Yes. Well I have started courses in interior decorating and design."
John	"You need to set it up… so when you are ready to say…"
Bonny	"It's over."
John	"I am not going to spend the rest of my life here… cuz you're not! So you might as well set it up so, you don't have to Bonny. Do you understand, what I am saying?"
Bonny	"Yes I do."

This is another conversation that John and I had on October 1, 1993.

After my reading was over, I went home and listened to my cassette tape. I could hear the loud sounds of a man's heavy breathing throughout certain parts of it. I was a bit alarmed over this because I absolutely knew who the man was, and I was sure, about what he was trying to say to me.

John   "Well you have made up your mind. You, are going to do it. You are going to be your own person. Well, now you have to deal with all of the guilt and all of the garbage that goes along with it, but you can handle that, can't you?"

Bonny   "Yes."

John   "That's going to be the hard part Bonny. There is so much junk that has been dumped in over the years and for you to suddenly say," "That's it, I'm going to do what I want to do."
            "You are going to do it, but you really have to deal with a lot of junk in accomplishing it. Okay?
            All the family comes into it. They are going to be nattering and yapping at you and whatever one doesn't think of, the other will."

Bonny   "Is this to do with my personal life?"

John   "Yes, it's your personal life. Okay. You are ready and it is time. But, I don't think that they totally disagree that you need to be your own person, but because they didn't think of it first.
            And Bonny, they have always, sort of dumped on you and, you are finally going to stand up and say, "Sorry, go find another junkyard."
            And, they are not going to like it. That's what it's all about, so if you can understand that. Okay?"

Bonny   "I know that I can't take anymore of the crap that is going on either."

John   "I know you can't, it's really getting heavy and thick since that man died. I tell ya. That is going to be a real mess before that's all finished. Anyway, what are doing for work and stuff? What are you doing?"

Bonny   "Right now I am working for the elections until the end of the month and I started my own business."

John   "Good! What are you doing?"

Bonny   "Interior decorating."

John   "OH WONDERFUL! WONDERFUL!"

Bonny   "I have my first job and I have a couple of others ones lined up and I am working for the commonwealth games for five months."

John   "That's wonderful. You are networking and you are making contacts and you are also getting your self confidence up. And you are thinking, I can do something worthwhile. You are going to do extremely well with them. I like your independent business. I do. I think that is the one that is going to hum.

You need your own business because you are not really somebody's, nine to five person. You know that. Plus you need something that will challenge the hell out of you, or you are going to get bored out of your mind, and drop it because you are very intelligent. And that, is what has been driving you nuts, sitting around raising children, you know."

Bonny   "Yea."

John   "So, I don't know how your other half is going to take this. He's not concerned about you taking a job, but what is going to happen is that you are becoming independent. You are going to create a business, you are going to run it well and you are going to have your own money to do what you want with it.

(The sound of a man breathing in the background of my tape begins.)

That, is what he is not going to handle well because he is not the boss anymore. He is NOT the controller anymore. Okay. And that is where the families come in because they have always thought that you were the nice, dutiful wife. And well… to a point, I guess that you were.

(There is breathing on my tape again.)

162

But, that was not you. You were not happy. And finally, you are doing something and when they find out that it is working, it is going to get worse. Okay. Do you understand what I am saying?"

Bonny   "Yes."

John   "But, the difference is, I think that you are ready to handle this now. When we first talked about this, I don't know if you could have handled all of the criticism. Now, you can!"

(A man breathing again.)

Bonny   "All of a sudden, I have this strength. I don't know where I got it from."

John   "From yourself. You've always had it. YOU just finally tapped into it, that's all. If you get angry enough or fed up enough, it's amazing what you can do."

Bonny   "Yea, I am."

John   "And it is the way a lot of men and women have started businesses."

Bonny   "Well I actually had gum surgery and I was in bed for four days and one night, at 2:30 a.m. I started watching this show, "How to start your own business." And I thought, I am going to go for it, this is what I am going to do and this is what I am going to name it."

John   "It'll work well. I have no problems here at all. The other thing that I like here as well is that you made some good friends. You have some good people around you, but you need more and you're going to make more. In these other two jobs, you are going to find out that you can get a rapport going with adults and keep it going. And that is the biggest thing that I see because you are going to make some friends and realize they like me. They like me because I am a person. Not because I am someone's mother or somebody's wife or belong to this family or to that religion or whatever. It's because I am a person. And, it is going to work. In some small way, this may strengthen your relationship."

Bonny   "Actually as far as I am concerned, it is really over. It is. I am not looking to fix it at all."

(A man is breathing again on the tape.)

John   "Okay that was your big decision."

Bonny   "He has dinner meetings all the time and he's sometimes away and once he didn't leave the phone number. So I told him, I can't wait to start my business because I'm going to have all of these meetings."
He said, "With Who?"
I said, "Oh don't worry, I'll find some people."

John   "I like it. I like it. I like it. I like it.

(The man is breathing very heavily now.)

I am going to put it another way to you as well too. There is a possibility that within three years, there is NOT a marriage. I mean permanently, you live here, and I live there."

Bonny   "Hmm."

John   "I think the three years is around it because of the ages of the kids. And as they get a bit older, you are going to feel, well, this will work.
Do you understand what I am saying?"

Bonny   "Yes."

John   "Because kids pick-up falsehoods, the nonsense and they pick-up the garbage that goes on. They know what is going on?"

(The breathing is much quicker now.)

Bonny   "Oh yea, they do."

John   "And finally, you'll get to a point of, why bother? Why keep the false front going here?"

Bonny   "Well, we lead pretty separate lives now."
     (The breathing begins again.)

John   "I understand that, but even more so, separate houses and the whole nine yards here.
     And, you have a pizzazz here? You have an ability to do something here and you can do it well."

Bonny   "And that's with the business?"

John   (Breathing again.) "It's with the business, very much so. I have never seen anybody so ready to get into a business and pull it off. And the thing is that, when it comes to actually meeting the needs of your clientele, I think that you are going to be very understanding, very compassionate and very good. But when it comes down to, this is what it is going to cost you… this is the way that it is. (The breathing starts again.)
     Do you understand what I am saying? That is the bottom end isn't it?"

Bonny   "Yes."

John   "That's what it is all about when you get through it all.
     And I want you to do something else, in your spare time. It's time that you sat down and wrote a book, about marriages, about marriages within your own community, your feelings, and different things like that.
     You are the first, and there is more, to come. An awful lot of ladies are looking around and going, well can I or can I not? You are sort of the first or the avant-garde. You might want to write that to help someone else."

Bonny   "It's funny I bought an empty book about a year ago and it's just sitting there. It's pink. And I don't know what I am supposed to do with it."
     (The breathing begins again.)

John   "Maybe that's what you are suppose to do with it, to help others. You see, when I read… well when your children are old

165

enough and I read for them, I am going to see the same things that I am seeing with other couples.

The kids are saying, "Are they going to arrange my marriage? Am I going to marry someone who is East Indian?"

And I am going, "No, no. I don't think so, unless you want to."

This is what has changed. (Breathing again.) And you are doing it, sort of, for your generation as well."

Bonny   "It's funny, I saw this program on television on East Indian arranged marriages. (The breathing is much louder and it is continuing throughout this entire part non-stop.) It was a satire on it and it made me so mad that after I finished watching it, I felt like clubbing someone. YOU KNOW WHAT I MEAN, I just COULDN'T STAND IT!"

(Very heavy breathing now.)

John   "And under certain circumstances, it worked well, but it doesn't work anymore. It's senseless in this country. (Heavy breathing again.) So I guess, that is what the empty book is for. You need to write, what your feelings were, what you went through, how hard it was to sort of, not rise above, but allow yourself, to be yourself and not subvert everything that you believe in. So, it'll come!"

Bonny   "I have a question. There is… I am just wondering, what is going on in my home. I sort of feel like…"

John   "Who's there?"

Bonny   "Well… I don't know who is there? I have a towel from off of my bathroom counter, that is always thrown in the sink. And I am the only one in that bathroom. And now, I have a couple of pictures on a desk in my kitchen and they are moved everyday. The pictures are of my dad and my children and the kids are saying that, they are not doing it."

John   "No.
Somebody wants to talk to you. Why don't you sit down and talk to them?"

Bonny   "Is that, what it is? You mean I just…"

John   "Yes. It's time!

Sit down and have a CHAT! Someone is trying to have a little talk with you, or tell you something, or help you with something along that line. It's time to sit down."

Bonny   "What if they don't come?"

John   "They WILL! When they move things around, what they are basically saying to you, is LOOK, we are trying to get your attention!"

Bonny   "Okay, so, it's not my husband doing it?"

John   "I don't think so."

Bonny   "You see, the pictures weren't moved when I left the kitchen for a phone call and he was the only one in the kitchen. Later he came down to get a drink of water and went back to bed. And when I went back into the kitchen, the pictures were moved.

I thought it was him trying to drive me crazy." (Laughing)

John   "No, I don't think that it is him. No. I think that is too obvious for this man. If he wanted to drive you crazy, he would be very subtle about it. But I think that you know him too well, he knows, he couldn't get away with it.

No, I think that someone is trying to chat with you… fair enough."

Bonny   "And, the way that they are turned, they are being done now, sort of, to me, like in a babyish way. It's not even… then I thought that it had to be my daughter."

John   "All it is, is a attention getting device. I read for a lady in Regina and she says she gets woken up at 3:00 in the morning with her mother's chair rocking. And I said, "Well fine, why don't you go talk to your mother."

"It's that's same idea. You know, whatever. This person may not have had a place to sort of sit in your house that would cause your attention, but moving things, he knows, WILL GET YOUR ATTENTION!"

Bonny   "OH YEA, because I know where everything is."

John   "Exactly because he knows your house, you know, it is an immaculate house."

Bonny   "But... it wouldn't be my dad though?"

John   "YOU, think NOT!"

Bonny   "I don't know, is it?"

John   "I think so! I think so. He's far from finished dear!"

Bonny   "HE'S WHAT?"

John   "He's far from finished. There is enough stuff going on here, that he is far from finished."

Bonny   "But, he wouldn't be MAD, if he came?"

John   "No, I don't think that he is mad at all. If he was mad, he would be throwing things around the house. He's not doing that. He's trying to get your attention, that's all."

Bonny   "Because I have... I sort of thought that I was over everything, but I have this deep resentment of the way that we brought up and everything. And it's just... coming out of my ears right now."

John   "Well, you're not alone, are you?"

Bonny   "No."

John   "I read for.......... And you are not alone, okay? SHE IS RIGHT!"

Bonny   "Well, there is a court case going on right now between some of my siblings regarding my dad's will. I just don't know. My mom is upset.

One of my sisters and myself had gone to see a lawyer and we had answered some questions about my dad's will, but the lawyer's office made a mistake and sent the papers to my brothers instead. And we weren't taking part in the court case, but these papers had to be filed within the year, just in case we were going to do anything. So everything is stopped now as far as we are concerned, but my mom is in the hospital and she doesn't want to see any of us girls. So you see, all of this is absolute crap!"

John   "Mother doesn't want to deal with it and yet, mother, can put an end to it. It is the silly part. She can stand up and put an end to it immediately. She won't do it because… I don't think that your dad is going to let her. I think that he is orchestrating it."

Bonny   "You think what?"

John   "I think that your dad is orchestrating it."

Bonny   "Oh really."

John   "I don't think that he knew what was going to happen until it did happen. (There is a man breathing on the tape at this point.)

And now, that he is looking at it, he's going, "NO, I made a mistake." "And I think that he's trying to fix it."

Bonny   "HOW IS HE GOING TO DO THAT?"

John   "Through his girls.

The only one that can fix it, stand up, make it stop, and make it come right, is your mother, by saying do this, do that… this is enough. And I don't know whether she is going to do it or not."

Bonny   "I don't think so. She just has these feelings for my brothers, that she has never had for her daughters."

John   "Well, it's the old thing that the girls aren't worth anything and the boys are. It's as simple as that."

Bonny   "It's exactly, that."

John   "The thing is, in this family the girls are more competent than the men are. Aren't they? And I think, daddy has begun to realize it. And you know, it is not without precedent, a lot of women have inherited and done a lot better than the sons ever well. But, the girls were shortchanged and you know it."

Bonny   "Yes, I know."

John   "It's another decision that you got to… where do YOU stand? It's a tough one. Okay?"

Bonny   "Well, I sort of backed out of it, but I resent it."

John   "I don't think that you have.
I think that dad is trying to tell you, not to, but I can't make your decisions for you Bonny. I can't. But it wouldn't hurt to sit down and have a little chat with dad because I am almost certain, that that is who is there."

Bonny   "I don't think that he would actually show up. Would he?"

John   "Aha. He would certainly guide you."

Bonny   "Can we do this through my thoughts?"

John   "Sure. Yea exactly. You, don't have to have him standing in front of you. No, that is not what I am meaning."

Bonny   "Oh yea, because I think that I would freak."

John   "The presence is there, but no… yea it'll come through your thoughts.   It'll be the way, that you are the most comfortable to meet him."

Bonny   "That's the way, that I do it."

John   "That'll be fine. Yea. So find some quiet time in that house and if he moves some pictures around, sit down and have a chat. It'll be interesting… real interesting." (Laughing)

Bonny   "It's such a mess. It's just unbelievable. My mom is in the hospital and we haven't gone over to see her because she said that she doesn't want to see us. The case is stopped. And we have to go over and see her cuz its awful that we haven't seen our own mother! I don't even know, what to do. So we thought that maybe one day next week if I'm not working, we'll go over and see her."

John   "I don't know, if you will ever get your mother to sit down and say okay, this is this and this is that, okay. Because I don't think that she will ever admit that, there is something wrong here. Okay. She has never dealt with those types of emotional issues in her life. She's never had to, she's never wanted to. Okay. You know, she raised you."

Bonny   "I know."

John   "And neither did your dad, but there is a point here now, that THE GIRLS, have had enough! Okay. Now, it is their decision what they are going to do and how far they are going to push the brothers. And the brothers are scared out of their minds because they know that they are going to lose."

Bonny   "I am thinking of my children also because they have always had a lot to do with their cousins and I don't want to wipe that out for them."

John   "Well think of your kids as well, in the fact, that, this is THEIR money too. This is their inheritance. Okay. Grandpa did not build, all, this up for a bunch of fools. He built it up for future generations okay? Because he never had anything. He wanted to make sure that he had left them something. He thought that he had. And I think it suddenly dawned on him when he looked at it, from over there… rather than from here… OOPS, I screwed UP! I left out half of my grandchildren!

You know. And it is a mess. It is a terrible mess, but in the old days, it would have been made right. Okay. Do you understand, what I am saying?"

Bonny   "Yes."

John   "The brothers would not have done this. But, mainly they would have made it right and that is what your dad was counting on, but it isn't happening is it?"

Bonny   "The brothers don't have the feelings that my dad had towards us. They don't! It's like we don't count for anything. We don't MEAN anything!"

John	"No. YOU DON"T!"
Bonny	"And that's what hurts so much too.
John	"Well look at them in their relationships. You're not the only ones that they don't care for. That's the way that they want things. But, you know, you are striking a blow for yourself and I think, THAT'S the most important issue at this point. Okay? Whatever you are going to do with the rest of the family, that is up to you, but I am letting you know that it is all blowing loose."
Bonny	"I am ready to say, go to hell to all of them!"
John	"THAT or get the other two girls and say, "Hey, we are going to stick together because we are fighting for more than just this, WE ARE FIGHTING for our kids too. So, it is up to you BUT, for yourself, YOU HAVE MADE THE STEP FORWARD and I think that you are going ahead. I don't think that you are turning back, now, dear."
Bonny	"No."
John	"I also know you, from reading you, over the years, that once you get your teeth into something you are not going to quit. YOU, are a very determined lady. You need to do a few things which you are doing, to get your self confidence up, to not be coerced, to not be threatened, to not be, put in your place, so to speak. But remember something, you have had twenty some odd years of having that hammered into your head. Just look at how you were brought up, what your parents did... that type of thing."
Bonny	"And, it didn't help being married to, who I am married to."
John	"NO! OF COURSE NOT! BUT, you are not ALONE! But, you are the ONE that is going to change it or begin to change it. Okay? I don't know, if you'll ever finish it but, you are the one that is doing it. And, you are not alone. Okay?

Your sisters are obviously doing the same things, more or less, if they don't get threatened again and even if they do, maybe, they have to keep going anyway. Because I am telling you, with starting this business, you are going to get threatened from everybody, aren't you? But, what do you want? That's what's most important here.

YOU ARE A PERSON, BONNY. And, that's what is important here and I think, that this is what you are finally standing up and I think everybody is. I think all of your sisters are as well in different ways. Now whether you support each other or not, that is something that you are going to have to come to a decision on. But I guarantee you, that no matter what happens, this family will never be the same again anyways."

Bonny   "Do you ever see it resolved?"

John   "Yes. Oh yes."
          It will get resolved in a courtroom, but it won't necessarily get resolved between each other."

Bonny   "It will end up in a courtroom... though?"

John   "I'm almost certain unless Mother intervenes. She is the only one who can say, "We do this, we do that, and you listen up."

Bonny   "Will it do any good for me to try and talk to her."

John   "You can try. You are one of the few... that she might listen to. It depends how valuable she feels this family is. It would keep it together, if she would step in and say, "Hey" at least till she goes. She is the strong one in this family, she always is.
          I also think that Mother has been ignored, especially by her sons. And, that hurts."

Bonny   "Oh yea, yea. But you see, they are the only ones that matter to her. It didn't matter that we were there for her all those weeks after my dad passed on. And I did everything that I could for her and later on, whenever she phoned me about anything, I was on the next ferry over to Vancouver."

John   "Oh no, of course not. That's what you are SUPPOSE TO DO!

It's your duty, right?"

Bonny   "If any of the girls do anything wrong, she always says, I'm not going to speak to them anymore, but the boys can do fifty million things wrong and they are still number one to her.
This is what... I can't TAKE IT ANYMORE!"

John   "But her grandchildren too."

Bonny   "Oh definitely. Definitely."

John   "Maybe it is time that you told her this. Okay? It's time that it maybe came out. I think that you have two sisters that don't disagree with you Bonny."

Bonny   "Oh no, they do! They do!"

John   "So maybe it's time for all the girls to stand up and say HEY!
This is a tough ONE, isn't it?"

Bonny   "Yea. Between this going on, and my husband, and than the whole family..."

John   "Yea, it's a tough one."

A Father's protection close at hand,
as he now sees, how his actions affected my soul.
His love would finally find its way to me,
for the first time in my life.
As parents, we must always consider,
how we can lessen our children from needless strife.

– BONNY BILLAN –

Unfinished Business

Chapter 12

The door lock on the driver's side of my mini van was not working properly for some time and my spouse refused to take it anywhere to get it fixed. I repeatedly told him about this problem, but he tuned me out. Consequently I couldn't get into the van through this door, so I first had to unlock the passenger door and then stretch across the seat with my umbrella to unlock it. This was unbelievable and very annoying to say the least.

I drove my children to different activities daily and I always had a lot of errands to do. And after a month of this scenario, I decided that I wasn't going to do it any longer. Therefore I began to leave my door unlocked, especially whenever I was out shopping at the Bay. I didn't care if someone had stolen the van or if perhaps, someone was hiding in it waiting for me to come back. I had reached my tolerance level and I thought whatever happens, happens.

However, one day something quite strange started happening. Whenever I came back to my van, somehow my driver's door was always locked. At first I thought that I had made a mistake and I had locked it out of habit, but then I made sure that I didn't lock it on purpose. However, each and every time that I came back to my van, the door was locked!

I wondered, how on earth this was happening?

Something very incredible was going on here and I knew that once again, someone was protecting me. Although, who could it be?

I thought that it must be my dad who was watching out for my safety, but it was so hard to comprehend, even though, a part of me knew that it was probably true! When I told others about this occurrence I don't know if they truly believed me and I wasn't even sure, if I should believe me!

I never wanted to buy this vehicle, but my spouse wouldn't listen to me. He went ahead and bought it anyway as he bought himself a new car. There was also a problem with the brakes and the only way that I could release them was by doing it by hand. Therefore I had to bend down and pull a lever forward and when I did this, the brake released, but the pedal would hit my hand very hard and it hurt a lot. I must mention, that the van did not have these problems when he first bought it.

I previously had a new car and this piece of metal was proving to be quite a lemon! I repeatedly pointed out to my spouse that there was a problem with the brakes, but he ignored me. When he finally took it to a mechanic, it was discovered that the brakes were almost gone. His dad joked to his friends that I was driving a vehicle with no brakes, but he should have added in, that I was also married to his son who lacked any common sense. I was worried about the safety of my children and it was very frustrating being married to a person who never listened or respected a word that I said.

One day as I was leaving the Mayfair mall parking lot with a girlfriend, I unlocked the passenger side door and after my friend got into the van, she unlocked my door. I knelt down to release the brake, but this time something different happened. The van bolted ahead and began moving and I started running beside it trying to catch up to it.

(As I am typing this out on September 28, 2004 there is a story on "Oprah" about a woman, who could not stop her car because she lost her brakes.)

I tried as hard as I could to get my foot inside of the van, but at this point it was moving very fast and the door opening was too high for me to climb in. My friend eventually reached her foot over and stomped on the brake and the van grounded to a halt. We sat there laughing for quite some time, even though, it would not have been funny if someone had been hurt. There were other cars in the parking lot and how my van avoided hitting anyone or anything was a miracle.

Since my dad's passing, so many strange things had begun to happen around me. I had some towels and pictures that somehow moved on their own, lights were turning on by themselves, and there was also the sound of someone walking upstairs quite frequently. I had light bulbs which popped and burnt out as I turned them on, and then, I had to replace them four hours later because they burnt out again. There was also the sound of a man breathing loudly on the cassette tapes of my readings. And he quite often made himself known to me, as I was watching a television show or a video tape which I had previously recorded. Also the time on my alarm clock would quite often slow down even though, there was a new battery in it. And I had some other things that moved as if by their own means and there was no human explanation.

I had been contemplating a divorce for the past few years, but now it was in the forefront of my thoughts. Furthermore I began having nightmares with my dad in them and I'd often wake up screaming. I was afraid that he was going to appear to me one day soon, and I believed that my father was around me because he was upset about my wishes regarding separating. Also I wasn't sure, if he was trying to stop me from going ahead with it, but I had no reason to think that he would be in favor of the idea. My life had suddenly turned terrifying and I didn't know how to stop it. It was one thing dealing with dominating males on earth, but now I had to deal with them in heaven too!

I often wondered why God wanted me to experience these spiritual situations and I truly thought that I knew the answer to this question.

Remember... I had repeatedly cried out to my dad, as I asked him why?

For many years I had quite happily accepted that I had a unique knowing within me, but when my dad first began reaching out to me I was really frightened. This was something completely new and hell, this was my DAD! It was very scary to think that he could actually come back to communicate with me. He was sometimes intimidating when he was alive, let alone, him now appearing to me from the other side where he could probably do anything that he wanted to me. I didn't know what his intentions were or what he was capable of doing. I just knew that he was reaching out to me from heaven and I was scared! Understand that in this situation, I didn't know if it was going to be a positive encounter or not, and I had no indication that my father was coming to me out of any real love.

Can you imagine how you would feel to re-unite with one of your parents or a loved one that had passed on? In addition, you didn't really know what to expect because your relationship with them had always been distant. Would you be in fear or would you feel very blessed and thankful to God for granting you this huge gift?

In the last year of my dad's life, he spoke about his wish to leave his estate equally divided amongst all of his children. He pointed this out to most of my siblings. However he was told that if he did, my mother would not be taken care of. Consequently in the past 1½ years, some of my siblings found themselves on opposite sides of a family court case which ensued over my father's will. And there was now a lot of turmoil in a once relatively close-knit family.

In an attempt to help settle the problem and for my male siblings to truly realize exactly how we were raised, I sent a letter to an East Indian magazine in Vancouver. It was in response to an article which was written regarding inequality issues between the genders within our culture. This subject had stirred something within me and angered me all over again regarding my childhood issues which I thought were somewhat dormant. The past few years of turmoil had created an uproar and a non-stop powerful reaction in me. This proved to be the end of any silence within myself and the beginning of my re-emergence, as the strong woman that I was when I first married eighteen years earlier.

In my reply to the magazine, I wrote about my upbringing and the favoritism of the males over the females in my family. The reaction to my correspondence from my male siblings was not favorable and as a result, one of my sisters and I also became involved in the proceedings. My heart was never into it and I didn't truly want to be a part of it, but my dad strongly wanted me to join the case. This was one of the reasons why he was around me so powerfully. However, before I did anything I checked repeatedly, that this was his final wish and what he absolutely wanted me to proceed with.

My dad had already suffered on his dying bed, as some people took a hold of his hand and signed his signature as an "X" on a legal document. My father was paralyzed and completely helpless to stop this from happening. All he could do was lie there, as he witnessed the betrayal of this situation. As this information came to light, I realized the hurt that he must have gone through and I just deeply wanted him to be at peace. A short time later, my Father made himself known to me and he explained some issues that he wanted me to be aware of.

One night on Sunday January 15, 1995 at 3:00 a.m. while I was trying to fall asleep, my dad appeared in my mind. When I first saw him, I couldn't believe what I was seeing, so I opened my eyes and then closed them again. He was still there. His appearance was the same as he had always looked and he looked friendly enough.

When he first began to speak to me, it was mind boggling to say the very least. I was shocked and I just stared at him, as I questioned if it was truly happening. As he continued conversing with me, I knew that he was really there, especially since he wasn't going away. I listened to him with great surprise and I understood that I wasn't dreaming because I hadn't gone to sleep yet.

At first I was lying down in the darkness, but after a short time I turned on my lamp. This was partly for comfort and partly so I could write down everything that he said. Once I came to my senses, I very quickly grabbed a journal and a pen off of my night table. I began writing down what he said to me, and then I stopped and covered my eyes with my hands, so I would be in darkness. I needed to do this, so I could see him clearly in my mind's eye. He responded and continued communicating with me and every few seconds, I had to uncover my eyes so I could write his messages down. This continued for a time and it was the most special extraordinary event that I had ever experienced in my life!

The following is a part of my conversation with my dad in spirit.

Dad   "You don't know, what they've done. Yea. You're smart... you'll figure it out."

Bonny   "I love you Dad. I really do."

Dad   "I know, nay bay. I love you too. Don't cry.

("In this moment, I truly wanted to be a part of his life, the part that I had missed out on. I didn't realize that I had emotional issues left with him, but I do. He used to say nay bay or something like that, whenever I cried as a child. I wasn't sure what it meant, but he was now saying it again.)

Bonny   Thanks for being around to help me out, cuz I wouldn't get through it."

Dad   "I'm sorry for what I did."

Bonny   (I started crying.)

Dad   (He wiped my tears away off both of my cheeks. And he rested his heavy hand on my face. I could feel the weight of his hand on me.)

Bonny   "I forgive you. I forgive you."
(I felt so close to him at that moment. I knew that I had to get through these issues, so we didn't spend much time on them. Besides... face to face, what does one say to their dad?)
(He's smiling at me and waves, as he half turns to go.)

Bonny   "I love you Dad."

Dad	(He nods his head and smiles.)
Bonny	"If only we could do this life all over. You're so close, I feel you so close. It feels wonderful. There is no feeling that I have ever felt that compares... almost glorious... so wonderful. Thank you for being... for being here."
	(When I said, that there is no feeling that compares to this, he said...")
Dad	"AHHHHHH COME ON!"
Bonny	("He always used this phrase when he was living.")
Dad	"Take care of Mother. She needs your help."
Bonny	"She... doesn't want me around."
Dad	"You were always there for her."
Bonny	"I feel so bad about her."
Dad	"I know, I know."

Once he left I turned my lamp off and I saw five or six lights soaring across my ceiling. They were yellow and purple in color and kept appearing and disappearing. The splashes of color were about the size of the moon and the only thing that I can equate this experience to is a light show. (In my notes I wrote the size of the moon, but I think it was more like the size of golf balls.) It was fantastic and it seemed that the feeling was very happy... that is whoever or whatever the light was... it was very happy. My dads visit touched me deeply and I surly felt his powerful strength with me now. I felt there was nothing that I couldn't conquer!

In regard to anyone who has a loved one who has passed over, I am sure that they are doing well because the peace, love, energy, and light that my dad gave to me when he visited was absolutely magnificent. His loving energy was so wonderful that a part of me wanted to go with him... maybe, even all of me. The force was so very loving, that I can fully understand, the sweet release of ones body passing on. There was only goodness and warmth... all around me. If you have a loved one in heaven, know that there are now in a closer state of pure love.

When my dad first appeared in my minds eye, it was so hard to believe that he could do this. And equally as hard to fathom that I could actually see and hear him, let alone, speak with him! I could communicate with him whenever I wanted to, and as soon as I thought of him, he appeared in my mind's eye. I would just close my eyes and there he was. Furthermore I accepted my dad communicating with me after I understood, that he was not upset with me for wanting to get a divorce.

I also asked him to pass on any of his messages to me through my dreams because I didn't want him to appear to me in a human form. I certainly wasn't ready for that, if ever I would be! I guess that I finally had my father's attention and maybe... just maybe, I thought that he cared a bit about me after all. This was the beginning of my healing with him and I was very fortunate to be granted such a huge concession in speaking with him. I was so lucky that he had heard my words and if he had not come back to talk with me, would I ever have truly had a chance to fully heal? You can't imagine, how immediately healing the words, "I'm sorry for what I did," helped to soothe the pain within me, and began to assist me in forgiving him.

Having someone acknowledge that they treated you unkindly is tremendously healing to your soul.

About two weeks later, a white angel like shape flashed across the kitchen ceiling. It was about a foot long and this time I wasn't alone because my daughter was watching television in the family room. On another day when I was in the shower, a white flash of light glided above me and then it disappeared. It was about fourteen to sixteen inches long. I had also begun to see white and dark shapes from time to time.

When I first thought about it, I was a bit unnerved, but then I later realized that it was a blessing and there was nothing to be afraid of. Before all of this happened, I'm not exactly sure what I really believed about life after death. I was so surprised when my dad first came into my mind's eye because I had never experienced anything like that ever before. And I certainly didn't know that it was even a part of me. Although I often had spiritual things happening to me, I never actually knew anyone personally who had reached out to me.

How did my dad know, that I was the one he could get through to on this level? Did something like this ever happen when I was younger and I just can't remember the circumstances surrounding it? Most likely if I had ever said anything of a spiritual nature, I would have been silenced because my dad never wanted any of us to stand out or to be different. Could this possibly be one of the reasons why he tried so hard to keep me in my place, especially when I was vocal about anything? He didn't want this to grow in any way, shape, or form.

The most ironic thing about this whole situation is that my dad never believed in anything of a supernatural nature, so it was very hard to even consider, that he could come back and communicate now. About five years earlier, he found out that I had gone with about ten other people to see a well known "Medium" and he flipped out on us. He said that when he was a young boy in India, there were people like that on every street corner. And he was told to stay away from them because they could go into your body. I guess he meant that they could possess you. I listened to what he said, but it didn't make any difference because my curiosity in this subject was just too great.

Now and then, my dad came to visit with me and the following was conveyed to me when I had a reading through an intuitive session in 1995.

"Your dad is doing fine now and he is in no pain and his legs are fine. He is up doing his thing, but he did have a period of adjustment that he is sort of coming out of now. He was a bit shocked because he didn't exactly realize, what he was going to wake up to. He's laughing when he said, that he was finding out that, "HE IS NOT THE BOSS!" His thinking is really being turned around, but it is taking time to adjust because it is not done overnight.

He said that he has a long way to go as far as really understanding, what he calls true values. His intentions were always good and he did not realize the effect some of his actions had on others. He knows that I am unhappy about the family split and he says that it has to be settled. He is going to do his best to stimulate the minds of my siblings. The only way that he can influence them is by getting through to their subconscious. It is a skill that he is learning or is trying to learn.

He is sitting with a wise counselor over there, who has shown him the effects of what has happened. He is being given some choices as to what he could try to do, but he has to learn how to do it. It is not easy to do, even though, he has quite a forceful mind. This involves using his mind in a completely different way. Even living in spirit is different because it is a thought world and you use your mind a lot, and he has had to learn it. He has had to project to this side to try to get some influence over here because it really bothers him that his family is split up. He also knows that is partly due to how his will was made out, and partly due to the traditional values and the stubbornness of everyone.

He thinks that it's a bit funny, that there are people that are a bit two-faced and they don't know which side of the fence to sit on. They are smiling to both sides of the family and are waiting to see what happens.

He also says, "The family as a unit, the family love that is important and not the money." The part that he is trying to bring forward to our minds is the family, the family, the family. The unit, the pride in the family, the love of the family, we need to pull together. He is working on this and he is saying that there will be a fair settlement. And it is almost likely it will be the lawyers that will come up with the compromise.

He's continuing with, you are someone who says, "I am who I am and if you don't like me too bad. I am not going to change" and you don't put on airs.

He added, "Do you realize that you will have to share the children from time to time when you divorce? You have to SHARE THEM BECAUSE IT IS IMPORTANT FOR THEM! Help them to understand, that it is not their fault. You may have to say this over and over again. People grow apart and it's nobody's fault.

When you got married, it was not really for the right reasons. You really didn't know him, but you didn't really know yourself either. Your children are important to you and they are really your joy. That is going to be the hard part.

It's almost like you have to gain your own self respect back and it'll take time to trust your own self, well enough. The bright mask that you put on hides a lot of stuff. There is a lot of pain inside of you, it is not just that you feel alone. It's like you're asking yourself, "What do I want to do with the rest of my life?"

You don't want to depend on anyone and you'd like to have somebody to share your life with… someone to lean on from time to time. You really are looking for a soul mate and there will be one. And he will walk into your life when you least expect it. He will be a person that will understand you.

Right now, the real you will have a hard time showing itself. It is when you can be free, relaxed, and happy that your real personality will come out. It is then, that you will be able to attract your soul mate. This person has depth, so he will see past your bright, happy self and see the depth that lies behind it. You cannot be with anybody that does not have depth and he does! You will be able to respect him because you are a person that needs to be able to respect. There is a lot of strength and a lot of gentleness in this man. It is your joy of living that will bring a smile to his face."

The legal proceedings regarding my dad's last will became a battle of the sexes, in fact, almost every part of my life had become one of females versus males on every level. One week before it was to begin in the Supreme Court of Vancouver, I decided that I could no longer be a part of something that I didn't truly believe in. When it came down to the nitty gritty I was not going to court to argue over money, so I dropped out of it. I hated what had happened to our family and I felt very strongly that if my dad wanted to leave his estate more equally, he should have done so himself. In addition, I felt like he was using me to help carry out his change of heart and new plans, and I just couldn't take part in something that wasn't truly me.

My lawyer's office called me repeatedly throughout the week, but I didn't take any of his calls or anyone else's because I had already made my decision. However, I still wanted to make a final attempt at trying to settle the situation, so about five days before it was to begin, I phoned one of my uncles. He was out of town, so I then called one of my brothers. This brother gave me his word, that I could trust him, but unfortunately it would turn out, that I had chosen to trust the wrong male again!

A relative conveyed to me, that this brother had spoken with his lawyer and told him that I had settled on behalf of my sisters. And to cancel our court date for the coming Monday. It was common knowledge that if it was cancelled, it would take another year before it would get to court again.

I was in utter shock when I heard what had transpired, because we only spoke about trying to get everyone together for a meeting. As his betrayal sunk into my heart, our bond to one another was severed and my trust with him was shattered forever. I became angry over what he had done and I rejoined the law suit the day that it began in court.

It seemed that the males in my life still believed that they could do whatever they wanted to without any consequences. He, along with my spouse would be the last two men within my world, that I would ever trust again for many years.

My three sisters and I were the only family members present throughout the proceedings. We had a female judge and the case was settled through a male mediator at the end of the first week or into the next week, when one of my brothers came to settle matters.

This entire matter had taken place over many months and my time sequence regarding going to court actually occurred a bit too early in my story. The next chapter happened before these legal proceedings and prior to any sort of settlement.

My mother's heart stayed with her sons and she had made it clear that she didn't want to see any of her daughters. However, I kept sending her Christmas, birthday, and Mother's Day cards hoping that she was receiving them. One year for Mother's Day, one of my sisters and I had sent our mom flowers. I heard that the same brother who had betrayed me earlier, had intercepted the floral arrangement and threw it in the garbage.

My life was splintered and my heart was constantly breaking over and over again because of the separation with my mother. We had a close relationship and my undying bond to her was very strong, and I really missed not being able to see her. Throughout the years I had always looked forward to visiting with my mother and now, that was just a memory which was a million miles away from me.

My soul was still taking blows and now it was dealing with the loss of my mother, my brothers, and their families. They meant the world to me and in the past whenever I went to Vancouver, I often spent a lot of time packing my things from one home to the next. I did this so I could spend at least one night at four different homes, so I could satisfy as many people as I could with my visit. I came back home rejuvenated, but I was always a bit tired. I continuously gave them the best that I had and now, I felt like I had just wasted my love on them!

The absence of my mother in my life was the biggest regret that I ever had in all that had taken place. However, I truly had no idea just how much sorrow and heartbreaking anguish was ahead for me, in regard to her, until five years from now.

It's Only Me!

Do not be alarmed, for it is only me!
I know that in the past, I was often harsh and then you'd leave,
but I am different now, as I am trying to set my soul free.
You have changed much too, I really do see,
and you must continue to release the past, as you also believe.
The spiritual things that you have seen,
are actually as you have perceived them to be.
As I reach out to you from beyond, please know that I come in peace,
so do not be alarmed for I come in love, and it is only me.
I can see many things and how they will actually be,
and as I come around, remember, you are a part of me.
I truly want you to be safe, happy, and live in harmony.
You've had enough of all the rest, this I absolutely know,
and you are creating a new life that will very soon show.
Bona, when you sense that I am near, please never have any fear,
whether you believe me or not, you have always been my inquiring dear.

Dad in Spirit

Why was he so dead inside,
and never cared when I was hurt or even cried?
If only I had known beforehand,
that the man I married was some kind of robot clone.
When we said goodbye, I had no doubts,
for I was so happy, that he was out of the house.
However I hoped that he would share more of himself,
for the sake of our children's happiness and emotional wellbeing.
Needless to say, they missed out on much with their dad,
and the situation turned into something that was quite sad.

– BONNY BILLAN –

The Inevitable Ending

Chapter 13

My disappointment in myself and my choice for a life partner had grown as the years went by. I had settled for a life with my children and a husband who was always busy doing something else. I was raising them alone, even though, I was married. This was especially true since the birth of our third child, who was born during a time period, when my spouse had a new promotion and his career was progressing steadily. He was working hard to prove himself and I was giving just as much time to the care, development, and parenting of our children.

Over the years, he continued to repeat his horrific phrase referring to my miscarriage. And as the sharpness of his vocabulary severed away at my spirit, it would eventually contribute to the downfall of our union. Every time that he flung his appalling words at me, my heart would overflow with such sorrow for my child that was not meant to be. And I could do absolutely nothing to silence him. Whenever I heard his hateful words, a piece of my tortured and brittle heart fell off and its jagged edges ripped and sunk into my soul repeatedly cutting it into shreds.

My soul had begun its slow death many years ago and now this cruelty within my life had penetrated and crucified me down to the deepest depths of my very being. Whatever was left of my core was hanging by a few threads as my life force was starting to shut down. I was unhappy and parts of myself had given up.

My immense pain began to show in my outward appearance, even though, I dressed well and my hair and make-up always looked good. I had stopped exercising because I no longer had the energy and the desire to look as good as I could anymore, for myself or him. The life inside of me had been rung inside out, as the tension and deep pain that I was carrying daily was harming my entire soul. If anyone truly looked at me, they could see that something was deeply wrong.

My eldest brother asked one of my sisters, "What's wrong with Bonny, why has she gained weight?"

The answer to this question was that my body had gone into self preservation mode and was taking care of itself, by shielding my anguished heart from anymore pain. It also became very cold and no matter what I did, I couldn't warm up. There were little squiggly things flying around in front of my eyes. I finally went to my doctor and he discovered through a blood test, that I had an under active thyroid. The thyroid is located at the bottom of the neck and my condition is called hypothyroidism. Everyone needs to have normal levels of the thyroid hormone in their body to maintain normal mental and physical activity. Weight gain and tiredness are also symptoms of an under active thyroid. All of the stress within my years had finally taken hold and exhausted my thyroid. My treatment for this was to take the smallest pill imaginable each day to keep my thyroid levels normal.

My spouse and I were from opposite sides of the spectrum and we were constantly in a battle regarding practically everything. I didn't understand his way of handling things and he didn't care to hear mine.

Whenever we were invited out for dinner or going anywhere, we were at least forty-five minutes late for each occasion every time. I gave our children their dinner, cleaned the kitchen, and got myself ready and I still found myself waiting for him by the front door. I asked him, to try getting ready an hour earlier than he usually did, so we could be on time. It was so very rude of us to walk into a dinner party and be so late. He had no regard for the hostess and over the years, he never changed because he just didn't care enough to.

One day a neighbor was going to come over to help him put together a playhouse and slide that I had bought for our children. Just before the neighbor was due at our place, my spouse told me that he was busy with a casino night for his work and I should help the neighbor build it.

I said to him, "He expects YOU to help him with the building NOT ME!"

I told him to cancel the project until he was available.

He said, "No" and then he left.

What was I to do now, since I knew that our children were looking forward to playing on it the next day. Our neighbor came and I helped him put this house together for a few hours. After we finished it, he looked very angry and refused to take any money that I offered him for his efforts.

As he was leaving he said, "Don't ever call me again!"

I was so embarrassed that I never looked at this neighbor again, even though, he lived almost right across the street from us. This was just one of the frustrating situations which I had to deal with. What sort of man would treat his wife like this? What sort of woman would endure it?

Sometimes when I wanted to explain my point of view to him regarding some matter, I wrote him a letter to clarify how I felt and I left it on his dresser. I found that this calm manner was always the best way to explain any issues which were plaguing me, and it always worked well with him. It gave him the chance to process whatever points I wanted to make. While recognizing exactly where I was coming from without me having to fight for his undivided attention or have him interrupt me or my train of thought.

On certain days, life had become unbearable and it seemed like I was just going through the motions of everyday living. My spouse left in the morning and he returned home sometime between 7:30 p.m. and midnight. He had ceased to be a very involved member of our family and it appeared like he was only concerned about himself, his career, and whatever praise that he could accumulate. I realized that he had work related activities which I mostly supported, but he always had a meeting to attend somewhere, at least that's what he told me. Quite often he would come home to shower and change his clothes and then he was off again.

The children and I began having dinner by ourselves almost nightly and on the days that he did come home for supper, he often arrived after mealtime was over. He said that he didn't want to hear the children's chattering during this time. I suppose that he believed himself to be exempt from any unpleasantness of parenthood. Our children needed an attentive father and on many occasions our daughter was normally sleeping by the time that he got home.

I was alone on many nights and once the children were in bed, I kept myself busy decorating or working on some other project. I was a single parent long before the word divorce was ever mentioned. It was a lonely time and this continued over a period of nine years, and all of this added to the frustration which I already felt within our marriage. My life mainly consisted of my children and I didn't really know who I was any more or what dreams I wanted to create for myself.

I truly wanted a loving, helpful, and unselfish spouse and some help anywhere in our lives. Furthermore, I am not saying that I was a fantastically, wonderful person for I was far from that. I yelled at my children at times, but I was also very irritated that there was such a huge missing element in my partnership.

Our lack of intimacy didn't help in our relationship either and years earlier, my soul could no longer bear the pain or the body contact of being with him. On that day of reckoning, I could no longer deny, ignore, or hide my emotions, or the silent tears that began trickling down my face when we were alone together. His harsh words had long ago set into motion the collapse of my feelings towards him. Our marriage had become fragile and getting professional help would possibly have been the solution to repair it, but I couldn't do it alone. I had asked him time and again about going to see a marriage counselor, but he never gave me a reply. Now I was very much imagining a different future for myself and my children and it was constantly on my mind.

Whenever a problem arose with one of the children or with anyone else, he always blamed me for it and I was very exhausted from being his all time scapegoat. He had chosen his lifestyle and that was his choice. Now I was also on the brink of making a different lifestyle choice for myself. I needed to leave my soul abuser, before the person who I was truly born to be completely failed to exist.

Do you have a soul abuser? Is there someone who depletes you of all of your energy? Is there anyone within your life who constantly puts you down? Do you live with somebody who never supports anything you say or wish to do? Is everything in your life a bloody battle with this person? Don't wait until you get to the point that I did, try to find the help and the solutions with your major problems one by one, as soon as you possibly can.

I had now been married for nineteen years, and for the past ten months or so, I had dug deep within myself and brought forth a renewed energy with a strength and vigor that I hadn't felt for quite some time. Today was the day that I had decided, I was ready at last to break my bondage with him once and for all. I had finally given myself permission to leave.

Writing had always been a big part of my life and I have always kept a diary. On Sunday February 5, 1995 the following was my journal entry. "As I am lying in bed watching "Living Single," I noticed that it is 12:30 a.m. and it's my birthday. Do I feel any differently? Hell NO! In fact, I feel pretty good. I look forward to the coming years (God willing) with an eagerness that I can barely contain. I feel pretty happy inwardly and it's a feeling that I haven't felt for quite a long time. Oh yes, the future will be something to write about. I know that it'll be a time to come into my own mentally, physically, and spiritually."

On February 14, 1995 the following was one of my journal entries.

"Mentally – I want to be at peace with myself and not feel such anger over certain situations that I have no control over. And to try and not be so hurt or feel betrayed, when a friend or relative hurts me… to try not to be so deeply hurt.

I have my daughter as my shadow, no matter what I do or say and I feel like I have very little freedom. I don't believe that I can even begin to realize my potential and my reason for being, in my present situation. Things need to change! Things have got to change!"

"Physically – I am determined to become the person that I use to be physically. What happened in my life to me… for so many years… for me to not take the care and the time that I once use to for myself? What? Why? When did I lose me?????"

"Spiritually – "I have become aware of a whole new sense of things to experience, a whole new sense of things to come. I can't believe the experiences that I have had so far. If I go with this, if I stay open for what is to come, what new feelings and experiences will I have? Will it help me to fully understand who I am, what I am, and what I can become? And from, where I came from? One thing I know, is that it will help me to advance to my next level."

A couple of months later, my spouse went out of town for a week long conference and when he returned home, he practically had a new wardrobe. Over the next week, he avoided contact with me and he couldn't look me in the eyes. I had sensed many things in my life in regard to certain people and I sensed something new within him. This was when I knew for sure, that our marriage was truly over and it was just a matter of when the best time to end it would be. The disrespect which I was receiving had come to its end, and I decided to conclude our union in the summer which was in three months time. However I must say, I had a whole new appreciation for him as I gave him credit for having the guts to go for whatever he wanted in his life. He had surprised me as a slight smile spread across my lips. It looked like our split was going to be easier then I thought it would be. There was no love left between us anyway.

A couple of weeks later, a small incident happened and when my spouse came home after midnight, he once again blamed me for it. It was so tiny in comparison to anything else that had occurred, but this was the last straw for me. And in the span of a second, my destiny had finally changed. My big decision to divorce had been cast into the heavens above, as I bellowed out, "I AM DONE!"

I said to him, "NO! I AM NOT GOING TO DO THIS ANYMORE!"

As I walked away, I threw my hands up in the air and I said, "I'M JUST

NOT GOING TO DO THIS ANY LONGER, I'M DONE!"

Ohhhhhhh did it ever feel good! I had so much strength and these few empowering words were the first step to regaining my self respect. In that moment, the love that I had lost for myself began its long journey back to my spirit, holding its arms out to me from the most sacred part of my soul.

I wanted to make sure that I wasn't being hasty in my decision, so I made an appointment with a counselor. My first visit was a tearful recollection of what I had experienced, as I recounted to her, what my spouse had called me for so many years. This kind looking woman was the first person that I had ever shared it with.

She replied, "It looks like you blamed yourself for it, all of these years too."

I had one more visit and it only lasted twenty minutes and she confirmed my decision as she said, "You've made your mind up."

I then made an appointment with a lawyer and the necessary papers were drawn up. In addition I spoke to my spouse about divorcing and he was honestly okay with the idea. I swear this, on my life! He didn't have any objections and he wasn't angry at all. Actually he didn't have much of a reaction and he just said that it was too bad, that we wouldn't be together for our grandchildren. This guy was unbelievable!

We decided on certain things in our divorce and I said that he could have the children whenever he wanted them, and he agreed to whatever we spoke about. Since things were quite calm I decided to wait until the end of June, so the children would be out of school before I legally acted on my decision. However, a week later my spouse became intolerable, so I called my lawyer's office to forward the official papers for our separation. After he received the correspondence, he went back on everything that he had agreed to. And he played the part of a wounded victim to our offspring.

He went running into the children's television room and screamed out to them, "Your Mother wants a divorce!"

He upset all of them and he made sure that they knew that I was the one who wanted this parting. And on some level, our children would begin to blame me too. I would have to bear the hurt and guilt for my decision and deal with the pain which this choice caused my children, because I wanted to escape from HIM! However, whatever this all involved, I was going to do it and create a new life for myself!

He propped up the letter which he had received from my lawyer on his bed side table, so our children would see it as they walked into our room. I kept taking the papers down and placing them into his top drawer, and he kept taking them back out again, and putting them back out on display. I don't know what the big deal was anyway? He had checked out of our union and his parenting role for quite a few years and we rarely ever saw him! Our marriage certainly wasn't something he ever cherished! Was he not man enough now, to stand up for himself and his life decisions, and face his consequences by telling our children and others, his real truth?

Did he honestly believe that I was going to continue living in our situation forever, as he was living a separate life from us? This was not, what marriage and fatherhood meant to me!

When I told a neighbor who lived beside us about our impending situation she said, "I'm not surprised because he was never home. It was always just you and the kids together all the time. We always knew how late he came home because we could hear his music blasting from his car before he turned the corner."

He wouldn't move out of our home until his lists of demands were met and it took almost five months to figure it all out. I really felt very sympathetic towards him for having to leave his home which he had created, even though, throughout this tension filled time, life was a complete hell to live through with him.

I even told him that if we moved, he could live in the downstairs of our home, if he didn't have a place of his own to move into. In our agreement, I ended up giving into him, on of course finances. And his threat to me was he was not leaving the family home until he received it. I was not and have never been a vindictive person and I wanted to be on friendly terms for our children's sake.

However, how could we be friends, when we had been enemies for so long and now he was absolutely livid! Though, I was still worried about how he was going to live and I kept pointing this out to my lawyer throughout our negotiations. I merely wanted kindness and harmony within my world and I couldn't understand manipulating and ruthless people. I was constantly giving them another chance to show that they had changed, and this was a big part of my ongoing dilemma with people within my world.

On the other hand, the disgust which we felt for each other could no longer be disguised. I had been repulsed by the sight of him for so very long. I simply wanted my freedom, while I was looking forward to a more loving existence and the chance to create a peaceful life with a gentleman who respected me and my children. Throughout my years I had most certainly missed out on having a loving connection with a positive partner.

We separated six weeks before our twentieth wedding anniversary and the only thing that was important to me was trying to make the transition of divorce easier for all of them. I didn't realize, what the cost would be for me in trying to help my family throughout this period of massive stress filled adjustments.

My ex husband just wouldn't admit that he had also agreed to end our marriage. I guess that he thought he would receive more sympathy if he portrayed himself as the injured partner. He never once said to me that he wanted to stay together and try to work our problems out through counseling, or whatever else was needed for the marriage to survive. Except, after we were into negotiations, he mumbled something about if there was something that he could change, he would. I looked at him and I never said a word. Freedom was finally at my doorstep and I wasn't about to let it go. And let's face it, he wasn't capable of changing anything, but his clothes!

I suppose that he wanted to keep the charade going for his benefit so he could present himself as having the whole package. He was someone who had truly succeeded at life and he had a marriage, healthy children, a nice home and a good job. However, he had also proven to be a cold-hearted person whose icy demeanor could chill even the cold artic wind.

The morning that he left, he got up early and carried all of his clothes out to his car. As I was lying in bed, I had my back turned to him. I don't think that he even knew that I was awake. He finished his packing before the children were awake. I must admit, I was very relieved and a bit excited and I couldn't quite believe that it was actually happening! Hurrah! He was moving into his parent's residence and that's where he would remain living for the next couple of years.

On that final day of our marriage, he was back home before long and he spent the day with the children. We all had dinner together and around 8:00 p.m. he said goodbye to our offspring and he left. My daughter slept with me in our king size bed and once she was sleeping, I allowed my tears to flow. They flowed and flowed and flowed. I had never in all my life, ever experienced such a deep throbbing that was gripping and pounding at my insides. The pain which I had buried within me was waiting to be broken apart as I cried non-stop throughout the entire night. After those moments, my tears subsided and never came back again. It was finally done and I had at last gotten rid of him! I could now breathe a great sigh of relief.

As each day passed by, I was becoming more at ease and as every week went by, I became even more so. I felt so free. For the first time in a long time, I felt like I could accomplish anything that I ever wanted to. I had spent twenty years with my spouse and he had been the only man who I had ever been with. My world hadn't exactly been overflowing with kindness from males and I had no idea, how very long it would take for me to fully trust another one again.

I remember thinking when my father passed on, that he was the first of a long line of people that I would eventually lose through death. However at this point in time, many of the relationships in my family were actually being severed and it felt like I was experiencing one death after the other, even though, they were all still alive.

Now I had to confront another giant loss, as the relationship which I had put my entire life force into had failed. Had I also failed because I just couldn't tolerate the pain of it any longer? He called me a quitter for wanting to divorce him, but I thought it was a rather courageous thing to do. I had given him all of the love and respect which I had within me and I had been totally faithful to him, but over the years he had stomped on it down to the crux of my very soul. He didn't want any of it and he didn't want me. I honestly didn't desire him throughout the past several years either, and as for loving him... nooooooooo, I didn't love him either. This was not how I had envisioned my life and it seemed as if love had mainly eluded my heart since the day of my birth. If God had not granted me children, I never would have known what real love was.

However, at this moment in time, I really didn't know if my heart could stand another death... and that was the final ending of my little family. My babies, who I had given life to, had been hurt so very badly and I had caused it. I had broken their hearts and devastated their worlds. And I felt terrible for creating this anguishing pain for them. I was feeling very deeply at fault for it all and it would take me years to overcome it.

My children who I would do absolutely anything for, had dreams of a family living all together. However, I had dismantled our family portrait and there wasn't enough cement to bond us back together again. My vision of a so called fairytale life had shattered and come to an abrupt end. I had held onto the hope of it for as long as I could, but there was nothing left to salvage as I gazed upon the crushed ruins of our marital foundation.

I had fought so many raging battles throughout my life, as I stood up for whatever I believed in. Now here I was on the battlegrounds once again, standing all alone as I looked out at the tattered bodies of my past, while clinging to my shredded heart within my unloved and ravaged soul.

My Fairytale Slipped Away

Our lives together had slipped away, as my fairytale had come to an abrupt end.
Our castle was left standing alone, as the reality of a divorce had finally materialized.
My crystal slippers had fallen off my feet and one by one,
they had shattered like my dreams into fragmented pieces.
The remnants had been sent swimming out to sea, amongst the ocean
of tears that I had shed, throughout my years of pain and loneliness.
The blazing crimson pumpkin which had been carrying us had tumbled
and crashed, sending squashed and smashed bits of our life flying all about.
Our footmen scattered away like frightened squirrels trying to hoard
their winter stash of nuts from intruders.
They all ran and were too frightened to become involved in this sad turn of events.
My prince had turned into an ugly beast with grotesque warts and his bumpy,
pimply skin had now blistered and popped open for the world to see.
The pus within him had ripened at last, and was now oozing out through the
rotting nucleus of his pores, as the blood that ran through his veins
raced and raged like the gushing of the white water rapids.
His neglected teeth which were evident from years of decadent decay,
had sprouted fangs and were now dripping with a dark poisonous venom,
as his mouth was spewing and sputtering away.
The reign of this roaring beast was finally over, so consequently in a need
to strike one final blow in vengeance, he sprang and pounced on his family
to make them suffer even further for his inadequacies.
Years earlier he had lost his way home, only to forfeit his maiden and now,
his kingdom had crumpled before his eyes and was gone from him forever.
His piercing wales could be heard throughout the darkening forest,
for he realized, that he'd never be able to regain what he had lost.
Many never knew about the callous nature which lived deep within him
and because of his cold heartedness towards his offspring,
his loss would be imminent and total.

Bonny Billan
1996

My soul was screaming, didn't you know,
and I wanted it to stop without any low blows.
However as hard as one tries, there are sometimes those that connive,
and use whatever ploys they can, to undermine another's life plan.
They blame and cover up, that they weren't much of a man,
for in life they were selfish and quite often ran.
Behind closed doors, many are actually frightened and sad men,
who simply don't understand, how to treat a woman.

– BONNY BILLAN –

The Aftermath

Chapter 14

The choice to divorce was quite a huge decision to make especially because of my strict and traditional upbringing which was so deeply embedded within me. My parent's expectation to always be proper and to live life in a respectful manner was constantly at the forefront of my thoughts. And even though I'd spent quite sometime considering the repercussions of a divorce, I had no idea of what was waiting for me, now that I had taken this step. I had expected that certain people would react to our divorce with surprise, but I never anticipated to be judged so harshly by my community which I soon discovered was very narrow minded and opinionated.

Years earlier, I had decided to wait until our children were a lot older before I made a change regarding my marriage. However, sometimes certain situations in one's home become so unbearable that your future wishes cannot be delayed. Hell was at my doorstep and it was not only snoring beside me in bed each night, but it was ugly and I felt like smothering it with my pillow. I simply wanted to stop the noise which was booming out of it all throughout every night.

Each night for quite a few years, I went to bed wearing headphones while listening to music in an attempt to drown out my spouses obnoxious and deafening noises. He was so loud that one could hear him quite well even when they were downstairs in the family room. And this was through two closed doors, let alone, being in the same room as him and this nauseating sound. I fell asleep in the wee hours of every morning out of exhaustion and I tried to sleep elsewhere, but it wasn't anywhere as comfortable as our bed.

My living on a daily basis with someone who I no longer respected simply added to my aggravation and it wasn't very healthy, loving, or respectful for me or to our children. If one is not in the best possible place for themselves or others, then something positive needs to occur to make a brave change in their life. And this should be done sooner rather than later.

My separation created an immediate improvement to my state of happiness and I found myself smiling throughout my days and nights. My energy and self confidence began returning as the old me was resurfacing.

I kept thinking, "I DID IT AND I'M ACTUALLY FREE OF HIM!"

One of my brother-in-laws commented to his wife that, "Bonny looks so happy… it's like the old Bonny again."

I was overjoyed after so many years of pain. Although, I could sense that it was going to take quite some time for my children to come to terms with it, that is if they were ever able to. I'm certain that they must have been experiencing a horrible gut wrenching pain from what had transpired between their parents. I put myself in their shoes as I considered, how I would feel if the same thing happened with my family when I was growing up. It would have been awful for me to bear.

I knew that I had to persevere and be especially strong for my children's sake, so I made a decision to not bring another man into their lives. They had suffered through much and I never wanted another male telling my children, what they could or couldn't do. Maybe this was a mistake, who knows for sure! I felt awful for the hurt that our separation created for them and I was determined that they would remain the number one priority in my life. I was their mother, I gave them life, and it was my responsibility to see my parenting through to the end, even if I had to do it alone. However it was more then that, it was simply because this was the type of parent that I had always been.

In our culture the most important expectation for a couple has always been to stay together, no matter how negative the circumstances may be that they are living within. It seemed like I came from a world where the word "divorce" was like a four letter word only to be whispered behind closed doors. I never truly wanted to resort to divorcing because this was very foreign to my beliefs also, but it was the only road to follow especially since my strength, self respect, and love were returning to me.

How on earth... had I endured so many years of such agony?

A woman in our culture taking the initiative to go ahead and begin divorce proceedings was not only virtually unheard of, it was completely unacceptable. There were only a handful of other divorced couples, that I knew of at that time in my ethnic background. Many people still believed in the old world thinking, that a female carries the blame for the failure of her marriage, while her male partner maintains his status in our society. A divorced woman is considered a social outcast as she is looked down upon with a stigma. Consequently females have a much harder time being accepted as a single woman, whereas males are readily accepted simply because they are born a male. They continue with their lives no matter what type of person they may be. And if there were any indiscretions on his part throughout the marriage, they are sweep under a rug to eventually be forgotten. This ancient philosophy and belief system are a huge part of my culture, and this appalling treatment of women has been passed down from one generation to another. What is wrong with this way of thinking?

Many people in my society including our friends and relatives didn't know how to handle our split. Several of those living not only in Victoria, but in Vancouver also had much to say about me, as the entire blame was put on my shoulders. No one seemed to understand my point of view at all regarding my decision to divorce and in some ways, I was even treated differently by those closest to me. I was being shown that I wasn't good enough, as my negative childhood and marriage memories were now repeating themselves to me once again, throughout my new found status.

One of my friends laughingly said to me, that in her youth she was not allowed to play with a girl in her neighborhood because she was from a divorced family. I knew that she didn't mean any harm by her comment, but I didn't like being singled out by yet another and given an example of non-acceptance because of my divorce.

Another friend of mine told an acquaintance of hers, that she was going to be meeting with me and the other woman asked her, "Why do you want to be with her?"

When she told me the story she had a bit of an attitude saying that, I should be grateful to her for sticking up for me.

I was shocked at her response as I wondered, if she even knew, what friendships were all about? What's more, I didn't realize that I had to be grateful to someone for being my friend. I felt so uncomfortable when I heard her words and my stomach felt sickened immediately. Within this moment I knew for sure that my new life wasn't going to be easy, especially since people simply couldn't mind their own business or accept this improved version of myself which I had created.

A different friend's mother asked me, "If your husband changes and starts to do certain things, will you stay with him then?"

My next friend questioned me, "Are you sure that you want to do this, maybe you are just upset over your dad's death?"

This friend had divorced a year or two earlier and I had fully supported her throughout and after her ordeal. She also knew about our daily problems. Other friends never said a word about our situation and simply disappeared from my life completely, as if I didn't exist anymore and some of them weren't even from our culture.

One day after I separated, I went to visit a relative and I had taken her a bouquet of flowers. She said that she was going to tell her husband that they were from a neighbor, so he wouldn't know that I had been over to their home. He hadn't been able to accept our split and I felt so awful when I heard this. I know that she didn't realize what she had said, but was I now suppose to pretend that I just didn't exist anymore?

My decision had not been made lightly and my friends knew that I had been terribly unhappy. Perhaps they didn't realize, that I had thought about it for years or what I had actually suffered through, but I hated having to defend my actions repeatedly.

I only had one family member who whole heartedly supported my position and this sister also lived on Vancouver Island. We always supported each other and she never questioned any of my decisions which I ever made.

My relationships were changing all around me because I wanted to stop the abuse and disrespect in my life and go in a new positive direction. However anywhere I turned it was difficult and these were just some of the cases of hurt which I had experienced.

When I told my mother-in-law that we were divorcing, she said to stay together because all men were the same. And I wouldn't find another guy that was any different.

I told her that "My decision was not up for debate."

She phoned me three days in a row to try and change my mind. The only person that I was worried about hearing this news was actually my mother, but since she stopped speaking to me I had no one to be concerned about. No one was going to stop me from proceeding with this and this part was actually as easy as saying, one, two, and three.

Of course I worried about my children, but the relationship with their father had reached a point of no return and when I came to this crossroad, I turned to the path of freedom. I had finally refused to be an outlet for his resentments any longer. He truly needed to go find the reasons and a cure for his anger and I needed to find all of the causes and the healing for mine. For the first time in many years, I thought of my needs and I honored the wishes of my soul. I had at last woken up and I had so much strength that I knew my father's spirit was walking with me, and perhaps, even carrying me.

Divorce was not a disease or an illness and it was not something contagious. It was simply a situation in my life and a road which I opted to take using the free will which God gave to me. It was my life, my decision, and it was not anyone else's concern, but when did toxic people ever stay out of other lives?

I didn't have more then six or seven people that truly supported me in my new situation, if even that. However it was a nice surprise when a close friend of my spouse's family gave me her support.

She said, "You were quite an asset to him and he never would have achieved as much as he did, had he not married you."

Yet it didn't seem to matter to other people within our community that I was a devoted wife and mother for twenty years, or that I always went above and beyond for the sake of my family. I was being trashed from one end of our city to the ends of Peat Meadows on the mainland, and some women even had the nerve to say it to my face.

Several of them had known me since I was a child and were familiar with how very strictly I was raised. They knew that I never really stepped out of line in the role that I was in. Yet they didn't stop for even a miniscule of a second to consider that my heart and spirit just might have been completely crushed, for me to have taken such drastic action. Also none of them bothered to hear that my husband may have contributed immensely in creating this bitter ending to our marriage. They just didn't care!

He was born and raised in Victoria and he had a good reputation and standing in the community. Many people had known him since he was born, but what they didn't know was that he was a major suck up, who did whatever he could for praise. He portrayed himself to be prim and proper, but I knew better then they, since I experienced first hand what his true character traits were. Outsiders weren't familiar with the other side of him and perhaps they didn't know of my compulsive side of cleanliness either, but I never tried to intentionally hurt a living soul. Furthermore, I certainly never tried to crush and destroy another human being's spirit.

My biggest offences were in keeping our home immaculate, enforcing my children to be the best that they could be, being strict with them, and constantly trying to get my spouse involved with his family. There was no quibbling about these matters and everyone that knew me, realized that this was a huge part of who I was, as I always tried to do the best for my family. I have always been a real person and my main character trait is that, whatever you see in me is what I truly am. Hence when I see someone who isn't genuine, I find it so hard to tolerate them, let alone, live with them. I rarely kept what I was thinking to myself and I very much wore my heart on my sleeve. My spouse told me himself, that I don't play favorites whether it is with a family member or not, because I see and say things the way that

205

they actually are.

My children's father also tried to do his best for his family and for a lot of years he did, but somewhere along the line his head got stuck in the clouds. And he considered himself to be far above most people especially me. As he succeeded in his work, he had acquired an air of total arrogance and it was impossible to tolerate his attitude long before the end of our marriage. I saw a totally different person then what he saw when he looked into the mirror, and I am sure that the same held true for him when he looked at me.

My life was never the same again and whenever I was out at any public engagement I felt that I now stood out more than ever. I didn't experience many women who were standing up and supporting another woman, even though I was feeling absolutely alone and quite misunderstood. There were many opinionated women who had no compassion or understanding at all. And the only thing that mattered to the gossip mongers of our community was that I was to blame for wanting out of my marriage. I had gone against the traditional values of an entire backward thinking society, and as I stood before a completely new lifestyle, it was somewhat scary as my culture had turned against me.

What disgusted me the most was the fact that even the younger women were not sympathetic to the needs of a now divorced woman. I must say that the males were not any better. However, one would hope that a female would be much more aware to another female's needs, especially if she truthfully looked at and admitted her discomfort in her own marital situation. These same women wouldn't ever consider leaving their marriages because of how they would be perceived by our community. And secondly, because it would change their social status and livelihood. They wouldn't want to be alone, different, or to be judged by others. Although the most important point is that they simply didn't have the fortitude to take a stand regardless, of how badly they were being disrespected in their relationships. As a result, instead of offering some consideration to another who has taken that big leap, they do the opposite. What was interesting was that several of these women were incapable of staying out of other peoples dilemma's and never spoke about anything which was happening within their own families. Their negative energy was deadly and if they were to ever harness it for anything good, our world would be a better place to live in.

Many people do not like it when someone else changes their life because they now pose a threat to them in some way. It forces them to look at themselves knowing full well, that they should alter something in their own lives and get out of the rut that they are in. Perhaps, they are even a bit jealous because they don't have the courage to take a stand on their own.

Divorce can happen at any time, to anyone, in any family and no one has a golden shield against this happening to them in their relationship. If it does occur to someone that you know, what is needed is love, understanding, and friendship and not dishonor, ridicule, and abandonment. One may need to dig deep into themselves to see how they might help ease someone else's pain and not add to it.

The manner in which I was treated hurt my feelings, but I made my mind up to be even stronger and follow through regardless of how hard my life was going to be. I didn't know what was still ahead for me, but I planned to not falter and to truly succeed in creating myself and the life that I deeply wanted, no matter what it required me to do.

Women must stand up for themselves and for whatever they believe in, regardless of what the world is saying about them and how little support they have. I only had a few women supporting my beliefs, but that is exactly what strength is all about. Besides, I knew that God was with me and I wasn't truly alone, so how could I ever fail? My dad had also reached out from the far depths of heaven to protect and assist me in this new uncertain part of my life. Yes, at last he was with me and my children. And at this point, it didn't matter to him any longer who I had married, but rather to assist me in every way that he could, to help me escape from him!

Why would I take the time to ever consider, what people on earth thought about me, when I was being shown love from heaven? What's more, I had been treated so unkindly by many people as they tried to repeatedly crush my heart. I really hadn't enjoyed the human experience for quite some time and a part of me was giving up on the human race. And from the moment that my father first communicated with me, I felt a wonderful love and a comfort that I had never known here on earth. I was certain that I was being guided by him and he already knew the outcome of my future. And if I had now made the wrong decision, he surely would have let me know. Thus as heaven reached out to me, I knew that everything would be all right... someday.

I was proud of myself for finally realizing that I wasn't going to tolerate anymore disrespect, especially from males and that I deserved so much better from my life!

DO YOU HEAR ME... FROM MY LIFE!

It wasn't my husband's or my children's life, it was my life! Yes, they were involved in it, but I came into this world with desires and a destiny to fulfill for myself, just like they would fulfill one for themselves. I finally took control of my situation because my soul had grown and become alive, as it began its plea and insistence on me making enormous changes. As I looked at my face in the mirror, I could see in my eyes that my soul was shifting. What's more, it seemed like the universe had begun to systematically eliminate all of the males and the male domination from my world. What did it all have to teach me about myself? Had all of the stinging pain and turmoil in my life actually been a blessing in disguise, as it had finally convinced me to scream out... I deserve to be treated so much better!

The truth and reality of separating is that good people do get divorced. It is much healthier for everyone involved if parents follow this path, so their children don't have to constantly listen to two adults battling away. All of which is very detrimental to their emotional, spiritual, and mental wellbeing. In most cases both parents try to find a balance for their children in this enormous loss, but in our situation that didn't happen. I was the only parent who was trying to show them that that their lives would continue to be consistent, that I loved them, and I would always be there for them.

I wanted to ease our children into this new situation, so their father came over to our home about two times a week for dinner. And as much as I wished for him to be out of my life, I wanted them to be able to see him as often as they could. Especially since he wasn't putting forth much of an effort in getting together on his own home turf. The children were happy to see him and maybe it gave them a bit of false hope of us getting back together again. However, I don't regret having him over because they needed to have some time together, as they became accustomed to our new state of affairs. Maybe I should have foreseen that since he was often an absentee father in marriage that he wouldn't be much different in divorce. Except I deeply believed that he would strive to maintain the connection that he had, and he would do whatever it took in this entire world to be a loving and caring father.

About five months later, I had planned a vacation to Disneyland with my children and their father was going to come along for five days, even though, we were going for ten days. When he discovered that I was going to pay for all of our expenses, he quickly extended his time to ten days. I even gave him $300.00 in U.S. funds so he wouldn't have to worry about any finances. He spent most of the entire time shopping for himself while the children were with me, even though, seven days before we were to leave for our trip I was in a car accident. A male driver accidentally crashed his vehicle into mine and the next vehicle hit him, and needless to say, I ended up with whiplash. As a result, my vacation wasn't exactly pain free. However, his selfishness with our children and with me, knew no bounds, whether it was in regard to our marriage, our divorce, my health, or fatherhood.

Consequently, my biggest problem in my divorce became my ex spouse, but truly, how surprising was this since he was also my biggest problem in my marriage. This became apparent as he chose not to accept all of his parental responsibilities which he demanded in our divorce agreement. This was in regard to the times which were stipulated for him to be with our children at his place.

I suppose that he thought of himself to be above the rules and regulations of parenting and the laws of our contract. Therefore, the inequality and male dominating situations of my marriage extended right into my divorce, as he did whatever he wanted to do and gave practicality nothing of himself.

He phoned and came for the children whenever it was convenient for him. And the more that I pleaded with him to take a more active part in their lives, the more that he tuned me out. I constantly tried to convince him that he was hurting them by not being further involved in their lives, but it fell on deaf ears.

I was deeply concerned as I repeatedly said to him, "Do not lose the bond that you have with the children."

Whenever their father was tired of hearing my much too often motherly sermons, he left.

He was a part of their lives for a few years, but that eventually fizzled out especially after he met a certain woman. You can't even imagine the hell that occurred at this point! However I was very fortunate as heaven reached out to help me once again. I'll continue with my savings grace in book two.

If you are going into a relationship with someone who has children from a previous marriage, perhaps you can see it in yourself to not be self-centered concerning the happiness and relationship of a parent with their children. What's more, certainly try to remember, you are thought to be an adult and the time for any immature game playing was suppose to be in your childhood.

I finally gave up on my pleadings to him after spending three years of my time, energy, and futile attempts of asking him to be an adult. I was perturbed, angry, and exhausted from this insensitive male. He now had his total freedom and I had an even bigger load than I did before. It was so unfair and he was unfair, but how often had my life ever been balanced and smooth flowing, especially where males in my culture were concerned? Egotistical and male dominated men had been a constant theme throughout my life and it seemed like it wasn't over yet. Except I must say, that throughout many parts of my life there has always been a kind male within my group of friends, relatives, or business associates that was especially nice to me. These men always treated me with respect and a gentleness which displayed the thoughtfulness and softer side of a male's traits and awareness.

Over the years it turned out that our children would live with me full time for 365 days a year, with my ex spouse still sending them child support which was based on them living with me part time. My children had to not only deal with the death of our family, but with the death of their father, despite the fact, that he was very much alive. It would be an understatement to say that he hurt them immensely and his steel-hearted callousness inflicted needless pain and weaved deep sorrow into their hearts. This would sadly be a part of their souls forever. I was absolutely helpless in this situation and it was upsetting that since our separating, he showed that fatherhood was not worth any amount of sacrifice. I wondered what the word "Father" meant to him. Was this his way to get back at me for the divorce… maybe, but he had always been self serving since I met him.

One day I said to him, "I forgive you, for being so mean to me throughout our marriage. I agreed to your demands throughout our divorce so we would remain friends, but where are we now? I did whatever you wanted to have done and I was taken in by you."

I finally came to the realization, that I would no longer waste my energy on him and his negativity had no room to grow in my world. As well, I decided to no longer listen to him regarding any blame which he was still casting at me regarding everything with the children. I recognized that I could never change him and the only person that I could truly change was me, so I put him out of my thoughts and our home.

Also, since I wasn't the only one who had brought our children into this world and considering his non-compliance with his total responsibilities towards them, I hated the fact that they still had his last name. I even considered changing it, but in light of what had happened with the males in my family, I really didn't want that last name either. I even considered beginning with a new last name for myself, but I finally decided to go back to my original family name. My ex spouse was very condescending towards me when he discovered that I went back to my maiden name.

Did he truly think that I would ever want to keep his name? If I hadn't insisted on having children, there wouldn't even be any grandsons on the male side of his clan to carry on their family name.

It is up to each and every one of us as parents to demonstrate to our children, that we are the most positive role model that we can be for them. Our children of today are tomorrow's future and if we haven't done a great job of raising and guiding them, then how encouraging will that future be? We can't abandon the offspring that we have brought into this world, the ones that we have nurtured, loved, and protected with our lives. They are entitled to have the time, support, and encouragement of both of their parents and if someone can't do that, then they should never have children.

If one decides to marry someone who would like to have children, they need to be truly honest with their fiancée and themselves in regard to how they feel about this major decision, before they take this crucial step. One will be doing their future offspring a tremendous favor by declining to spread their seed, if they can't see themselves in an unselfish role of navigating parenting through to the very end. It's perfectly acceptable to feel this way and its better to be truthful at the beginning, rather then hiding it until after one is married. It's your choice, so be proud and straightforward about it.

I had given so much of myself throughout my marriage and motherhood, and now I had the full responsibility of complete double duty in our divorce with three children. How on earth was I ever going to begin in my process of self discovery, when I didn't even know how to stop giving or how to begin to take back for myself? I had no extra time for a personal life because I always put the children first and I was so busy with them. I was constantly driving one of them somewhere and giving a part of myself to another within my many moments of time.

Many women sacrifice their lives for their family's welfare to the extent that they lose their true identities and they become someone's wife or mother. Many females are taught or notice at a very young age, that their own mothers are continually sacrificing themselves for the sake of their families. I thought that I was so different from my mother, but as I had watched her during my childhood, this concept was deeply implanted in me. Sometimes I felt like I was Mother Earth herself.

Even a few years after divorcing, one of the hardest parts you have to come to terms with is the fact that many of your annoyances don't end because you are still dealing with your ex husband because of your children. This is the main reason to strive to get along with each other. However, it can't be done if only one of you is trying and the other one is still wanting to get even with you, for asking him to leave the marriage. The children's happiness, well being, and adjustment to a new life are the most important issues in any divorce, and this is what couples should keep reminding themselves.

At times you may find yourself in a struggle with ex husband because he is trying to use his last means of power over you, so he may send his support payments late. Other times, he may try to control the situation by picking up and returning the children whenever he feels like it, that is, if he even shows up in the first place. In my case, he came whenever he chose to, he was always late, and he cancelled whenever it suited him. In this way, he knew that any plans which I had would be effected and he wasn't about to forgo anything which he had planned in his life.

When one separates from their spouse, their friends and families can't possibly know or understand how lonely they may be at times. When one's children are out and about living their lives, your time still revolves around them especially if any plans change. At some point one needs to work towards building a life that is beneficial to their mental, physical, and spiritual wellbeing and incorporate that into their daily routine. I spent most of my free time re-creating my thoughts and inner self by reading many books regarding self improvement and spirituality. I also went to seminars and speakers regarding much of the same. I exercised every day and each night after dinner, I went for a long walk with my daughter.

I also enrolled in a bi-weekly three hour sales and business class at a college. One evening as I was getting ready to leave for my class, the "ex" called to say that he wasn't able to take one of our children to their game. This was not the first time that he had done this and since my life was becoming too much of a juggling act, I decided to drop out of my class. Shortly afterwards, he phoned to say that he would come by after all. I could rarely rely on him to help out and as I was trying to get ahead with creating a new life, his hand kept trying to pull me back. Therefore I decided to concentrate on the wellbeing of myself and my children, so I put my decorating business and classes on hold for awhile. I had just finished a basic course for the computer, an enlightening one on "Angels," and one on preserving family photos.

I was also in the middle of a small renovation of our home. It sure felt good to have my carpenter rip out a few things, that my ex spouse had insisted on having installed nine years earlier. I simply hated the wood stove, brick fireplace surround, and our bedroom carpet. It all had to go. Also I spent hours scraping off wallpaper in the kitchen, large family room, and powder room. I then had everything repainted including the hallways, laundry room, and computer room. I also had a railing taken out and added in two pillars, a mantel fireplace, new carpeting, and had new blinds installed into the family room. As well as, new flooring put into the kitchen, staircase, and upstairs hallway. I changed the playroom into a black and white theme of a "I Love Lucy" home office, and redecorated the large sitting room for the children's computer and television area. Of course, I began everything in the master bedroom and the first items to go were the bed, carpet, furniture, and drapes. On the main floor of our home, I draped sheer white material on brass rods and puddled them on the floor, and now our home had a very Grecian feel and look to it. I loved it. It took a couple of months to complete everything, and once it was all finished it was a totally different home. It was now a very calm and peaceful environment because the energy had shifted and the old stale and harmful forces were gone. My soul… had also shifted.

I had also taken Feng Shui courses which consisted of shifting energy to create a balance of peace and harmony in your living environment, between all of the elements in a room, home, or building inside and outside. This was one of the best courses which I ever took and I discovered, that I was already living with parts of it in my life already.

I also bought a sage smudge stick and cleansed the energy within every room in and outside of our home and garage, by walking through each room with it lit. Once everything was done, I had never known such peace in my life ever before. This was all a part of my healing process which I had begun at one section of my life and continued through to every part, so I could understand, rearrange, heal, and create a new sacred growth with myself. I was creating my peaceful sanctuary here on earth, to house my heart, mind, body and soul in white light and love.

Along with our new serene surroundings the idea to write a book about my marriage was constantly on my mind. And since I wanted to be home for my daughter at lunchtime and my sons after school, I stayed home and began my story. The enjoyment that I received from my writings was great as the words just flowed out of me. I was never happier as I wrote about my issues and my past union. This was also one of the best things that I ever did in order to continue in my positive and beneficial course of action in nurturing my soul towards wholeness. I also went to the movies once a week and out to dinner with a friend every Saturday night.

When I absolutely needed to have some time for myself, I went to my favorite book store at Hillside Mall. I'd gather up as many angel and spiritual books as I could, and I'd sit in a comfortable chair and read for a few hours. I enjoyed this time so much and I treasured every book that I ever read. These moments of relaxation had always been my savior and throughout the coming years it would increase even more so. I think that it reminded me of my childhood days at the library.

I would never wish divorce upon anybody, but in the event that it is happening to you, I wanted to shed some light in regard to what you may expect as you are going through this process. I had a desire to make the issues and the pitfalls of my divorce known to other women, so they would have the benefit of what I learnt. Therefore I have added in a few guidelines and suggestions to help make life a smoother one for the future welfare of yourself and your children.

I had a desire for women to know, that whatever they are experiencing, they are not all alone, and that there is help to guide them throughout any times of despair. I wanted them to feel supported, especially when they thought that no one understands them or even cares.

Everyone needs a support system and if you can confide in one or two trustworthy friends, then I suggest that you do so. There are also support groups for separated and divorced women and this may be a benefit to you, if you decide to join one or drop in from time to time. Don't go through this disturbing time on your own or feel ashamed for the split, and please find some kindness for yourself. If you have divorced, it was probably the best thing that you possibly could have done in loving yourself and for the growth of your soul.

It certainly helps in this type of situation if a woman is in a good financial position before she decides to separate, but quite often this is not the case. In fact, this is usually what keeps a woman married in the first place. Every woman is going to need money for living and paying for her expenses. If her spouse is not in agreement with her decision to separate, she may have to rely solely on herself for this. If one has cash available, now would be the time to take that money and put it in a safe place for yourself and your children because you are going to need it. What starts out as a calm divorce can very quickly turn into a heated one and trust me, spouses love to hold monetary matters over their partners head.

There are lawyers available that will look at your case for a minimal fee. However before you do anything, I suggest that you speak with a counselor at least once or twice, so they can help you put things into a proper perspective. Different lawyers have different fees, so it's best to look around and compare fees. Also check with your friends, just in case they know of a lawyer that you can use. Your first visit is a consultation so I don't think that there is a fee, but be sure of this before you schedule with anyone.

Over the years, some women in my culture have come to speak with me before they went ahead with their divorce proceedings. I shared everything that I had learnt with them, while cautioning them regarding different factors within their various scenarios. I also added that it never hurts to consider every word which passes through their spouse's mouths and to try and cover themselves for every type of event.

Once a lawyer is found, you will need to give him your income tax returns, your spouse's tax returns, retirement savings plans, financial statements, insurance policies, and stock holdings etc. You also need to look over your will and have that changed. Any joint bank accounts or credit cards that you have together must be capped off, so you are not responsible if he adds any debt to it. I hope that throughout your marriage, you made sure that your name was listed on everything jointly, especially if you bought any large items such as a house or car etc.

If you are fortunate enough to be able to buy your spouse out of his portion of your house, the title will be changed into your name when this is done. Don't leave anything to chance because depending on the type of insurance you have, you may have to get him to sign a separate document for the liability and the contents of the home back to you. This will be done after he has removed his portion of things from the home. Everything that you have both accumulated must be looked at. And if either spouse has had an inheritance left to them, it doesn't become a joint family asset unless some of that money has been used for the family. This may have changed over the years, but this is how it was when I divorced.

There are some other issues to consider when you are drawing up your divorce agreement. Most divorce orders are based on joint custody and each parent sharing time spent with their children. However, consider what will happen if your spouse doesn't live up to certain conditions of your agreement. Decide what consequences that he will have to bear in this event, and make sure that it is a part of your order. And please find a way to fit this into your agreement.

If he has insisted on joint custody, but he doesn't live up to that, then perhaps it should be reverted to sole custody for you. Also the amount of child support per child will have to be readjusted for him to pay a higher amount. Remember to take into consideration all holidays especially the two months in the summertime. The extra amount of maintenance should be calculated from the time that your agreement began, and you need to factor in the lifestyle which your children grew up in also. Furthermore, try to add in that once you have sole custody, it cannot be changed back to joint custody. I would not recommend sharing custody with your spouse because if you want to go away for the weekend or a trip, you'll have to get a letter of consent from him to do so. If he is an unhappy man, he is going to add even more stress to your life in these situations and may make life as agonizing as he can for you. And depending on your spouse, you may want to deal with him as little as possible.

When drawing up your divorce agreement, if you get child support payments every two weeks instead of twice a month, you will get a couple of extra payments per year.

Most importantly, if your spouse was not a great father while you were married, he may not be any better after your divorce. I gave into my spouse on huge issues and I thought that he would do his best within his role of parenting towards our children, but I was wrong!

He based our entire divorce on the court case regarding my dad's will and he insisted that if there was a settlement, then he wanted to stop paying me alimony. I was going to add in, that it had to be over a certain dollar amount, but I didn't want my lawyer to think I was being petty. This was my mistake! My counsel told me that if I wanted to get alimony for life I probably could, since another woman was granted this from a judges ruling. However I didn't want to do that and as it turned out, my ex spouse only had to pay me alimony for four to five months. And then he was let off the hook, even though, I was married to him for twenty years. This never should have happened!

He refused to leave our family home until his requests were met and our agreement was signed, sealed, and delivered to his satisfaction. I absolutely needed to be rid of him as quickly as possible from the deepest part of my soul, for he was making life quite unbearable at home. He was also saying things about me to the children that weren't true. They were being emotionally mistreated and he was upsetting them as much as he could, as he tried to keep matters brewing away. This man certainly needed extreme counseling in how to love and nurture his own children! He was absolutely hell to live with, but then again, this was probably part of his plan.

I missed out on two major issues which I should have legally received in our settlement, but I was dealing with such a shrewd person. In hindsight I was so kind to him in our settlement, even though, he tortured and symbolically dismantled my soul repeatedly for many years. I owed HIM NOTHING, but I just couldn't be as heartless as he had been to me. I was either very stupid or quite compassionate!

However I wasn't married to a nice soul of any sort and since money had been the only important thing to him in our marriage, he of course fought for it to the bitter end in our divorce. Except five months later, the tables of destiny had turned and I was now in a position to buy him out of our home. Can you imagine how that felt? I was very fortunate and grateful and I treated him with so much dignity and respect regarding these matters.

Therefore women you decide, what is the price you are willing to pay for your FREEDOM?

I realize that when one is in the middle of a mind boggling event such as a divorce and there are children involved, it's not easy to think clearly. Also, if you are coming off of decades of mistreatment and hate, it's difficult to not take short cuts. However, you have to stay as strong as you can and look out for the future and security of you and your children. When you go to your lawyer appointments, it's probably not a bad idea to take a friend with you. They will keep you strong and may alert you to something that you can't see, for this process can become shocking and very overwhelming at times.

There is an invaluable service with the Attorney General's office called the Family Maintenance Enforcement Program and it is offered here in Victoria, B.C. It is a no cost government funded service which I highly recommend to any woman, who has divorced and is having problems with her spouse sending payments. It is one of the most important things that you will have on your side in your new found situation.

I believe that in order to access this service, your divorce agreement must be filed with the court system from when you divorced. I don't know if this is still operated this way, but if you are having any problems in this area please check this option out. Also I suggest that before any woman divorces, she checks into the regulations of this program especially if she isn't considering filing her order with the court system. One day you may need the security that this option provides, so I strongly urge all women to have their divorce orders filed or comply with whatever the rules are for enrollment. Your spouse may not want to go this way because it is to YOUR benefit to file your order, not his! If he defaults on his payments, this choice gives you something to fall back onto!

One begins this process by phoning in to speak with a representative and if your situation falls under the required criteria, they then mail the necessary forms out to you. Also, for each pay period your support payments are sent into the board by your ex spouse, they are recorded, and then they are forwarded to you by mail or directly deposited into your bank account. This takes a few extra days, but in the long haul you will be grateful that this service is even available. The board can only send the payments to you after they are received in their office, so if an ex spouse sends them in late, you will receive them late. He may do this to use whatever control he has left in your situation, and this surly gives him a sense of power.

Normally when you divorce, your ex husband gives you post dated cheques for the year to cover the support payments to you or your children, and he should continue to do the same for this procedure. The enforcement of very late payments is followed up with a letter from the board to him regarding any tardiness and everything is on file. Thus something for you to consider when drawing up your divorce agreement would be to add in a stipulation which says, that if you require the services of the Family Maintenance Board, the same rule applies as it did in your divorce order. The board will be sent one year's worth of cheques before January 1st of every year.

Lastly if you ever intend to register your children for scholarships which they will receive when they attend a post secondary school, make sure that your name is also listed on each form, for each agreement, for each child. When you first set up this agreement, one is asked for a principal signature and then a secondary signature. Check to see if you are able to be the principal signature on each form and if by chance you happen to be the major earner in your home, this should be quite easy to do. You'll avoid problems in the future if you can do it this way, for if your children are living with you full time, you will be the one paying for their entire daily expenses and post secondary schooling etc. Your children's requirements have to be addressed day to day and if one parent is not readily available, the children's funds must be at your disposal when you may need to access them.

When I divorced it was such a huge step that I had taken and I somehow thought that my life would be smooth sailing from that point onwards. However, I was so wrong again and I had no idea that my spouse would not honor all of the terms of our agreement.

If you decide to divorce, you can choose to put your children ahead of yourself or yourself ahead of your children, but in the long run the best way is to find a balance on all fronts or as close to one that you can possibly create. Parenting has never been a very easy job and as your children are going through their teenage years, you sometimes wonder, what the hell you signed up for! The fact of the matter is that you have taken on a huge undertaking, and you must do the very best job that you possibly can in raising them, until they are mature enough to continue on their own. One day that moment will come, but right now, it doesn't seem soon enough.

I caution anyone intending to marry another, to be completely convinced about the person that they are involved with, and about to wed. I realize that there are many different types of marriages, but ONE MUST be as sure as they possibly can be and have no doubts or unanswered questions about their intended partner.

You should look at his life and his accomplishments and speak to others that know him. Spend as much time as you can observing him in many types of different situations to see how he reacts, and responds in positive and negative scenarios with you and others. Listen to yourself and your gut feelings about him, and hear what your soul has to say to you. How do you truly feel, when you are around him? Is there anything that makes you uncomfortable about him? There is no need to rush into a relationship with anyone, let alone marriage, especially in normal dating circumstances. If one is seriously considering a certain person to be a major part of their life, then I don't think that it is out of line to have a background check done on them.

I haven't had any experience regarding prenuptial agreements, but all women need to take care of themselves and their wellbeing. This is especially so, if a woman has assets and even more so, if she has greater assets than the man that she is moving in with or marrying.

I didn't look at my divorce as a crushing defeat, but rather as a positive move taken by me in order to regain my own sense of self respect, self love, and a new chance to strive for a happier, fulfilling existence. Also I felt within my soul, that my true potential was untapped and my future possibilities were boundless, as I had now given myself a tremendous opportunity for my greater growth. If I hadn't divorced, I probably would have ended up being a shriveled soul barely existing, that is if I were still alive.

How is your life progressing for you? Do you think that it's the best one that you can create for yourself? Are you happy, somewhat happy, or do you wish at times that you were dead? How many of my experiences can you relate to?

Males are constantly being empowered throughout their work and various activities and in some ways the opposite began happening to me. I know that I should never have allowed it to occur, but as one grows, they learn and change for the better. The potential for many females would be great, if they were given the same equal opportunities from their births onwards as many males are granted. However, if this has not happened for you, females of all age groups must continue to persevere and work that much harder with the belief, that they can achieve whatever they wish to.

There may be others that will regard my book as a negative move for myself, but I hope that by bringing my issues to the forefront, there will be many more females that will see it as an opportunity. One which will give them clarity and the awareness to clearly look at, who they are, and what they would like to create within their lives. Along with considering, that if their situations warrant it, they do have the strength and the courage to stand up for whatever they believe in, even though, they may not have the support of their families and friends with them.

Females of all ages truly need to stop and reflect on whether or not, they are being honored, respected, and treated well by ALL of the people within their lives. Furthermore, listening to another woman speaking about matters which are plaguing women all around our world may make you feel uncomfortable. However, it may also force you to look at your own reality to determine, if anything is missing within YOU and YOUR life. Listen to any aching feelings which are screaming deep within you.

I hope that I have helped awaken something within your soul, which will encourage you to truly TAKE CHARGE OF YOUR DESTINY, and then extend your power out to assist others within their lives.

Did You Ever Consider
I Had A Good Reason?

You unjustly ostracized me because I wanted a divorce,
did you ever consider, I had a good reason, oh of course?
You were cruel and as gossipy as could be,
and I was not proud of you, who were of the same nationality.
You know exactly, who you are,
for your minds are often closed, and your spirits very far,
and you show no compassion, and never see beauty in a shining star.
You really should have the truth, before you judge another,
for you haven't walked in their shoes or know what they've discovered.
Think back to the times when you were talked about.
Didn't you wish you could silence all those hateful shouts?
For you see, I was a woman who definitely wanted out,
and I could no longer see myself living with him in our house.
I had enough of my spouse having another life,
while I was blamed for every bit of marital strife.
That's it, my pain I finally put a stop,
as many from my culture, their eyes did pop.
Now years later, I wish to share,
one need never stay with someone who is selfish and doesn't even care.
If you ever decide the very same route, I hope others are nicer to you.
Now as you are reading my words,
what will you do, with whatever you have learnt?
Will you turn to those to gossip some more,
or try to understand that a man is not the ultimate being,
and begin to support other women in situations sight unseen.
Look back to the time of our ancestors, haven't we progressed further,
than always blaming our universal sisters?
Hope you'll see the light, long before me, & don't disregard your needs,
but end your charade rather than continuing to live in misery.
Also, God sees all, and he even loves those whose thoughts are small.
The next time a woman decides to divorce, maybe you can show
some kindness, and help her throughout a lonely and painful course.
Then truthfully look into your eyes, to see your anguishing lies,
and do something positive to silence your soul's screaming cries,
before it truly dies.

Bonny Billan,
1996

Shattered Dreams

My childhood was full of laughs, chaos, and tears,
and many changes that left my heart pounding and broken.
He left without hesitation, screaming, and slamming the door,
and as it flew shut, I sat alone.

In those days I use to cry thinking my life would never be the same.
Although I walked around thinking that maybe it was a dream,
but in reality it was my life.

Since then I have smiled again, knowing I will be okay.
I have seen my Mom try to love again, but still to succeed.
My brother has grown stronger, and my other brother yet to tell.

We have moved on and started fresh.
All kinds of miracles I have yet to experience.
The family I have now, is all my heart needs.

Janessa S.
Grade 7
November 3, 2000

What Is A Man?

A man is someone, who sometimes simply can't understand,
that he may need to alter himself, as he works on his life plan.
And discover what it takes to be first rate, especially with his mate.
No male needs to define a woman or tell them what to do,
and it's actually true, females have an important purpose here on earth too.
A man's occupation, life, and recreation time,
are not the only significant things that matter, and need to shine.
He should add to his relationships and not bruise or abuse ones self-esteem,
so WOMEN seize your opportunities and don't allow your life to merely be.
DO NOT settle for a partner who is selfish and only takes, takes, takes,
and thinks he is supreme, because the more money he does make.
If your spouse demeans you... this is not, what a husband should be,
you must stay alert and attain the awareness to always see.
I tried to keep everything together at a huge cost to me,
and in the end, it almost completely destroyed me.
Everyone must strive to be with one, who truly believes,
that their mates can also achieve, absolutely anything they want to be.
We must all have respect, kindness, friendship, and wisdom with love,
no matter whose company we are in, even if they are no white doves.
In the end, we don't want to be bitter and have quarreled our lives away,
so we must strive to be with only those, who will stand beside us in pure love,
and support our authentic beliefs on any given day.
If anyone expects us to truly exist with them in the healthiest way,
then all of these characteristics they must daily display.
If they don't, goodbye we must honestly say, even if they are a relative,
a sibling, or an old friend, it's not good if we are with them till the very end.
Cuz when you feel what is in your heart, you need never sell yourself short,
as you trust in your soul, in this moment of your lifetime.

Bonny Billan

Being A Woman

Being a woman for me, has never been an easy place to be,
as my life from the beginning was a fast restless pace.
Each day many tasks I always had to do,
and it continued when I wed, cuz he was crude.
When I truly needed him, he didn't treat me very well,
but that's my past and for him, at last I did cast.
For my soul would no longer allow me, of having no place on his list,
guess I showed him and did he ever hiss!
My heart had awakened and screamed, "I will no longer be forsaken,"
and as I finally honored my soul, I listened to what it was saying.

Many males in my life have been domineering,
and so self involved that they felt only their needs mattered.
One day I decided to deal with my buried issues of pain,
and face my fears which they actually helped me to create.
Even though it may take me years, and I may shed many a tear,
the day will finally come, when I will say with no blame, I have won.
If your life is similar to mine, you had better wake up,
and decide what to do, if you truly give him the boot.
You have an equal right to happiness and to leave a life that is untrue.

I have now chosen to be in the company of kind and trusting individuals,
who know women are indeed very special beings,
who should be treasured, and not abused by those who don't have a clue.
For a woman is sacred and there is no one else that compares,
as she gives and gives and sacrifices, just look at what she has endured,
because of that male beast who thinks he is supreme,
when in fact, he truly needs a lot of deep healing.

Who told him that he was so damm wonderful?
Oh no… was it a woman who didn't know any better?
Guess there are many of both genders who need to understand,
that the ultimate are not, all those darn men.
For where would they be without females?
I know… somewhere deep in hell.
As you make positive changes, you must alter yourself and your thinking,
and the next time you believe, that a man is so swell,
look at your inner beauty and remember, you too, are a great belle.

Bonny Billan

Abuse... It's Easy For One To Do

No matter what one says, it's never okay,
to hurt someone, even in the smallest way.
Even if it's only by flipping your slipper,
at a not so pleasant teen!
It still counts, even if you miss,
or yelling at your kids.
Yes I admit... that I was guilty of this,
now I feel so remorseful for it.
It's easy for one to do,
ABUSE THAT IS!

There are many kinds to it all,
but it's never right to make someone feel small.
Whether it is verbal, spiritual, physical, or emotional,
it will eventually hurt their precious soul,
and no one deserves that at all.

For each of us, it is our own call,
to not do this and prevent it from happening to another.
God wanted us to truly discover, if we are ever abused,
we must find the tools, to properly recover.
Yes this all comes in good time, it's true,
to understand this vicious cycle in the human race.
Please don't give up, don't be a disgrace,
we must stop abuse, before we pass it to the next generation.
Continue to work at being a kind and whole person,
so one day you'll be proud for learning the biggest human lesson.

Bonny Billan

The Stifling Of A Soul

There were many who tried to stifle my soul,
but they did not truly know, that heaven was at my side.
God was just waiting for my mind, body, and soul to coincide,
so I would listen to my heart, which one day would awaken.
And force me to change from a life which I hated,
and to depart from my world which I had participated.
I heard a voice along the way, which actually tried to stir me,
and I thought it might go away, but instead it became stronger.
Until the day I could no longer stay in a place, where I was truly dying,
and the truth of the matter, was that I could no longer deny my lying.
The time finally came to make a great change, so one day I could be free,
it was that simple, so you see, now great possibilities could come to me.
Once I began to clear the way, I guess you could say, my face was happy,
brighter, and full of life, just cuz I was no longer somebody's wife.
It takes a lot of strength and courage, while others do detest you so,
but I didn't worry for my soul was beginning to come alive.
I knew more, than I could ever share, though many didn't care to hear.
I saw that they were still locked up in their sad lies,
and it was clear as I looked deeply into their pain filled eyes,
that they did not want to listen to my truth with their closed minds.
However I finally did it, oh yes I did,
and you can too, before you flip your lid.
Oh yes you can, come on… cuz I'm waiting for you.

Bonny Billan

229

What Will People Think?

Does it really matter, what people think?
Since whatever you do, they may never believe.
Don't worry about their judgment calls,
for in their lives, they are often thinking small.
It only matters, what you truly feel.

What do you really want to do?
For when you are old and gray,
they'll already be gone anyway.
You know, all of those people that you worried so much about,
and always thought, what on earth will they say of me?

Humans hide themselves, cuz for heavens sake,
if they let their guard down and let their wishes known,
what will people think?
They try to never expose, what is truly in their hearts,
you know, all that stuff that humans often dread.
They feel it's better to hide it all, and bury it with their death.

We have all been raised with some restrictions,
and it was enforced that we live under certain conditions.
Except our world is now, in quite another time and place,
and one needs to make great changes, no matter what their race.

For in this new phase that we are beginning now,
you must set a different pace in a world that is your stage.
What do you say?
It is worth a try, to perhaps touch the sky?
And to know in the end, that your existence stopped being a lie,
because you gave it all, from deep down inside.

Though you often sighed, as life made you cry,
you took a magnificent leap, as you looked God in the eyes.
You had no fear, as you both joined hands,
for you were no longer alone, as you set about your new plans.

I truly let it be known, what my heart and soul deeply felt,
and so what, if I am judged, as the one who exposed it all.
Some may ask, was it just some kind of vengeance call?
I hope they'll recognize, I wanted to inspire others along their way.

And I used my life that often made me quiver, deep down to my liver,
as a way to help others grow, so they would also one day know.
If she could do it, then maybe I can too,
and rid myself of a life that's not so cool.

If your years have been filled with horrendous screams,
that's truly not, what life should be,
for your heart shouldn't have to suffer, endless pleas for needed relief.
Hence say yes, I'll listen to the stirrings of my soul and aim to achieve this,
so one day, I can possibly reach inner and outer simultaneous bliss.

For in the end, it doesn't matter what anyone truly thinks, but you,
and the best that one can do, is to send others great love and healing.
You know, when I look in the mirror, I'm pretty happy as I grin,
guess in life… I truly did win.

Bonny Billan

232

The rules and regulations of every culture that need to be re-evaluated,
are the areas that do not consider females equal to their male counterparts.
All of the guidelines, that disrespect a woman and deprive her
of any of her human rights, need to be completely abolished.
Each woman needs to find her own philosophy which is unique to the calling
of her individual heart and soul, and than live that on her own terms.
Both genders need to create an existence with others,
who truthfully respect them on all levels.

– BONNY BILLAN –

A New Dawning

Chapter 15

*E*very step that I have taken has been a constant one-sided crusade for me, as I have edged towards being treated as an equal to the domineering men which I have encountered in my life. I feel as if I have been through the battlefields of war while trying to emerge from the quick sands of a lifelong struggle for gender equality, as I pleaded for my voice to be heard. My life made a warrior out of me as I have continually fought for my beliefs, my desires, and my human right to simply be myself.

I was to have no forewarning of the conflicts that I would entail throughout my years, other than my struggle at birth which actually became the foreshadowing of my entire existence. I have always honored my beliefs while supporting whoever else needed my help whenever the occasion arose. And much of the time, the only ally which I had to draw upon has been my own inner force. I have been a worthy opponent much to the displeasure of my rivals for without exception, I have always defended my convictions.

233

My battle cries have sometimes been loud, but they also gave me much strength and power. I had no idea, that my years would be so full of unimportance, sorrow, short-lived happiness, jealousy, betrayal, ridicule, divorce, sole parenthood, and finally total abandonment. It is truly amazing just how much heartache and pain, one's heart can endure.

Along our pathways we may encounter those of either gender, who are only at their best if they are dominating others that they perceive to be weaker than they. Sometimes they try to frighten people when in reality, they are actually the frightened ones. Their main goal in life is to attempt to bring people down to their level of thinking and they thrive on causing others pain. They seem to possess quite a negative force and the selfish thoughts which they perceive of themselves, gives their sense of worth an egotistical boost. They are the most important person in their world, and any unhappiness that they may have caused to others is irrelevant to their way of thinking. The fact that they have added to the demise of another's life doesn't even enter into their psyche.

These types of people are truly unhappy themselves and need a lot of deep healing, but they are usually incapable of seeing this. As well, they are quite unaware that their victim's weaknesses began, took root, and grew stems because of their negative attitude, deplorable behavior, and constant abuse in how they treated them.

These offenders may be family members, friends, or others which you perceived to be supporting you. People that you have encouraged to be a part of your life and who you thought you could really trust. However, whether you realized it or not, what you actually received from them is their disrespect, arrogance, and betrayal.

We select many of the people that we invite into our lives, so we need to truly consider who we invite into ours! If you have discovered anyone in your life who is like this, then you must try your utmost to stay away from them. If you can't at this very moment don't give up, but wait for the day when you can break away from them.

Will any negative people ever realize, that when they are emotionally, spiritually, verbally, mentally, physically or sexually abusing their wife, sister, daughter, mother, aunt, grandmother, girlfriend or any other female or male, that this is their disturbing contribution that they have given our world? This is the painful legacy that they have left in their name which may continue to grow generation after generation.

It is sometimes hard for us to understand the actions or the pain caused by others or ourselves. However let it be known, that everyone shall one day meet the energy and the karma which they have given and created in a positive or negative manner. For as sure as the sun rises, none of us shall ever be able to evade, but rather be forced to shake the hands of our own destinies straight on.

My views regarding the equality of the sexes within our culture were very different from that of my parents and even though I was a strong female, I had inhaled a bottomless amount of cultural debris and hurt during my lifetime. I never really comprehended all of the damage which had crept in and bonded itself to hinder my sense of self-worth, despite the fact, that I refused to accept any of their old world beliefs. As well as constantly fighting the very foundation which they were made from. It also took me quite some time to realize, that I didn't have the knowledge to recognize, nor had I truly grasped how very much this infringement was carried within every cell of my body in relation to every second that I had lived.

When my marriage began, a different kind of control freak surfaced. He would look different than that of my childhood because I thought that I loved it, but the continuation of control regenerated itself immediately. I had endured twenty years of a very structured and regimented childhood, and I had survived another twenty long grueling years of marriage to a very cruel person. Though I had known for a long time that I was terribly unhappy in my painful situation, I wasn't sure what to do about it?

However one day, I had at last woken myself up and realized that I had been lying in the deep, dark trenches of a deadly relationship which I needed to escape from immediately. I managed to believe that I could pull myself away from the cruel clutches of my captor and leave my imprisonment forever. Along with allowing myself to imagine what taking flight might feel like, I had finally decided to flee.

I had made the decision that my spirit would no longer be stifled, demeaned, or inflicted with the stinging pain which I had endured in my past. It seemed that throughout the years, I had merely traded one sort of dilemma for another. Happiness was just a memory and I hadn't experienced it for quite some time. Was I not on earth to be happy? I deserved joy, but would I ever truly find it within me?

Could my soul not soar high off the ground like a beautiful white dove flying with her wings spread full span soaring high above the ocean, against a brilliantly colored sunset in freedom... ahhhhhh... to be free! This would be true happiness!

My freedom was so near as my heart was pounding and a new sense of living was emerging in me. All that I had imagined which I wanted to accomplish in my life was mine for the taking.

For the first time in a long while I knew that my life was going to change forever. I was going to do it! I had survived through much and I would carry on for myself and for my children! My decision had finally been made and I would begin a cleansing pathway to find and love, the child within me which was abandoned and lost many years earlier.

As I began my new passage, it turned into quite a spiritual one and I discovered that I had not journeyed here alone. I discovered that I had never been alone, and I had support and help especially in the most agonizing and loneliest of times. I would soon learn that as I continued in my life, my world would be surrounded with the blessings of the heavens above. I may have been deserted by many human beings, but God would continue to reach out to me with loving arms filled with the healing miracles, which I needed to fill the hollow gashes within the depths of my soul.

Our lives are only as limited as our thinking is and until one allows a new thought process into their psyche to create a different future for them, they may be stuck in their present situations. Sometimes we believe that our choices are limited in regard to our chances of true happiness because we are in a certain relationship or marriage. I realize that there are relatively happy couples living everywhere, but are you one of them? If you aren't, will you simply continue in your unhappiness?

Ask yourself, "What do I really want out of my life? Do I truly want changes?"

Perhaps truly consider one last time, if there are any other options for you and your partner to try and transform your lives together? This is a decision that you must make very carefully. If there are no other ways, then ask yourself, can I or can't I separate? Do I actually want to do this and uproot my entire family? Also no matter what the case may be, you must not stay in any dangerous situations whatsoever.

I ask you, can you look into a mirror and face your fears or are you going to keep looking past them and pretend that they just don't exist? Why not listen to your soul for the first time in many years? Your spirit will let you know, what the answer is. If you deeply crave a change than within this transforming moment, your positive attitude and actions will begin generating your new destiny. You can then, expand that out to other avenues and your intentions will create a new flow into your life.

If you are a self-sacrificing woman, your heart is not exactly going to be into separating, although your soul and your belief system will give you the strength which you need, if you ask it to. You should make a list of your priorities and options, but please put yourself on that list also. I only had two or three people that honestly supported my decision at the very beginning of my parting and one of them lived out of town. If your situation is similar to mine, the benefits to separating will be numerous and what you gain cannot be exaggerated. You can dig deeply and pull your strength to the surface and yes, there will be challenges, but I never once regretted my decision even for a second. The peace and happiness that I felt could not be mistaken and no one deserves to live in misery and negativity, let alone, lying beside it in your bed.

You must not deny yourself the chance to recognize and discover your true potential and even surpass what you believe you are capable of accomplishing in this lifetime.

Remember MOTHERHOOD IS A FULL-TIME OCCUPATION and I gave it all that I had, as I surrendered my soul into it. I choose to be a mother who gave up everything for the sake of her children for many years. I had watched my mother as she sacrificed herself for her family and maybe I was living too far behind in the past and not progressing forward. At times, I knew that it wasn't the healthiest way to live, but I still kept myself on the back burner. My mission of motherhood was the most important undertaking that I had ever taken on. The love, development, and shaping of my child's spirit, self esteem, and importance was not a responsibility that I had ever taken lightly, and it was deeply embedded within my heart.

How will you handle it, if you decide to divorce and your spouse does not partake in any of the responsibilities with your children? Do you have anyone that can help you from time to time, so you can take a much needed break? Please believe me when I say, that being a single parent with no one to lend a hand is an absolutely tremendous undertaking which doesn't stop for many years. It is very time consuming, quite often frustrating, and a never ending job as you now have the entire responsibility for the wellbeing of your children.

If you decide to go this route, you need to do everything that you can do, to get into the healthiest state of mind, body, and spirit, not only for your sake, but for the best interests of your children. It certainly is not the time to start thinking about bringing a new person or partner into your children's lives. Your children must be your first priority and try not to be selfish where they are concerned. Also remember, they just had their worlds blown apart and that has to be quite a scary place for them to be in. You truly should be putting this part of your life on hold, at least until their sense of security and structure to their new living arrangements has had time to resurface in a loving environment. My children needed to observe that it was not acceptable for anyone, be it their father, relative, or friend to treat them or me with any disrespect whatsoever, therefore they experienced and witnessed the ending of some of our relationships.

My next step was to begin a soul searching journey towards healing my spirit and discovering the woman who was hidden and waiting for me, while creating the woman that I truly wanted to become.

When my soul first began to stir I wanted to find out what my purpose for coming to earth was. I also needed to know, what I ever could have done in my past life to have created such heart breaking situations and such a turbulent ride for myself in this lifetime. I could not understand why so much negativity came to me from different people, especially since I only tried to help them. It was everywhere. I was a good person and I wanted to know why and how, I kept drawing these situations to myself. It was not happening to anyone else that I knew and I was being hurt, betrayed, and my heart was repeatedly being stomped on.

Were my standards just too high for others?

I certainly wasn't exactly enjoying this whole human experience which I had decided to come and try once again!

I realized that somewhere along the line, that God tied into all of this. What was God trying to show me about myself and the people who were around me, and why was disrespect and anguish continuing to resurface in my life? What had I said, that I wanted to accomplish in this lifetime? What could it be? How did all of this connect together? I needed to know!

Have you ever asked yourself, any of these questions?

Is it time for a major change and overhaul of your life? It's not an easy road to take, but what in life is easy?

I decided to take my life in a spiritual direction because this was the only way which I knew to receive the answers, that I had contemplated for so very long. I needed to know about my past in order for me to understand my present, decide what I wanted to create in my future, and what type of individuals I wanted in my life. As a result, I spent the next decade dealing with and saying goodbye to the old, as I was given a chance to build a new life. I began delving throughout my fragments and trying to purify my spirit. And as I did, I truly looked at the people who were around me and I saw them in a whole different light. I went through many phases and along the way as my inner issues surfaced, they needed to be looked at and dealt with differently. While I began a new way of thinking in order to create a major shift in my old soul.

My soul was carrying strength, negativity, fear, anger, hate, anguish, loneliness, despair, sacrifice, and courage from all that had transpired throughout the years. Over time my deep rooted pain would continue to make its way through my body, as I was about to travel on a passage to heal my toxic wounds which began many lifetimes ago.

I would come to understand, how my unloving history had impacted my life from all that was denied to me, and how my deep embedded agony would challenge the healing of my soul. Also I realized that the ghosts from my past and present were lingering deep within me, alongside the self imposed restrictions which I had placed upon myself. What's more, I knew that I had to look at my inner workings, anger, and change myself before I could even think about truly being with another man.

My heart, mind, body, and soul needed so much love, nurturing, and healing and throughout the coming years, this is what I worked on as I cultivated the same growth in my children. I wanted to become a fully healed and self reliant woman and most certainly so, before I ever entered into another relationship with any male, that is, if I could truthfully believe in another one again. Only my children really mattered to me throughout this time period. And as I sifted through my dreary past with the intention of discovering what I truly wanted out of my life, I began to form a new relationship with myself. If I hadn't been awakened and pushed to the breaking point, I may never have known what my true potential could ever be.

I wanted to start enjoying life and to experience new and different things that were denied to me in my past. It was time to live and easily laugh again, and I looked forward to it with a yearning pleasure that I hadn't felt in years. I intensely wanted to create an existence in which I was absolutely free, and I never wanted to be with anyone who I ever had to answer to again. However, I had no idea what deep obstacles lay ahead for me. The spiritual process which I went through would surprisingly become the greatest part of my healing journey, as I began a search for the love that had darted past me throughout my life.

I shall never cease to forget, where I have come from, and what I have lived through for I proudly pay homage to my passage, which was built on my trials and tribulations for equality, freedom, and my right to free speech. I realize that my soul has led me towards plights which were paved on the roads of the less traveled. And I hope to never succumb until I have scaled my highest mountain for my greatest purpose. I could not have foreseen the solitude, the tormenting pain which lived within, or the miracles which God would bring to me over the course of the next decade or know, that the discovery of self-love would be my biggest triumph and change my world forever.

Take A Chance And Change

Our actions tell us many things,
it shows us, what's in our souls.

Have you been kind to others today
or have you purposely tried to hurt another human being?

Truly consider, "Why you are so angry?"
Can you possibly see, that your soul is saying something to you?
Perhaps it's time to create a major transformation,
that will make a difference to your present and your future.

For the first time in a long while, actually listen to yourself.
Are the situations in your life, really someone else's fault?
Perhaps... it is you, that needs to change.

CHANGE HOW YOU VIEW THE WORLD.
CHANGE YOUR DAILY PURPOSE FOR BEING.
CHANGE YOUR VIBRATIONAL ENERGY, BY CHANGING
YOUR THOUGHTS, YOUR ACTIONS, AND YOUR REACTIONS.

CHANGE YOUR MIND AND BODY,
AS THIS IN TURN, WILL ALTER YOUR HEART & SOUL.
CHANGE YOURSELF IN EVERY WHICH WAY.

CHANGE INTO A TRUE SPIRITUAL BEING,
WHO IS LIVING OUT THIS HUMAN EXPERIENCE,
CHOOSING EACH MOMENT OF TIME, WITH LOVE, & COMPASSION.
YOU HAVE MUCH TO GAIN AND GIVE.

TAKE A CHANCE AND CHANGE,
SO YOUR BIRTH AND PRESENCE HERE ON EARTH,
WILL HAVE MADE A DIFFERENCE TO YOUR SOUL,
AND OUR UNIVERSE!

Bonny Billan

What Does It Mean To Be A Human Being?

We travel to earth once again, to be a human being,
but what does this logically, truly all mean?
We live our life in another human body,
that we constantly want to change, so we won't look sloppy.

We experience its pain and all of its earthly sensations,
and we often feel it's not good enough, for us to be seen in.
Therefore we alter it, for the good of our soul,
at least that's what we tell others, and hope they are sold.

We are all created and connected by one great God,
so I must ask, "Why the hell are we fighting over pieces of sod?"
What is it, what have humans truly created here on earth?
Is it a world that we are truthfully proud of?

Look around, what have we honestly done?
Created much Warfare, Death, Poverty, and made many Guns!
Is killing an innocent human, what we were truly meant to do?
A lot of people on our globe, don't even have a clue.

Do we honor all people in regard to their human rights?
It's not okay to take another's life, in the name of any war,
let alone, taking control of or destroying their sacred homes,
for this is NOT THE WORLD, GOD WANTED US TO CREATE!
And one day, our souls may face an overwhelming fate.

Before we were born, we were all heavenly loving beings,
now many of us are portraying the traits of human unintelligence with no brains!
In this moment, WE ARE STILL, THAT SAME SPIRITUAL LOVING SOUL,
who consisted of PURE LOVE and who could CONQUER MANY THINGS!

We do not need to treat another with Abuse, Inequality, Domination, or Violence,
for in our true souls, lives the same love that traveled with us from heaven.
In the hope, we'd heal our world with Love, Light, Compassion, & Prayers,
and all of us can generate this love in any given second, without any flares.
PLEASE LISTEN, NOW IS THE TIME, for you to share and spread your energy
throughout our universe, from the VERY HEART OF YOUR UNIQUE SOUL!

Bonny Billan

Upon A Fairer Shore

I once met Angels upon a fairer shore,
and they told my soul, that I'd never be alone.
One day, they'd very likely appear,
as I'd anticipate for them to be near.

And within every step, that I would take,
I'd somehow know, that our bond, they'd never forsake.
However, I would forget for a time, within this new body of mine,
that they had been with me from birth,
and God had not sent me alone to earth.

It would take me years to recall our sacred connection,
and to realize, that they'd help me in my resurrection.
Though my soul always knew about this secret pact,
it never told me, but I never really lacked.
Some day I'll return with them to heavenly bliss,
but for now they stay, or their presence I'd surely miss.

Have you remembered, what your soul's agreement is?
Close your eyes and breathe deeply within.
Let your mind roam free, wherever it wants to be.
Can you feel or see, what you should truly do?
Don't worry, one day… it'll come to you.

Bonny Billan

Angels dancing, messengers on our grounds,
hear their voices, as they bless and visit all around.
They've come to alert us, as they love us so much,
accept their help, as you feel their loving touch.

– BONNY BILLAN –

Have You Invited Angels Into Your Life Yet?

Chapter 16

*A*ngels love and protect us, while our Spiritual Guides help raise our level of spiritual awareness, as they all guide and assist in making our lives easier for ourselves and others. When my Angel visited me years ago, she had extended her loving arms out to me at a time when I was deeply questioning, if I was actually worthwhile. Though I didn't quite comprehend the blessing and magnitude of it all for many years. I was extremely fortunate to have been granted the privilege of actually seeing my protector, let alone, being able to speak with her.

I had been deeply lacking loving and respectful people throughout parts of my life and meeting my Angelic Guardian created a somewhat new perception into my world. It pushed and expanded my beliefs even further into a realm which I was very fascinated with, as new doors stood open in anticipation of me crossing over into their loving threshold and stepping into their reality. I was standing on a whole new horizon of a miraculous entryway into furthering my experiences, insights, and healing.

Angels have protected me and my children throughout our lives and they have also taken care of you, even though, you may be unaware of their presence. Your Spiritual Guides and Angels are waiting for you to welcome them into your world. One can ask for love, healing, strength, clarity, understanding, or help at any time for themselves or others.

I was given an example of their protection one afternoon around 1:25 p.m. when I was beginning to back my car out of the garage. I heard a voice very loudly say to me, "Be careful or you are going to run your daughter down."

I was puzzled as I wondered, how that could possibly happen since school was still in session and she was suppose to be in attendance there. However, I listened to the warning, and I slowly backed my car out of the garage. As I got to the edge of the driveway, I looked to my right and my daughter was standing beside the garage door smiling and waving at me. I was so shocked to see her there and I was very grateful for this huge warning. There would be many more to come in the following years.

I had no conceivable idea to what extent God would bestow gifts upon us to convince me, that the four of us were not all alone in this world. I was being shown that I needed to have faith that we were being protected. And one of the biggest messages which I would receive was, that I could request assistance from heaven in the span of a moment.

In a completely different type of scenario, if you sense an unknown energy around you, try not to be frightened about it. Always ask God or whatever you believe in as your source of protection, to surround you in love and white light. And by doing this, you'll know that you are being protected.

Secondly, you might want to ask this energy to give you a sign, as to who they are. Chances are, it quite possibly may be a loved one of yours from the Spiritual Realm. Ask for a confirmation of who is reaching out to you, and then let it go for awhile, and perhaps they'll draw closer to you when they are ready to do so. They may come and give you a symbol of something that they did when they were living as a human being. You may be a bit weary to do this and I can certainly understand and relate to this reaction, for I had many of my own to deal with. Also remember, that whenever my Angels spoke with me, I never felt one moment of fear with them. If you are experiencing anything of a spiritual nature, try to be calm and don't forget to say your protection, before you do anything.

When I had my initial experience over twenty-five years ago it was really mind boggling and incredible at the same time, as I often wondered if it was truly happening. On some level I was questioning it and on the other hand, I accepted it as just a part of my normal way of living. However, it would take me years to truly realize that I was taking part in a great miracle.

I shared my information with a number of people, but over the years some of their reactions were very disappointing. And I spent a lot of energy trying to convince them of my miraculous happenings. After a time, I only shared it with a few people and even then, I didn't know if they actually believed what I was describing to them. I had no support from my spouse regarding my paranormal occurrences and he continuously ridiculed me about them. However this was a part of my world and a part of who I was, so in effect, he had totally rejected me on every level.

In these moments I truly missed not having a close loving relationship with a compassionate male partner to share my world with, let alone, my divine experiences. I had deeply yearned for many lonely years, for that special someone who would understand me, my way of thinking, and my past, while sharing in the joys and everyday living with my children. I truly desired to meet a kind hearted gentleman, who could accept my spiritual life without me having to repeatedly explain my situations, while feeling so awkwardly different from others. Actually I really wanted a man who would not tell me that I was "crazy" regarding the encounters which I was having. I never once considered meeting someone who was on the same spiritual wave length as me because in my wildest dreams, I never contemplated that this type of man could ever exist. It was simply not possible! In being realistic, I was just hoping to meet a handsome and kind soul, who had a great outlook on life and who could accept my heavenly blessings in a positive manner. Time would tell, what type of man would eventually appear in my life.

I discovered, that I not only had premonitions and insights about different things that were occurring in someone's life, but my extra sensory perception also extended to feeling spiritual energy around me.

In May 1996 I wrote in my diary, "Lately when I am sleeping for an hour or so, I'm waking up in a cold sweat. And I can sense that someone is in my room. I can feel their energy coming closer to me, so I say, "OH PLEASE... DON'T APPEAR TO ME!"

I know that they are about to appear because I can feel their energy come to a peak, so I say again, "OH DON"T APPEAR... DON"T APPEAR!"

I can feel their energy withdrawing from me and leaving. I realize that this is the next stage in my development, but at this point I am not ready for this!"

As my third eye was truly becoming alive I actually didn't have many things in common with those who were around me, nor was this side of my life easily explained or smooth flowing. My soul had taken me in a different direction and since I lived without a partner, it gave me the opportunity to explore this avenue. And it provided me with the chance to be myself without constantly being dragged down for my convictions. I had been able to forge ahead in a relatively peaceful manner, even though, some people including one of my sons regarded me as strange. Thank goodness I had one of my children to share these events with, because over time, some of their own inner gifts would also come to the surface, and on some level be stronger than mine.

People are often weary and frightened by something that they have never been exposed to before and I'll attest to that. Fear of the unknown is a valid feeling and it has been a bit daring to keep exploring this sometimes scary, but intriguing realm. Although, it had a complete force of its own and I could not have prevented it from coming into my life.

There are many people who can identify with my experiences whether it relates to women's issues, inequality, abuse, motherhood, divorce, beginning anew or embarking on a spiritual pathway. I am also certain that there are a large amount of people who have had spiritual experiences happen to them, and they aren't sure how to understand it, how to cope with or accept it, and integrate it into their lives. As I began my spiritual pathway of healing which I so readily sought, these questions and many more were answered for me, and perhaps some of yours will be answered for you also.

One never knows, how God will show us our life's purpose or what we as human beings have agreed to experience in this lifetime, or even what karma we have accumulated. I know that a great majority of the public have also had these very same thoughts. Nevertheless because of the way that my life had transpired, I desperately needed these answers revealed to me as soon as possible. I was frantic to discover, what led me into this life which I was experiencing and in the greater scheme of things, I knew that God was at the helm of the whole show. At times as I truly wondered, "WHAT THE HELL WAS GOING ON," I remembered within me, that I was much more then just a girl who had been born, grew up and married. There was a part of me that knew a great deal more, but as hard as I tried, I couldn't quite recall what it was.

I felt at moments, that I must have agreed to do too much as a human being for I didn't seem to making much progress in my world. And I deeply wondered why my heart was repeatedly been hurt. However, I was about to truly discover on my journey of awareness and understanding, the different facets of our soul's pathway. As I would learn beyond any shadow of a doubt, that we are all spiritual beings just living the human experience. Life within our human existence is never very easy for any of us, and for most, there are several challenges and struggles which we must all undergo. Although I sometimes wondered, why it seemed that some people came away free from every negative incident which they inflicted onto others.

Now that I see my past in front of me, I understand how my human and spiritual side all interlaced and connected together, for the pure sake of my soul's growth. And also, what the purposes of my pain filled life were all about. I would soon discover, that I was asking myself the wrong question.

It wasn't actually, what I had done negatively in my previous life to have created this life, it was more in keeping with, what had I failed to fully learn? Therefore, this lifetime of events were created, so I could try to overcome any traits which I never fully conquered before. And all of my life experiences were for the greatest growth of my spirit.

Over time my spiritual teacher would explain to me, what my biggest issue to shift and overcome was. I was to stop any lack of respect which I had for myself by halting any mistreatments which I was receiving from any others.

I needed to stand up against all odds and stop every disrespectful and abusive occurrence within my life.

Yes… once and for all! I needed to truly love myself at all times and repeatedly say, "NO" to any offender of any negativity directed at me.

Furthermore, my soul had been preparing me to accept a responsibility and bring forth all of the information which I gathered, into the light of others to witness for themselves. The healing benefits and knowledge of my journey were just too great to not share with anyone else who wanted to enrich themselves.

I was given an extraordinary gift from God. And it took me years to have the courage to say out loud, that I have quite an intuitive side to myself whereby, I feel, I see, I sense, and I know things about others. This is part of my TRUTH! I truly have another part to me, that is alive, genuine, and living inside of me and it is within every waking and sleeping moment that I have. It was finally time for me to admit out loud, "I Am Psychic!" I have extrasensory perception, I get premonitions, I am telepathic, and I am "An Intuitive." Whatever word that one wants to call it… I was all of them! The word "psychic" sometimes has an odd connotation associated with it, but any which way that I looked at it, this is what I was and for many years I couldn't openly admit it to others.

I know that there must be many other people who also have their own special gifts which they are keeping a secret from others too. As well as, I have recognized that as I read certain books or hear some well-known people speak publicly, that they are psychic also. I understand that at this point in their lives, that they are not ready to have this information openly known about themselves. However, they need to look at it differently and know, that they don't need to hide this part of themselves any longer or be embarrassed of it, because it is truly A MAGNIFICIENT GIFT FROM GOD!

If this gift is a part of you, then you need to change your thoughts regarding your inner self because in your denial, you are in fact, denying your own truth and your soul's truth. You must honor this side of yourself before your soul rebels against you, by tossing your life into an immense struggle and pounding your heart to the very core until you finally do. Your time could very well be here now, for you to ACKNOWLEDGE, ACCEPT, and LIVE THE TRUTH OF YOUR SOUL!

My gift began to greatly expand in the year 2001 and on February 26, I told my children that our city was going to have an earthquake. I was met with their head shaking, laughter, and protests as I went through our earthquake procedures. Throughout the evening I was continually frustrated as I questioned my children about what they would do in the event of an earthquake, but it seemed like I was talking to the wall. That night I put all of the necessary provisions back into my car which included a large assortment of medical supplies, water, food, a shovel, and my boots. I also had an identical medical duffle bag and an escape ladder for inside of our home.

The next morning on February 28, when I was in the shower, the city of Victoria experienced an earthquake. It caused a fair amount of damage for some people, but we received none at all since our home was built on and surrounded by rock.

My children were speechless and they avoided looking at me, when I said to them, "I told you!"

I considered my knowing to be remarkable, but I had no indication that my world was about to be shaken and truly turned upside down, as my soul's awakening delved me even further into a major world event.

It would occur on September 11, 2001.

During the middle of the night, I woke up in horror from a nightmare where I was all alone in a large airplane. I had been able to see right through to the front of the airliner which was only a few yards away from crashing into a tall building. My heart raced uncontrollably as the metal bird inched its way closer and closer to the huge skyscraper, while every other part of my being was pounding away. There was no way to stop it from happening nor was there any way for me to escape, as I sat all by myself in my seat completely terrified.

Just after I screamed out, "GOD, WHY IS THIS HAPPENING TO ME?" a window on the right side of the plane blew out and I scrambled from my seat. I very quickly climbed out of the window and as I did, I flapped my arms up and down and flew away in the sky.

I immediately awakened in a sweat and I said to myself, "WHAT THE HELL WAS THAT?"

I was deeply traumatized as I went to get a damp facecloth to wipe off my face. I was too scared to go back to sleep and I stayed awake wondering, what my horrible dream meant as I huddled in my bed. I had had accurate omens in my dreams before, but I couldn't relate anything in my life to this one, and it was just too scary not to mean something.

A few hours later I feel asleep only to be awoken by the sound of my telephone ringing. It was my youngest son calling from college and he was yelling out, "Someone is attacking the United States and the airports are all closed."

I just couldn't understand what he was trying to say, so I turned on the television. I was absolutely horrified when I discovered the true life reality of it all, as the lives of so many people had been shattered. And I was truly sickened that something like this had actually taken place! What the hell had our world come too! Wasn't there something out there, that could have stopped this?

Later that evening as I was getting ready to go for a shower, I was thinking to myself, "How come I didn't have an inkling, as to what was going to happen in New York? How come," I asked myself?

Just then a voice in my mind said to me, "YOU DID KNOW, YOU HAD A DREAM!"

That's when I remembered, my nightmare that I had earlier that morning.

WHY and HOW did I ever dream about this horrendous event? Over the next month I was truly alarmed and felt nauseated right down to my stomach, as I continually contemplated what was happening to our world and within me!

I asked God, "What on earth was going on and why did you not stop it from occurring?"

I didn't receive an answer.

I tried to comprehend the significance of the magnitude of it all, as this not only changed the lives of so many people around our world, but it also changed my everyday life forever! God wanted me to experience this completely devastating event almost to the very end, but why?

I must also say, that I do recognize, what it felt like to sit there completely helpless with no control over the situation. There wasn't even a pilot flying the airplane which I was on! It was absolutely the most ghastly thing that I had ever undergone and it was so very frightening. I was so thankful when I woke up to find out that it wasn't real, but little did I realize… it was.

The only comfort that I can give to anyone who lost a loved one or friend on that devastating day, was that they were not alone. They all had each other. And they also had many loving and beautiful Angels and some of their loved ones from heaven, to help them make their transition to the next realm an easier one. All of their Angelic Spiritual Helpers would have made sure that everyone's loved ones period of adjustment from earth to heaven was as tender and caring, as it possibility could have been for each and every one of them.

My premonition on September 11th was my biggest insight so far and since this event was so colossal, I could no longer deny another part of my truth. Somehow and for some reason, I was now having premonitions about events outside of my personal world. I had been searching for years, and now God had shown me something in a huge manner. I couldn't keep myself a secret any longer and whether I was ready for it or not, it was time for me to embrace my true destiny. God had spoken and the truth of my soul… was now here. And… I was very alarmed!

Could I actually have agreed and consented upon this at some time before my soul's birth? WHAT... HAD I BEEN THINKING! What was the reason for my soul to experience this event? How did I tie into it and what was the connection? Maybe I was suppose to do something with the gifts that I had within me? Would they grow even stronger over the years? I knew that one day... the answers would come to me.

In book two, there would be much more for me to face as the universe and my soul steered me into the direction of a gut wrenching passage to purify my entire being! Various parts of my experiences would terrify me and make me cringe, and I could do nothing to stop it from entering... into my consciousness.

I also experienced further torment from new present life situations as I dug amongst the ruins of the aftermath from my past chaotic years. At this juncture I truly needed to accept and begin using the methods, which I was about to learn from my spiritual teacher. All of his lessons were to help my spirit confront, cleanse, and heal from my innermost secret wounds, which I had deeply buried in a grave within my several centuries old and curious soul.

I had no idea that the spiritual journey which I was about to embark on would lead me into a new learning stage of understanding the human, the soul, and the spiritual relationship. This would be the heart, mind, body and soul connection which is very much a part of us all. And throughout the coming years, I would be absolutely shocked over the memory, depth, and knowledge, that every heart and soul carries deep within it.

Furthermore, I discovered, lived, and experienced the most profound traits within my soul, which was filled with ABSOLUTE MAGIC. I was surrounded with completely PHENOMENAL GIFTS, which each of our souls consist of and have to offer us all. If at any point, you too decide to board upon a voyage such as this, you will eventually have the same potential as I did, while inviting these magical new joys and moments into your life also.

Have you ever thought about, what your soul has experienced, what path it is headed towards, or how you could purify your soul?

As I set about creating a new serene way of living, Angels and the Spiritual Realm would reach out to me with their love, as my senses were pushed onto an emotional roller coaster ride which careened out of control at times. I would be thrust into experiencing a new growing intuitive side to myself via the forces residing in heaven. This new process would very slowly helped me to face and begin to pulverize my pain, as it edged me towards the restoration of my shattered heart.

For the first time, I needed to carefully considered the reasons for this contact which I was about to receive from heaven, and to truly understand that they were reaching OUT TO ME IN LOVE. It was TRUE. I needed to realize and to accept, that there were others in our universe, that actually LOVED ME.

They loved me, for who I was, and I didn't need to explain anything about myself to them. They came to me… in pure love. All I had to do was to expand my thoughts and allow their love to flow through my mind and body, so one day I would be a whole and healed human being. Yes, one day my soul would be reborn.

Incredibly, the love which was denied to me throughout my life was about to greet me through the greatest powers of God, as it began to touch and encircle the pain within my entire being. This love in it's supreme form would do its utmost to try and heal the horrific damage inside my shredded soul, till it reached its way to the very core of my brutally damaged and broken heart. It would continue until it penetrated through my layers of fear and armor which I had surrounded myself in.

My Angels and some others from the Spiritual Realm were not about to leave my side, until piece by piece, my heart and soul were together and flourishing in harmony with one another. They would be my greatest assistance in helping me to heal from all of my past issues and any current ones, as they guided me into creating the life which I truly desired. They supported me to the highest degree and there is also help and support for you!

Can you allow Angels to bless and help you to heal your thoughts regarding your past and present, so the spiritual and human side of your heart, mind, body, and soul can joyously merge together?

When one passes over, their soul continues on in their spirit form which is very much alive and well. This soul carries on working continuously towards an even higher consciousness for the benefit and growth of its soul, whether it is in heaven or on earth. Once they are in the spiritual realm, they are closer to a purer state of love, as they have shed the human characteristics which often weighed them down.

It is now time in this state of our world, for us all to learn more about compassion, love, and healing and to use every resource that is available to us. We are at a grave time of need, whereby as many of us as possible, must become involved in order to calm and heal our absolute turbulent world of unrest.

We can ask God, our Angels, and our loved ones in Spirit, to help us send pink healing love, especially to those that need it the most and to help us envelope our entire world in a white protective light. We can continuously send this love, while we ask God to help everyone's soul to awaken and receive this love which their souls need to grow. We must also ask for help in dealing with our own issues and souls too.

All of us create our own destinies, which was our past, is our present, and will be our future. Every one of our actions and every one of our thoughts have an effect and a consequence held within them. If at any given point, we alter our thoughts in the present, then we have changed a part of our future. If we look at our pasts with a new attitude and understanding, then we begin to release the past. We all have great healing power and gifts deep within us. Isn't it time to let your gifts come forth?

Each moment of our lives are filled with opportunities and we are given the choice to react to any given situation with our grace or with our ego. We are all role models for someone and it is our personal option whether we chose to be the most positive one that we can be. It doesn't matter what gender we are or if we haven't been treated with very much kindness. Within a moment of time, we can always change ourselves for the better, for everyone's heart holds a place for KINDNESS. Quite simply, just because someone treated us very heartlessly, we don't need to pass that negativity onto anyone else. Perhaps, you are more aware and higher developed and evolved, then their traits are.

In order to begin creating a more peaceful life, you need to first know what you want out of your life, what direction you want to go in, and what changes you need to make. You also need to look at your own negativities and start changing them. And keep clearing your path, so one day, you will eventually see a new person standing before you. It may take five, ten, or fifteen years, but it can be done. Don't let anyone, any longer, destroy your spirit! Stand tall, don't give up, and start climbing your highest mountain. Dare to imagine yourself in a different and happier life, for you were granted a destiny to create... so go create it!

I needed to get through decades of thick blocks which were obstructing my pathway to happiness. As I did, I discovered more sacred gifts which were buried and lying dormant inside of me, waiting to be uncovered for their ascent upwards.

What dreams do you have buried deep within you? Would you like your soul to exceed its slated growth possible for this lifetime? In order to do so, you must work through your past issues and as agonizing as that may be, it is, what is standing in your way. It's never too late for one to transform themselves and it's a lot of deep painful work, but it is possible to accomplish, if this is what you truly want to do. Perhaps one day, you'll discover the sacred gifts which lay resting within your soul.

All of our lives have a great significance to them. What was your reason for being? What kind of imprint will you leave behind on earth to say that you were here? Have you ever considered, how your presence affects those who are around you, and the people that you live with? What influence have you had on your community, country, and world. What positive changes took place, merely because you were born?

I have fulfilled my soul's desire to create a book which would in some way help other females and I hope that I have accomplished this. In some way,

I also hope that it may shed some light and be of help to men. I certainly didn't want this to be a male bashing book and I know that there are millions of men that cherish their families. My wish was to simply speak about my personal experiences and observations of my life which would lead into, how I had to greatly alter myself. What's more I wanted to say, how greatly some people in both genders need to alter their cultural way of thinking.

I know that there are many loving and kind men that solely care for their children as their situation may or may not be similar to mine. They must be recognized, and admired for undertaking and fulfilling the parenting role of bringing up their children alone. I congratulate them on their successes of accomplishing such an unselfish feat, and carrying through with their responsibilities towards their offspring, even though, their challenges were many.

"I am certain that one day when you look into a mirror, you will see joy beaming on your faces and feel pride radiating from your souls for your selfless deeds. You have done a fine thing for your children and you can be proud of yourselves for doing your utmost for them, in their greatest time of need for love and security. You have completed your job as a positive role model during the most important and formative years of your children's lives. Also you have ALL given our world, your best with loving and balanced human beings which you created. Your courage and strength, like that of all women in similar situations must be applauded, alongside women and men of all cultures who have given their supreme towards the shaping of children for the encouraging sake of their growth and well being. You have all added to our world immensely.

This book was not written or meant to offend others, be it women, men or children. It is purely a reflection of my thoughts and observations that I have observed throughout my life. If you are a woman or a man in a respectful and happy marriage or relationship, you are very fortunate. This book was not meant for you or maybe it was, maybe it was intended for you to think about others who are less fortunate then you. Perhaps to even remind you, to truly appreciate what you have, who you are with, and to prompt you to make a difference in another's existence. It may possibly alert you to get involved and help someone else out... someone who may greatly need your support. It may be through talking, understanding, acknowledging, hugging, or just by giving of yourself physically, in any way that you can in order to assist them.

My pathway was invaluable for me and I wished to share its healing qualities to help others transform themselves and create never-ending possibilities in their lives. I also wished to assist them in increasing their thoughts regarding, what they believe about human life, what happens to their soul after death, and the different phases of the soul's cycle.

Many centuries ago, when my existence first began, my soul began carrying deep with it, every moment of every lifetime that I'd ever experience. Therefore as a result, in this life, my soul already understood and remembered everything that had ever happened to me. It also knew the true intention of my birth this time around. And it had purposely created a chaos within my world as it was convincing me, that the time had finally arrived to begin my major transformation towards my soul's greatest growth and eventual rebirth.

My crucial moment was now here, as my destiny had come to a crossroad and a page in my life was about to be turned. My soul was not about to take "NO" for an answer, as it was demanding that I begin my biggest mission yet, and honor the blueprint of my pre-arranged agreement with God.

I began my search on August 5, 1995, and as I was about to explore deep into uncharted territories, the questions which I had pondered regarding my past, present, and future would come alive and be answered for me over the course of the next decade. And even though, I had already experienced some extremely incredible things, I had no conceivable idea of what was about to occur for me spiritually, emotionally, mentally, physically, and psychically throughout the coming years. Nor did I realize that I was about to take part in another huge marvel which was granted to me, as the hidden truths within the core of my soul would roar and begin to greatly interfere in my life. My heart and world would twist upside down as a force inched its way and propelled itself to the surface of my very being. And as my soul's veil of long forgotten innocence was about to be lifted, my ancient wisdom was about to pounce on me as God entered my soul. My other senses would scream out for it to stop, but there was nowhere to flee! He wasn't listening to me… it just kept coming!

I was in pursuit of my truth and not only would I discover it, but I would also find the truth which lies within each and every soul, living in every human body, here on earth. It was a part of us all. And it didn't matter what culture, color, creed, or belief system that anyone was a part of… for their "TRUTH," was now here as well. They too, had no way to escape from it! One day they would without a doubt, confront it also.

My way of thinking was about to be greatly altered as I stepped into a new reality of spiritual consciousness. I climbed aboard only to be rocketed into a world which was beyond the stars, one which at times would completely tremble my entire being. It was a realm which we have all come from and where we will one day all return. A new pathway showed itself and as my soul started to unfold, I listened to the stirrings deep within and this is where it led.

To Be Continued In Book Two.

Dedicated To The Memory
Of All The BRAVE SOULS
Who Gave Their Lives On September 11, 2001

What the hell was that!
I had a nightmare in the middle of the night,
and I woke up sweating and was scared as a bat.
I washed my face, but sleep I couldn't take,
so I lay awake frightened, the rest of the night.

I was alone and I wondered, what could it mean?
This kind of dream doesn't just come,
it meant something, but I couldn't think what.

In the morning my son called from school,
and he was rather appalled, as he yelled
about some people breaking the golden rules.
He was trying to explain, but what did it all mean?
I could not understand him, so I put on the TV.

After I saw the news, I was troubled for many months,
if I could have helped, I certainly would have.
Except I did not understand, what it all meant,
for I think I had my nightmare, at the same time as impact.

I want you to know, that you are all VERY BRAVE SOULS,
to agree for that, as a way to go... WOW I truly just don't know.
I surly would have tried to give you a call,
for at least a chance to save you all.
Though I didn't have that opportunity to play with your fate,
for by this stage it was late, and I was too far behind the gate.

I later asked God, "Why I didn't have an inkling?"
Out of the blue a voice said, "You did, with your dream."
It was then that I thought back, and I remembered,
and I felt so utterly devastated.
It was very hard to truly comprehend,
that maybe, I could have put an end.
Of course, I didn't have the power to do that!
For I am not God, a Saint, or an Angel,
and we now know, it would have taken that great miracle.

Bombs, wars, soldiers dead, is this what we have actually slated?
Guns and ammunition, all over the place,
is this blackness, what out true destiny is?
All of these men and women, were someone's precious children,
what have we done, have we all gone wild?
Peace & Compassion for humanity, cannot be achieved overnight,
and our planet's chaos has formed a colossal plight.

We must ALL learn from that day forward,
and send our entire world, healing love and support.
Was this call for us to wake up and see our shame,
so these souls did not surrender their lives in vain?
What have we done to this great place of ours,
will we do the same bloody thing up on Mars?

Now years later, what changes have truly been created?
If we keep the same awareness, that we have always had,
and stay with the same gender, who are in command,
what chance will we have, to unite and progress ahead?

We are all from various races, whereby males are mainly at the helm,
it's time for a change, so we have an opportunity to end global hate,
and stop the hostile competitive need, for some countries to be number one.
Observe the news and see how a few, produce other's blues,
it's up to us, to show them how, to exist with continuous mutual respect.

It must begin within you, here and now,
for there is another way, to bring harmony to all.
Consider if each and every night,
we all prayed for others to see the golden light.
This can be done, without hurting another soul,
simply by spreading positive energy, instead of anger anymore.

We need to surround their souls, with loving pink light,
and visualize, which will help calm and start to heal their insides,
but we must absolutely, use all our might.

Ask God for their souls to truly awaken,
so they can actually feel and see, what has truthfully taken place.
And perhaps realize, that their actions were not the best,
and begin to wonder, why their hearts now feel more caring?

I urge you all, it's really not too late,
to save earth from some awful fate.
If things continue the way that they are,
the demise of our universe, may not be very far.

Please try to heal those, who are so in need of pure love.
I vow to you from my personal experience,
you can make a difference into your life and others.

Just by sending your heartfelt prayers and beams of light,
so one day they will eventually, feel your energy, without a fight.
For your love is needed to help free their souls towards peace,
and as a result, they will carry on, to emit that love onto others.

Thus pay tribute to those, who lost their life,
that it was not for some needless, conflict & culture fight.
It was really for us to be sent a very HUGE MESSAGE,
that in the beginning, middle, and end, it is PURE LOVE,
which will Rescue Us and Clear Our Passage.

To The Very Brave Souls, Who Gave Their Lives on September 11, 2001
To Help Rescue The Human Race... From Ourselves,
We Thank You, For You Showed, The Greatest Love & Courage Of Us All.

Bonny Billan

Isn't It Time?

As females, we start off in life, as fragile young beings,
who quite often, don't want anyone, to tell us a thing.
And mature as we do, this is the way life goes,
as living progresses with many woes.

However strong are we, as we often climb many trees,
till one day, they turn into huge mountains.
Although that's all right, for independent are we,
as we handle everything, that comes our way.

It's very clear to me, many women can perceive,
through the rugged terrain and all the rough seas,
and sort out, what our world truly needs.

Males in power, isn't it time, to step aside,
for you've shown, what you can actually do,
with your egos, dominance, decisions, and wars.

And just for once, calmly observe, how females live and display,
how it's done, without any violence, weapons, or machine guns,
and view our different ways of handling various problems.

Women, the world over, I say much is up to us,
to assist in creating a planet of harmony.
We must connect with others, who support our beliefs for world peace,
and speak up and demonstrate change, while we establish our new place,
and pray for the rest, to someday understand & accept this transformation.
One day, without a doubt, we will have an equal amount of influence,
and may even surpass, those, who wouldn't support or acknowledge us.

YOU CHOOSE, which it will be!
A world with tranquility or millions of people continuing in misery,
because of the choices and rage, many controlling males have made.

Bonny Billan

World Peace

Where is the love that God planted in you, on that special day?
Allow it out, so you can show others, how easy it is to display.
Our world wasn't supposed to be like this,
and now it is troubled and quite amiss.
Let's come together, as we continue in a whole new start,
and this can be done, for we really are that smart.

Dig deep so it can all begin, and give the love that you have within,
so our universe can truly win.
No matter who you are, let others know,
that you were born to share this abundant supply,
and I believe that in every religion, this is the bottom line.
We must end HATE, for this is what WE ALL TRULY WANT!
Let's change our fate and do this, before we make our last fatal mistake.

Somewhere in time, we stopped loving our earth and started destroying it,
and at this point it is angry and has rebelled, as it is now destroying us.
Whatever your color brown, black, yellow, or white,
try to do this, with all your might.
For we are all here for the same reason, and that is to discover,
what love we can give, for the sake of all others.

Also to all parents, you must rise to the challenge of raising healthy children.
Whom you have shown love and given self-esteem, as you give them the knowledge,
that they will someday be in charge, and must persist to spread love and peace,
however hard, that may be, for them to truly achieve.

We must leave them a world, that we are very proud of,
so they'll continue to generate, what they are blessed and happy to be from.
Know, that with your awareness, you all helped to create this.

This will certainly be the highest mountain, which billions of us will climb,
as we look down from the top, we can truly see, what has been achieved,
WHAT A MIRACLE… IT'S WORLD PEACE!

Bonny Billan

A Child Is Born

A child is born.
At the beginning not a great life to be,
except one day so blessed, they would foresee,
and show that out of heartache, great things could be achieved.

They will share and help many on their way,
to expand their thoughts of, what they believe of human life to be,
as they truly touch hands with the great divine.

One day they will speak with others, but only with their mind,
for not a word will they have to utter, on a planet filled with much clutter.
For their truth and spiritual self will truly have arrived,
welcome and love the true you, and never again, let yourself be deprived.

Could this child possibly be you?
Will you one day help transform the thoughts of our universe,
as we all reach further into a new truth and existence?

Touch hands with the heavenly realm, as they help you to progress,
grow as you truly become alive, and know your soul is blessed.
Create the destiny, and live the dream, you were meant to be,
till the moment your Angel comes... to guide you back, to your gentle home.

Bonny Billan

Share Your Heart and Soul

REACH BEYOND, whatever you IMAGINED for yourself,
realize that this is the WISH that God has for you.
Your HOPES and DREAMS are all in place,
for this is what YOU were GRANTED within this lifetime.
You have many BLESSINGS to look forward to,
ACCEPT YOUR GIFTS and let your HEART TOUCH YOUR DESTINY.
Watch your SOUL UNFOLD, GROW, and SOAR, than share it,
and use your INSPIRATIONS TO ENCOURAGE and GUIDE those
of both genders, in all different cultures around our universe.
You will be a great role model as you share your HEART and SOUL
for the IMPORTANCE, RESCUING, and GROWTH of our
NEW SPIRITUAL AND INTUITIVE WORLD.

Bonny Billan

A Testimony Of My Love

My children, the happiest and finest moments of my life were your births.
You have had my love, long before you were born and most especially,
from the moment I first cradled you in my arms.
I have continually thanked God for my precious gifts from him,
and I will always carry you in the deepest part of my heart.

You have been my driving life force and my anchor throughout our years together.
I hope that someday, you will understand that I came to a crossroad in my life.
One which demanded, that I start loving myself by putting a halt to my pain
and the disrespect which I was receiving.
When we divorced, your world changed forever.
Perhaps one day, you will forgive me and feel the truth within your hearts,
by recognizing and understanding, why my action was so necessary,
for me to partake in.
And come to know, that I have always persevered because of my love for you.

I hope that if I have taught you anything at all, it is that you must always
stand up for yourselves, especially in the face of any type of adversity.
Whether it is harming you, spiritually, emotionally, mentally, and most
certainly physically, you must stop it, and even say goodbye, if need be.

I have reached a place of living out the truth of my soul for myself
and in all of my relationships, for it is, who I am and what I must exhale.
I now recognize and understand myself better than I did, when we first met.
I know that most of the time we spent together, it was just the four of us,
and I tried so very hard to make up for the missing link.
Please forgive me for any injustices which I placed upon you,
and one day… forgive him too.

My children, you have been the primary reason for my purpose on earth
and my dedication towards you has been boundless.
Our connection has had the greatest of importance deep within me,
and my commanding bond with you has been invoked from the core of my soul.
I must continue on my path that I have chosen, so I can truly fulfill my purpose
to God, and to my soul towards it's utmost freedom and happiness.

I shall love you while I am here on earth, and then I will continue to love
and take care of you, as I watch over you from heaven.
Know that I shall never leave you and our destined love,
shall live within my heart and soul… forever.
I Thank You, for giving me the greatest Joy and for all of the Love, Kindness,
Understanding, and Support which you gave to me on our passage together.

From My Heart to Yours,
Mom

Epilogue

*T*hank you for joining me on this part of my journey.

I hope that everyone who reads my story takes into consideration whether or not, they need to look at our world, themselves, or others in a different light and make some changes.

My wish is for females of all ages to make every effort possible to never give up on their dreams. And to strive towards changing any abusive beliefs, disrespect, or outdated behaviors within their families and cultures.

Each one of you must continue in creating your future. Keep updating your course of action of the different stages which you will follow through, towards the greatest growth and happiness for your hearts and souls.

I am counting on all of you, to give some thought to this because you have a life of your own to fulfill. Many of you have suffered through horrendous atrocities which never should have occurred, especially in this day and age. Together, we can work towards changing this for others.

Imagine my arms around you, throughout the course of your plights as you keep stepping towards your new life. Visualize Angels surrounding, guiding, and protecting you, with pink healing love and white light. Feel and Listen, to what they have to say to you… YOU ARE NOT ALONE! Will you allow them into your life?

As you go through your process try your utmost to keep your faith and hope alive. Always remember… Equality, Respect, and Kindness for yourself and from others, must be at the forefront of your thoughts and actions, each and every second of your life.

God Bless You All.
My Deepest Love, Blessings, & Light Go Out to All Of You.

Bonny Billan

Acknowledgments

My heartfelt gratitude is to you GOD, my heavenly Father. I would not have survived my heart wrenching times, if your golden scepter had not encircled me and my world and blessed me with your divine love and healing. I thank you for your love, blessings, miraculous gifts, kindness, support, protection, insights, abundance, guidance and messages for myself. I truly wish to thank you for your blessings of love, kindness, abundance, and protection towards my children as well.

I also wish to extend my deepest appreciation for the gifts of Angels that you sent to guide me on my lonely journey. They shone their light on my pathway and as they shielded me with their wings, I began to feel what unconditional love was.

Although it has taken many years for me to fully awaken, accept, and embrace my destiny, I now realize that since the moment of my birth, my soul had been weaving a path towards my most sacred promises and desires. Through your grace and blessings, you have shown me repeatedly that I was never alone, as I proceeded to create a new relationship with myself and build a new life with my children.

I always knew that in the midst of everything, I was a very fortunate woman, but the incredible gifts which you granted me were absolutely astounding. Your grace has humbled me and I feel very foolish for ever having doubted our bond. I shall never break the connection which has been created between us again.

My spiritual path first began by being awakened by the impact of the very wise, loving, and life altering affirmations of Dr. Deepak Chopra and later on, with the transforming words of enlightenment of Dr.Wayne Dyer. I must extend my deepest gratitude towards both of you, for your inspiration has influenced my soul so greatly, that I have amended my views on life. You have shown me, how I can always further myself onto a higher level of consciousness towards myself and every person that I meet. And your thoughts have left deep lasting imprints on my soul. Both of you have positively added to my destiny and that of millions of others. Your words will continue to change our world on grand scales into that of new found knowledge, as we carry on to reach further towards a new reality and existence. Our universe is privileged to have you.

I also wish to thank you Dad, for reaching out to me with your guidance, protection, and warnings. When you touched me with your love, you began my healing process which slowly changed my thoughts and pain, as it started to heal the wounds in my soul. The greatest gift which you have given to me in this lifetime and something that I can share with others, is the knowledge

275

and proof, that a human being's life does not end, but rather continues on, after one passes over to the other side. This isn't the end of our time together or our story. Until we meet again… my deepest love.

With My Deepest Gratitude,

Bonny

Excerpts from Book 2 – "Conversations With A Tibetan Monk."

When I met Emily Watcher on August 5, 1995 I had no idea that I had found one of two souls, who could truly help me find the answers to my present day questions. And some of my future ones too. I had found my destined pathway to her and over time, I'd come to understand the greatest parts of my destiny which had already begun unfolding since before my birth.

Emily partakes in trance channeling and this involves her going into a trance, and one from the spirit realm speaks through her, regarding the person who is there for a session. In this meeting, a three hundred year old Tibetan Monk, who is in spirit, emerges and he speaks through Emily. As this happens her whole demeanor takes on a complete change, as does her voice. One can see the process for themselves, as she begins to sit very straight in her chair with her head held high. She also has a great look of authority upon her face. The Monk has come to be, as he nods his head up and down in acknowledgment, regarding information which he has somehow received about myself. He has processed it, for less than a span of a minute, even though, neither of us has said a word.

My reading begins by him saying, "Hello, my friend," and he speaks to me about my world, and what he sees regarding the growth of my soul on a spiritual level. He knows all about my past, present, and future and my experiences with everyone that I've ever met, while also knowing, what my soul's purpose is.

My spiritual teacher had finally appeared in my life, and his "SPIRITUAL SCHOOL FOR SOULS, LIVING THE HUMAN EXPERIENCE," was now in session. The only thing was… I was the only student. My long sought after answers, and my soul's purification was about to begin. It would take place over the span of the next ten years, as I was led into completely mind boggling experiences and the incredible purpose of my birth and lesson filled life.

Today I was feeling a bit apprehensive about this new experience which I was about to partake in, but here I was, waiting for my spiritual consultation to begin. I was dreading what the monk was going to say to me, and I prepared myself for the worst. I thought that he was going to put me down for divorcing, like so many other people had already done. However, as his messages started to flow, I was pleasantly surprised by his point of view and his words of wisdom. I had been led to a loving, positive, and spiritual friend in a safe environment.

He was someone who I could trust and confide in over the coming years. And it didn't matter that this male spirit was over 300 years old, for somehow, he knew and understood me. I truly honored and respected him. And even though, he often aggravated me, and I told myself that I was never going to see him again, something drew me back each and every time. You can't imagine my shock at the end of our ten year session, when he told me, who he actually was… to me.

School begins completely anew.
What will I be learning?
Ahhhhh… just wait and see!

August 5, 1995

Monk   "My Friend, I come to you with much love and much respect for you. The strength that you have shown in the past, to deal with and overcome, such trials and tribulations in your life. We come to you with respect, for the efforts that you have had in the past to grow, to grow for you.

You need only to be responsible for you and your efforts. You know this my friend, and we come to you to say again, BE GOOD TO YOU, in this! You cannot take on the responsibility of someone else's life.

What you do for you, effects all those around you, close to you, beside you. Your strength pours over all. You need only to recognize, that you at times, are the core, within the circle of your life. So, what you do for you, sets precedence, as you say, for others to see. Those little ones that look up to you for guidance, they see your strength. They see, that you model, one to be respected and loved. You need only to recognize this within yourself.

The energy that you have poured forth till now, to accomplish, what it is you have set out to accomplish, has not been wasted. Only at times it seems, this way for you. It seems, that, as you might say, you have been hitting your head against the wall and not going anywhere. It only seems that way my friend.

You needed to do all those things, to get where you are today, even at times, when you feel, that you have been wrong, as you might say, in your world, there is no right or wrong. It is how you felt at the time. And you did, what you felt was right, at the time. Who is to say, that you are right or wrong, but you.

And than again, my friend, you must never forget, that you are, but a human. You are a spirit within a body. And because, you have this restriction upon you, you might not be able to do all the things, that you feel that you could or should.

You must remember, that you are restricted in this way but, you can help others, at a distance, with your mind, my friend, send them loving thoughts, ask the higher being within you, to send healing to them, to send love, to them.

279

And my friend, love is the strength, within you. So you see, even, when you think, that you cannot help, you can. You are not restricted, within you mind, within the power within you. You need only to ask, for help to go to those, that you know need help, need love, and healing. Send those thoughts to those. My friend, it is a test of trust, for you, to trust that higher being, within you, that link between you, and your GOD, that is where your strength has come from in the past. Now, my friend, you are being tested, to trust again.

Do trust that all will be well, for all concerned, that all within your situation, at this time, will learn the lessons, that they need to learn, from what is taking place within your lives. I know that you wonder, what your outcome may be, of this, but, if I were to tell you that, you know within your heart, you would not learn, what you need to learn.

You are a wise soul, you have lived many lives. You have gathered, much knowledge, but the human side of you, my friend, creates this mistrust, at times. The spirit within you, knows, that whatever the outcome to be, is to be. And, you can deal with whatever, that is, but the human, the human with all of the emotions that go with it, feels a mistrust, at times.

So my friend, you must turn within to be in touch with that spirit within you, that GOD force within you, that gives you the strength and the energy and the faith, to continue, in the direction, that you have been going. And know, without, as you say, controlling, what happens because you know, you can't, but trusting, in the outcome.

Take each day, as it comes to you, and encourage those, that you are within this situation with, encourage them too, to have faith and trust to look within, and draw from the strength, that they have within them. It is the same source as yours, because all are connected, as you know. You can be as well as one close to you, examples, of that strength and trust for others not only in this situation, but others, to come. You, and one close to you, as you say, are breaking the ice, for others, allowing the waters to flow, as they may.

This is, what life is all about, learning the lessons, going with the flow. Growing from each and every trial and tribulation, that you need to need to conquer. Growing, and learning, and gathering more wisdom as you experience life, today, in the now.

At this time, it is, as you are being judged for who you are. It is, as you are been judged, for what you might deserve, for

280

what you might want, for what you might be respected for, but it comes down to, who you are. Who you are in the eyes, of others?

What is important my friend, and I will remind you of this, with great love, is to remember who you are, for you. This will carry you through, with strength and nourishment, and love, for you. Love for you, will bring love from others. Respect, who you are!

You have much love around you, even though at times, you feel, that you should have more. You have all that you need. You have support and understanding, of those who understand and accept you, for you, that is the love, that you want, deserve, and need. It will grow and grow, as time goes on, as you love yourself, more and more, others will love and respect you, for that.

The time has come my friend, for you to trust, you. To know you, to be you, being and trusting and loving you, is being and trusting and loving, the GOD force within you. The connection, is what, will carry you through, you need only, to trust as I have said before. And have faith, in your abilities.

My friend, do you have questions, of me?"

Bonny   "Do you see if my psychic abilities are getting stronger right now?"

Monk   "Oh my friend, I need not tell you that, it is, what you know. Again, do you trust who you are?

Do you trust your abilities? That is what confirms, what you can do, and not do, my friend. There are those that you can turn to, to verify what you think, might be true. Those are the ones, that have as you say, in your world, are experienced at this. I can encourage you as I have said before to continue in the direction that you are going. From that my friend, you have the knowledge, that you asked for.

Does this help you, my friend?"

Bonny   "Yes.

Am I meeting any of the challenges that I set out for myself before I came to earth?"

Monk   "Ohooooo, what is in your heart, my friend? What is in your heart?

Do you feel that you are?

281

In your confusion, you do not know, but as that confusion, becomes unruffled and as you listen to what you call, your gut feelings, listen to your heart. If you feel good, in what it is that you are doing. If you feel good and secure, and worthwhile, you must, know, that, what it is you do, gives you that, sense of worth.

And if it does, my friend, this will tell you, if you are going in the right direction. If it does not fulfill you, if you have no peace, within you, as you do, than you will know, it is not. And as you, turn to those, that, have been traveling in the same direction, as you, who have the trust and the faith, that you, look for, search for, desire for, as you communicate with some, that are doing what it is that you choose to do, you share, the goodness of it, you share, the love that comes back to you, because of it.

You will know my friend. You will know within your heart, that you are, accomplishing what it is, you want to accomplish. And, with your trust and faith, in your GOD source within you, asking to be guided in the direction, that you should be, that is best for you.

My friend, if you remain on the path, that you are going and your gut feelings do not take you elsewhere, than I think you know, what the answer is. You are going, in the direction that you should be.

Does this help you, my friend?"

Bonny

"Yes, it does. Thank you.

Is there anything that I should know about, that I should avoid?"

Monk

"My friend, there is but, a behavior, that is damaging to you. I might call it, your ego. One, who, puts upon you, the feeling of, may I say failure, may I say insecurity, may I say lack of self-worth and self-esteem. There is a behavior, that speaks to you, with pain and hurt, and lack of respect, and you know, what this behavior is.

I must stress to you my friend, that at the time, that you hear it with your ears and see it with your eyes, when you read between the lines and understand the true meaning of what is being said to you, by one's actions, than my friend, you must learn to detach from that.

You must learn again, to turn within, to be centered within who you are. To trust the GOD force, and ask for the assistance, to deal with this in the proper way, but my friend what is important is, that you detach, and know, that you are not what someone is making you out to be!

Know yourself, respect yourself, and love yourself. And know, that you do not deserve to be, as you might say stifled, restricted, constricted, held within the rules and regulations of someone else. Someone else's insecurities, someone else's ego, that is out of balance.

Do you understand?"

Bonny   "Yes."

Monk   "The freedom of being who you are. The spirit, that has gathered, all this knowledge and wisdom, along the way. The spirit that is restricted by the physical being, need not be restricted, by others, who only want to restrict you, for their own selfish reasons.

The spirit within you, has a great need to be free, to be who they are. So, this behavior, that I speak, you must hear between the lines. Words can manipulate you, as you say, can hurt you; can destroy you, because you allow them to. You allow the words and the actions of others to harm you, to bring you down. I say to you now, to be cautious of such behavior in your life.

And when you recognize, that behavior happening at the time, that it is happening, it only takes a thought away for you, my friend, to speak, to the GOD force, and ask, for the strength to deal with this, as you should deal with this. To ask for the right action, to be guided, for you, so you will know within your heart, that what you say, is needed to be said, and what you do is needed to be done to protect you. And to protect, those, little ones around you, this too, you must know this too. You must understand your responsibility as well, there. We, in the spirit realm know, we know that you choose to be, but a good model. So, do not be afraid, do not doubt, that when you turn to your GOD force, for guidance, for help, that it is there, for you.

Yes, you have accomplished much, that you have set out to accomplish. Yes, you have, but you have much work to do yet, as all humans, do.

I must caution you with patience, my friend. You need to know, that everything happens, at the right moment, for you, if you allow it to. And patience, is what you learn, even if you try, to rush that river, to rush that flow of life, you will lose your patience and become frustrated, and waste your energy, in a way that is useless. So patience my friend, is of great use for you to learn. And at times, my friend when you feel impatient, it is at, that time, that you need to look within, to find out why you are impatient. Your answers are within for you, at all times, this you know.

Do you understand, my friend?"

Bonny   "Yes."

Monk   "You have much love and support around you. You have little ones, that need you, that look up to you. Little ones within your immediate family and little ones within your big family, even though, at times you seem not to be noticed by those others, you are. You bring a smile to their faces at times. A smile within shines out, allow it to come, allow it to be. Know within your heart, those that truly love you for you. Be with them, around them.

Do you have but, any more questions, for me?"

Bonny   "Have I been with my husband before in another lifetime?"

Monk   "Oh, my friend. All of those within your life this time, you have been with, before. Knowing that, does not change, what has been going on today, for you. It only, enriches, it. It only gives you information. What is today, is today. This is what you need to deal with, but yes, I answer with yes. If this helps you, for some reason than, it is information for you to use.

Anything else my friend?"

Bonny   "No that's all. Thank you."

Monk   "You are a wise soul. You will use this information, that you have received today, to continue on your journey, in a positive way. This we trust for you. This we know, as truth.

We are here for you, at all times. You have many guides around you, my friend, those, that are there for you, at times when you least, expect help. They are there, for you."

Bonny   "May I ask you one more question?"

Monk   "Sure."

Bonny   "Do you see my Father around me? And is he trying to communicate something to me?"

Monk   "My friend, I understand that this is information that would be of importance to you, but, I ask you, do you feel that he is?"

Bonny   "Yes."

Monk   "My friend, do you need me to tell you, what you already know?"

Bonny   "No."

Monk   "I did not think so. Again, that, my friend, this is where your trust comes in.

     You are, but a sensitive one, that you know that you are. I believe, that too, answers a question you have asked. Trust, in who you are. Your feelings are correct. He comes to you and others, that are close to you, with great love. And at times in the past he has felt great sorrow because his understanding of life, served him well, as he grew, but he knows now, that those ways do not necessarily serve, his family well.

     Today, in today's world, he says to you, and other's that you can pass the message to, and you know who they are, to live their lives according to their own happiness, to their strengths, to their desires, today, in the world. He has only love. He has had much love in the past, as well, but love was not shown, in the same ways, it is today. It was not understood in his time, as it is today.

     Your understanding of giving, receiving, loving, and being, is much different than what your Father, as you say, has been in the past. He recognizes this, he understands this, and he says to you, and to those close to you, again you know who they are, that is important for you all, to be you, to follow your heart.

     Do not allow, that behavior to restrict you and take your freedom away from you, be the spirit of who you are, the essence of your life. He wants you all to live, in a world that brings you happiness, not sorrow, but happiness.

     Does this help you?"

Bonny   "Yes, it does. Thank You."

Monk	"He is with you, he is with you all. You, and those close to you. And I might say, as he says to you, he is there to help you in this situation, as well, to give you the strength and the encouragement to be you.
	I must leave you now, my friend. You are, but a good student in this lifetime. I must tell you, so that you know."
Bonny	"Thank You."
Monk	"Continue to ask for the information.
	Continue to accept the knowledge that comes to you, however it comes to you.
	Continue to share the wisdom that you have gathered with others.
	Continue on your journey, with love and light and may the God force within protect and surround you on your way.
	Go in peace, my friend. Go in peace."

Join me in "Book 2," "Conversations With A Tibetan Monk," if you would like a better understanding of your soul's journey and the heavenly world of love, healing, and growth from an intriguing realm. And discover, how to create your own miracles by allowing the light into your life.

Her Soul, His Soul

There once was a soul, that was split into two,
and then, again, again, and again.
Many ions long ago, this was actually quite so,
they were cast into the universe to evolve and grow,
to experience all facets of human life, and be repeatedly reborn.

They'd each partake in many different things,
and encounter a great deal of human pain.
And feel very lonely and misunderstood at times,
for they craved to reunite, with their molecules of long ago.

Oh the SOUL'S journey... such a long and painful fight,
several stages to travel and persevere with all one's might.
Even though, the soul often longs for heavenly flight,
no peace will come, till it achieves it's purpose, each and every life.

Where and when, would they meet again?
And in how many lifetimes, would their atoms reappear?
Would they come to recognize one another,
since their soul was a part, of specific individuals on sight?
What human being, could possibly know,
this knowledge could only be conveyed, through one's ancient soul?

Who would be the first, to finish their lessons on earth,
and release all the sensations, known to burden man?
To be finally free... without a fear or a problem,
for only their soul's completion, would allow them to breathe easily.
When would two halves be whole, for the two original souls?

In 2005 she deeply desired to re-unite, with her dearest soul mate,
and that is when and why, she took a chance with fate.
She dreamed, imagined, and believed,
for the opposite sides to coincide.
And tossed the thought into the universe,
hoping it may be answered, oh of course.

A few days later, her wish was granted and so you see,
once they reunited, her heart recognized thee.
When he smiled at her, his face was aglow,
she knew she'd seen his expression, somewhere before.

She was breathless whenever they met,
and he sent her essence into quite a whirlwind.
As she looked into his colorful eyes, her soul disclosed,
how closely connected, they truly were.
It was incredible to hear and perceive,
he had a somewhat parallel life with she.

Her stirrings told her, how deeply she must have cared,
for this dark haired soul, who didn't appear centuries old.
The instant attraction was certainly intriguing,
how could all of this truthfully be?

Here he had finally appeared,
and as she gazed ahead, she contemplated starting again,
since she was happy and healed, and no longer confined.

How should she tell him, that she knows,
his kind and appealing, very aged soul?
And it was once a great part of her whole heavenly being,
and that she sees, senses, and hears him, sight unseen.

What will his reaction actually be,
to something so unique, on the earthly plane?
And about her promise to God, that she made,
to share the Human and Spiritual Soul Ways,
before she dated or participated with he.

Perhaps his heart would also convey,
their tender bond for one another,
that lived within the gentleness of their souls.

Thus apart, they would be,
as she worked on her project, for God to see.
It was truly difficult to concentrate,
since she had re-connected with this mate.
Once again, she was bound and enslaved,
because all she wanted to do, was play.
However life continues for us all, and now he wasn't free to be.

Her hidden memories had come alive,
and though she tried, they didn't fade.
They were once again revitalized,
as his presence and absence, touched her insides.

Too many dedicated years to her work,
and now book one, was dreary to complete.
Consequently she conceded to defeat,
and started anew, with book number three.
This was a good thing, cuz meeting him,
inspired something loving, deep within.

She was amazed, it was second nature to feel,
many parts of his precious soul.
And since they were both at a distance,
how was she going to control her desires and resistance?

Possibly one day, she shall be daring,
and take a chance, and reveal the past.
Maybe he'll also come to remember,
the love they shared, in the realms of their passion,
in another lifetime, filled with much rapture.

However, amazingly though apart, these two souls reunited,
throughout the wee hours of many nights.
As their bodies slept, their romantic spirits took flight,
and roamed into a state, where it wonderful to embrace,
and elevated one another, to immense and grand heights.

They caressed each other, as they ascended through space,
something very special to experience within the human race.
One of the happiest encounters, for any person to come across,
to be amongst the stars with their soul's mirror image, on a solar date.

Miracles, it's plain to see.
They astral traveled, to simply be,
the vast loving force, that of course can't escape,
a great part of their closely entwined and developed souls.

Could it truly be, two souls can reunite, on the crest of the milky way,
and have their spiritual reunion, in the universe's glorious continuum?
How many roles, divisions, & characteristics, does one's soul compose?

The feminine and masculine, had found one another,
even though, the human beings had barriers in the way.
Their ying and yang came together and communicated,
and danced on waves throughout the luminous cosmos.

What more, is there to say?
Two human beings can rendezvous on a extraordinary plane.
It's apparent if one perseveres, clears, and expands their soul,
their body can experience bliss, without a single human kiss.
As their twin energy seeks them out, and merges to be as one,
till the day their shells they'll cast, and be together forever... at last.
The SOUL'S GRAND PURPOSE... is to one day, BE WHOLE!

Now she had met two, what would she do,
with a couple of handsome souls, that touched her core?
Which one in the end, might she chose,
to keep her heart, from endless blues?
She didn't have a clue, and it may possibly be,
a different gentleman, who was somewhat new.
Yet she was setting her past & long ago desires free,
and now that she had expressed them, her spirit felt at peace.

Over the earth and through the universe, soaring high as they often do,
the magnificent soul, though old, always finds someone new to woo.
A heart connection to another... something rare to discover,
her soul, his soul, many souls linked together... all from one soul.

Gazing in their eyes, it was hard to deny... she knew their sacred souls,
she had experienced a loving connection with two past life, soul loves.

Bonny Billan

We were drawn to one another from the very beginning and at this moment, the stars and the atmosphere around us were filled with a powerful force aligning itself within our exhilarated souls.

Today as we stood in his parlour with only inches between us, our hearts were smiling as we took note of each other's body language. I didn't trust myself to say a word to him because my senses were shouting out loud enough. And any conversation between us would have interrupted the flow, and some of my naughty and tantalizing thoughts. The echoes within his soul were also very clear and inviting, while making their way towards the very essence of who I was. The room was far from quiet, as our intimate rendezvous and soul's dance had begun.

As our mischievous eyes met, the moments and memories from our past suddenly came flooding back to me, and his alluring charm began enticing me in. I tried to keep my composure, but I sensed the heat of our bodies swirling between us. Whatever happened next would be entirely up to him because I wasn't about to make the first gesture. Although, the passion within me was rapidly rising as I felt his hot and sizzling breathe near to my tingling neck. It sent shivers up and down my bronzed spine.

He reached out to me in his usual playful and teasing mood, and gently ran his fingers throughout my lightly, scented, and tousled curls. I stroked my hand throughout his dark head of hair and leisurely, massaged the nape of his neck which I deeply wanted to nuzzle within. My soon to be lover began whispering sweet little nothings into my ear, and then continued with some very intimate and suggestive thoughts. I blushed as my heart rate quickened. He was enjoying himself, while it was having quite an affect on me. And, he absolutely knew it.

Next he sensuously traced the outline of my mouth with one of his tanned fingertips. And oh so lightly, he took liberties and allowed them to wander up and down my naked neck. He stopped just a bare centimeter short of my low plunging neckline on my silky, pink camisole. I followed suit and slowly ran one of my fingers around the curves of his luscious lips. And as my finger glided over his skin, I couldn't resist lustfully inserting it into his mouth with undue care.

His eyes suddenly popped wide open. I had surprised him a bit! I could hear his heart beginning to accelerate and race away.

He softly cupped my face into his hands. And in an urgent need, he leaned in and placed his soft and sexy lips upon mine. He lingered there for a time as he explored all about. I wanted to fall into his arms as I started to melt into him.

I could feel the intense warmth which was radiating deep within me, and as his mouth continued downwards, his sensual movements swept me away. Every part of my very being was longing, throbbing, and screaming, and oh so ready for his manly touch.

My ripened breasts rose up to welcome him as a bead of perspiration trickled down between my cleavage, and met with his breathless gaze. He beamed with anticipation and pulled me even closer. I felt his energy wrap itself around my body as if he had enveloped me with a sacred heavenly force. Any remaining self-control which I had within, quickly vanished as his soul drew me in rapidly.

We picked up momentum and began devouring each others lips as our hands felt its way through our clothing. Neither one of us could restrain ourselves any longer, let alone, resist one another's magnetic and mesmerizing chi. We had toyed with each other for long enough.

My silky hair fell within the folds of his open shirt as I softly fondled, nipped, and kissed his chest all over. He was touching, awakening, and thrilling my body in a similar type of pleasing arousal. I lost all sense of balance as I tumbled into his body.

He wrapped his strong arms around me so closely and with such strength and tenderness... as if to say, "Let me care for you, I'll never let anyone hurt you again."

I looked into his dreamy and soulful eyes and sensually whispered, "I desire to share my soul... with you."

He swiftly picked me up and lovingly caressed me, as he carried me to his masculine scented bedroom. At long last, I would be his and he would be mine, as our predestined date with destiny was now here.

Every step that we had ever taken, had brought us to this point. Oh God... why did this take so long, for us to manifest?

Here he was finally... right in front of me. A special, charismatic, and compassionate man. My heart was yearning to entwine with his.

To be continued.

New Excerpt

This was the moment for me to release any existing inner inhibitions which still lingered within me, and allow myself the experience of this man in all of his universal vibrations. I was a woman, and there was nothing left to say. Throughout the past years, I had used every excuse in the book as I shielded my heart and denied myself love from another man.

Why had I not allowed myself to pick up on this part of my life again or to let another man into my world? I knew deep down inside of me, that I needed to understand, accept, and love my entire soul before I could once again... love and trust another.

Over the years, I had chosen to exist somewhat in seclusion as I lived my past moments in celibacy and hid myself away from life. I toiled endlessly into the wee hours of each and every night, as my dedication to my writing took presence over all. I was like a monk on a lonely mountain top, striving to reach the epitome of one's greatest growth, without the outside world infringing upon his soul's intentions and utmost purpose of reaching nirvana. Solitude was the only haven which my soul required at this time, as I reacquainted myself with God. And somehow through a blessed soul's purpose, I became connected into God's divine realm. My soul purged itself in some isolated ritual of cleansing, down to the ugliest depths of my very being, as it searched for spiritual knowledge and the tools to heal and forgive others, while discovering soul love in its various forms.

And indeed my soul grew... to extreme heights and in every way imaginable. It went beyond my wildest dreams and higher, then I could ever possibly have imagined it to go! However, I was lonely at times. I didn't know of anyone else within my circle of friends, who had attained the same psychic and spiritual awareness as me. I longed to share my life and experiences with someone who could truthfully accept and appreciate my gifted side. Especially since, I was a bit hesitant about having to explain my heavenly encounters to another, after figuring out if their belief system was "New Age" or not?

I also wished for my everyday life to be very near to my heart's ultimate desires. I wanted to be living on my own with my children on their way, and my entire book publishing process to be completed. Actually, I didn't want a care in the world. I just wanted my total freedom for me, and the time to reintroduce myself to the masculine gender. And if I wanted to go on hiatus for a week or more, then I wanted to do that without worrying about anything else. I had most certainly earned this desire to be granted to me and my heart wouldn't stop until it had it.

Now I knew, who I truly was, and what I wanted out of my life. I also discovered, how sacred my soul was. And I desired to be with a man who had done his soul work to the core of his being too.

Time would tell me, if there was any man that my heart and soul could totally connect and celebrate with. And since my years of hard work on myself, my children, and my books were now completed, life's pleasures were awaiting me. It was at last... time to play. My moment was now here, for me to share my love and discover my new world that I had created... one of loving and kindhearted gentlemen.

Over the span of all of one's lifetimes, each of us have encountered many of our different soul mates. I now wanted to reunite with my very dearest one. The one that would know and understand me, and my ways, since much of me... was also much of him. I intensely wanted to meet the man, who was the first division of me... of us... the masculine side of my soul.

Upon my reunion with two of my soul mates, I recognized one immediately, and the other one, not until many months later. I decided to keep this recognition to myself for awhile and not share this gift with either of them. I wanted each one to feel whatever.... deep within their hearts. And if they desired to reveal it to me, I hoped that some day soon, they would.

I also wanted to explore this area of my life for a time. I was in no rush to make any great decisions regarding any man, and the fun, exciting, and passionate side of living was finally upon me. And I would accept nothing less, than the most respectful, compatible, and well-balanced relationship possible, for this lifetime.

New Excerpt.

As I looked into his vibrant eyes, my heart reminded me, that I already knew his caring soul. Many centuries long ago, we were once romantic lovers deeply in love. And at that time, he was... just mine.

Now here we were in a new century, meeting once again, as if for the first time, even though, our hearts already knew one another. I felt that on some level, a part of him recognized me, and he was the only one who could fully understand my soul. My greatest wish for this reunion with my most important soul mate was now before me. I waited much too long for this moment to come.

Our connection to one another had continued throughout our countless lifetimes, and our souls had dealt with every imaginable event known to man. In this life, we had both healed and evolved our souls to great dimensions throughout the universe. And because of this healing, our heart waves were able to penetrate through the deepest layers within our soul's entire core, and through all of the different lifetimes that were living within us. They had affectionately surfaced, while leisurely floating on the pores of our very beings, just waiting for us to notice them.

When I first saw my crystal, clear, energy waves in front of me, they were beginning to move towards him. And they must have arrived at their destination because within seconds, he reached out to me. A miracle was taking place and we were both a part of it. The various things that occurred whenever he was near or far from me... were simply incredible.

Our immense souls were permitted to remember, our thousands of years of ongoing history, as the thin veil between heaven's vast stamp of forgetting one another on earth, opened and parted way. Angels helped to unlock the nostalgic and reminiscent flood gates within us, so our soul were able to find and reveal our greatest loving feelings and memories for one another.

God had granted us the utmost gift of all. Our whole souls had finally come full circle on the earthly plane, and were now bestowed... freedom!

It also meant something else too. We would never be back on earth again as human beings, for we had graduated to our next level.

How blessed could two human beings possibly get? We had much to celebrate and be grateful for, and parts of our spirits were rejoicing and flowing in happiness. The heart of our souls were given a second chance at love, not only on earth, but on the cosmic plane too. The rest of our story was up to us… for as you know, everyone has free will!

However, I still had a big dilemma. Even though, I could follow the workings of our connected souls, I had not shared any of this with him. I certainly planned on telling him everything, except I needed to honor my soul's purpose first. Now, maybe it was just too late to share it with him at all. Yet, whenever I thought of him, it was hard to forget, he was my longtime, cherished friend. And my intense bond with him was a part of my heart, soul, and truth.

Could this kindhearted gentleman be the one, that my soul had been craving and impatiently waiting for all these past years? Was it destiny when we met or did I play with fate and manifest him too early? Was I falling for him or was I purely remembering our loving moments from our past lifetimes? Were we now truly meant to be together for all of eternity?

How about my first soul mate that I reunited with? Was our time over or were there any moments left for us? Was there a previous life connection between all three of us and if so, what could it be?

Only our free will, and all of our hearts, could answer these questions for any of us. Though I must say, I often receive premonitions regarding my future and it appeared that my world was about to get intensely daring and exhilarating.

In the greatest design of love, was there still another similar male in the universe whose soul's imprint was on my star, and he was just waiting for our pathways to meet also? It was a chance and a possibility to consider.

Now that my soul had accomplished its hardest work, I was weaving the tapestry of my future filled with my deepest wishes and desires. Was my love scene for real or was I creating and inviting my yearnings into my life, by visualizing and writing about them first?

Connect with me in "Book 3," "Desires, Destiny, and Love," as my journey of love enters into an exciting phase. And my heart leaps into the most romantic feelings, that every soul looks forward to encountering… love, lust, and sensuous desires. Stand back, observe the steps to take, and proceed with faith, as you too consider, how to create your future of truth, light, purpose, passion, and the purest of love… into your soul's magnificent and infinite existence.

About The Author

$\mathcal{B}$onny was born and raised in Vancouver, British Columbia and moved to Victoria, B.C. thirty years ago. She resides on Vancouver Island and has three children, 2 boys and 1 girl who are ages 28, 25, and 20 years old.

She is an interior decorator whose creative passion has stemmed from her youth and has now branched into other areas of her life. The most important concept of her decorating is based on the art of Feng Shui, and she enjoys creating peaceful environments with a balanced feeling of harmony and tranquility. These beliefs have become a part of her every waking moment throughout every segment of her life.

Bonny has always supported equality issues for women and wishes to continue bringing awareness of these matters, on behalf of others from all cultures and faiths. She is concentrating her attention on the plights of females of all ages, especially those who are currently suffering through the heartless difficulties concerning gender inequality. Her focus will be towards their well-being and prosperity, and sharing her awareness on this subject with those of both genders. She also gives her support for peaceful steps to be taken towards the freeing of Tibet, and its humane return back to the Tibetan people.

Fifteen years ago she began a journey of self discovery and throughout this process was led into a search for her own spirituality. This guided her into personal experiences regarding "The Path of Our Souls" in heaven and on earth, and its link with the Mind, Body, and Soul Connection which is covered in Book 2. She is continuing in her pursuit with the further exploration of the Different Stages of the Soul, and delves into "The Soul's Past Life Memory" in regard to the Heart and Soul Connection in Book 3.

Bonny's newest passion has grown into a business of giving Intuitive Consultations to nurture one's soul. She provides insightful "Soul Readings," to help others recognize and overcome obstacles in their lives. She also integrates all of her soul's experiences into Interior Decorating and her main objective is to reflect the inner essence within one's heart and soul into their home.

Bonny looks forward to meeting new people and traveling the world with the promoting of her books. Her humor and sensitivity are a part of everything that she does, and she considers that some of the essential things in life are laughter, love, great friendships, martinis, and of course chocolate. She has discovered throughout her journey of healing, the truest goals that every soul should strive to achieve in order to be free and happy. If one can find the pathways to purify their entire soul, and integrate their soul's purpose within their heart, mind, body, and soul connection, they will create their greatest state of serenity that they have ever known.

This passage has led her into her greatest peace and happiness thus far, and she hopes that your life will also be changed forever, as she shares with you, "The Truths of her Soul."

Any inquiries contact the author at:
Serenity Publications
P.O. Box 41045
Victoria, B.C.
Canada
V8Y 3C8

ISBN 1425118495-6